Luis Alberto Ambroggio
Golden collection
Long Island Al Dia Editores

First Edition: August 2017

Graphic Design: Daniel Walter Lencinas Cautela
Cover design: Daniel Walter Lencinas Cautela
Cover photo: Lucy Lencinas

© Luis Alberto Ambroggio
© Long Island Al Dia Inc.

ISBN: 9781974587216

Golden Collection includes authors who are also regular columnists of the digital newspaper, Long Island al Día. www.lialdia.com

Printed in USA- Printed in the United States of America

# THE HISPANIC UNITED STATES

## STATES

(Deeply Woven into the Nation's Tapestry)

LUIS ALBERTO AMBROGGIO

2017

# THE HISPANIC UNITED STATES

## (Deeply Woven into the Nation's Tapestry)

LUIS ALBERTO AMBROGGIO

Translated by Gilbert Grasselly

**2017**

# TABLE OF CONTENTS

## ACKNOWLEDGEMENTS

I wish to thank the following individuals:

Those who have given me the rich, impressive heritage of history, culture and the Spanish language, all of which have been the inspiration for this work. I thank my parents, my family, my roots extending into the past, the present and the future; my teachers, my friends—all the different components of my identity as well as all those who have shaped history, produced statistics and shared the visions and dreams talked about in these pages.

The North American Academy of the Spanish Language, its Director Gerardo Piña-Rosales for his encouragement and good wishes. My colleagues and persistent researchers and editors: Carlos Paldao, librarian and director of the collection of ANLE publications, Rosa Tezanos-Pinto, Director of the Center for Latino Studies at the University of Indiana.

The Director of the publishing house and the New York digital diary *Long Island al Día*, Jesús Ríos, for his promotion of valuable literature and his commitment to spreading the knowledge of Hispanic heritage.

Author Madelín Longoria for her careful, critical review of my manuscript, for her invaluable suggestions and editorial help. To Prof. Carmen Benito Vessel of the University of Maryland for her valued assistance.

The International Society of Writers, Poets and Artists, its founders Manuel Leyva and Elizabeth Leyva and all the institutions, individuals, voices and people at large who have contributed to the reality of Hispanic contributions to the tapestry that is the United States.

# INTRODUCTION

In life, one can set out on the adventure of sharing discoveries. In this book our purpose is to refer to essays, speeches and articles about the Hispanic imprint on the United States as lived and expressed from varying points of view, giving them all a somewhat formal cohesion to exemplify the title of the book. The autobiographic "I" of the militant and enthusiast will show up, as will the unifying "we" It is intended that each name referred to will serve as ample reference and call for a deeper and more thorough inquiry, since the reader's space and patience sometimes make it necessary to include only scant and sometimes insufficient data. There is no focus on or highlighting of this reality by digging into the abundant details of its rich history, but rather a focus on a cultural and literary presence, even though the book's paragraphs are sprinkled with quotes and other data within the range of what is possible to cover, including economic, political and social issues. This realization and efforts being made to reclaim the Hispanic contribution to the making of the United States is bearing fruit as shown by the popularity of the recent Spanish-language work of Ray Suárez:*Latinoamericanos: El legado de 500 años que dió forma a una nación*("Latin Americans: The 500-year legacy that helped form a nation)".[1] Those documents the confluence of Hispanic diversity in the United States; and that of Felipe Fernández-Armesto, **Our America: An Hispanic History of the United States**[2] that also contains poems to illustrate considerations of injustice, immigration, inequalities and the importance of conserving the Spanish language, beginning with an epigraph attributed to Pablo Neruda entitled *Toda la piel de América es nuestra piel*(The entire skin of America is our skin); also an older publication by Matt S. Mier and Feliciano Ribero entitled **Mexican-American/American Mexican - From Conquistadores to Chicanos**[3] and the revised edition of the volume that opened so many eyes with its narrative of

1 - New York, Calebra, Penguin Group, 2013
2 - New York, W. W. Warton and Company, 2014
3 - Hill and Wang, Rev. Sub edition, 1994

500 years of Hispanic history from a unique and dynamic perspective entitled, *Harvest of Empire: a History of Latinos in America*[4] by Juan González, to name just a few of the most successful publications as judged by reader interest. My impetuous, although not exhaustive documentation of this subject matter, will have a complementary role to the above mentioned works by using a somewhat encyclopedic style when touching on certain specific cultural and sociolinguistic matters and literary production—a kind of testimonial sketch which purposely assumes the attraction, anecdotal erudition and approximation—which is neither orderly nor scientific—by adding illustrative surprises in the most unexpected of places without logic or formal academic thoroughness. However, I will not be careless in transcribing long quotes from those who have written about the topics I am covering herein because their expertise, their language and the level of information they share, surpasses my own, bearing in mind the Borgian consolation that life and writing permanently improve on the repetition and rebelliousness of the plagiarist. Although along the pathway of these pages I will allow myself to refer to—but not stop to delve into—the minor details of certain proud historic milestones with abundant (but sometimes not well-known) chronicles of a sacrosanct but peripheral presence. For example, it is worth the trouble to look at the impressive list of the vast areas of the States that make up the United States which were previously territories of Hispanic nations (Spain or Mexico), even after the declaration of independence in 1776—a proven fact of the fundamental Hispanic presence at the very foundation of our nation: Alabama, under Spain until 1873; Arizona, under Spain until 1821 and Mexican territory until 1848; Arkansas, under Spain until 1800 and French territory until 1803; California, under Spain until 1821 and part of Mexico until 1848; Colorado, under Spain until 1821 and part of Mexico until 1848; Florida, under Spain until 1819; Louisiana, under Spain until 1800, and French territory until 1803; Mississippi, under Spain until 1783; Nevada, under Spain until 1821 and part of Mexico until 1848; New Mexico, under Spain until 1821 and part of Mexico until 1848; Texas, under Spain and independent until 1836, and part of Mexico until 1848; Utah, under Spain until 1821 and part of Mexico until 1848. The names of these States and regions point to their Spanish origins as well as those of many of their cities El Paso, Los Angeles, Sacramento, San Antonio (St. Anthony), San Diego (St. James), San Francisco (St. Francis), San José (St. Joseph), San Luis (St. Louis), Santa Fe (Holy Faith), etc.) (Note: A large number of States incorporated into the US in 1848 were part of the Guada-

---

4 - New York Penguin books, revised edition, 2011

lupe-Hidalgo treaty at the end of the Mexican-American war). It has been noted that the name California may have come from a book on chivalry entitled, **Las Sergas de Explandian**(1510) which refers to a fictitious kingdom governed by the shadowy queen **Calafia**. At the present time, in terms of population, the State with the highest percentage of Spanish-speakers is New Mexico (46.3%), followed by Texas (37.3%), California (37.6%), noted in charts presented in the next chapter. The incidence of the Spanish language differs in each State, as does that of the different nationalities that make them up. In the Southwest, Mexicans are a majority; in Florida, Cubans; in the Northeast, Puerto Ricans and Dominicans; in the Washington, DC metropolitan area, Salvadorans. As a matter of fact, one fourth of the Capital area's inhabitants are Spanish-speakers with an impressive history of public figures among them[5]. Specially noteworthy is the fact that in the largest iconic city in the United States—New York—one of every three persons speaks Spanish. Even Manhattan is referred to as **Central Boricua** by Puerto Ricans who celebrate their annual parade in that city. Another example is San Francisco, (once known as *Yerba Buena* - excellent herb), so-labeled by the much-admired Juana Briones. Data such as this will reveal a one-by-one as well as a multifaceted Hispanic presence with an eloquent profusion of parameters in the chapters that follow.

Predictions indicate that by the year 2030, Hispanics will be the most numerous ethnic group in the country, larger even than Anglos and African Americans. This will have an important social impact that is already beginning to be felt, for example, in the large number of Spanish-language news media active in the US today with over 13 daily newspapers, 150 non-daily publications, 125 magazines, some 600 radio stations and 100 TV channels, all in Spanish.

We also point to a recent report by Noam Scheiber in an article he wrote for *The New York Times* on March 8, 2015, which highlighted the fact that the Hispanic labor force is growing faster than that of other groups. These are also the conclusions reached in a study by IHS Economics—a global firm specializing in economic analysis and perspectives, commissioned by **Univisión,** which affirms that an Hispanics labor force is needed in the United States. Its clear conclusion is that with so-called baby boomers about to retire and with the Anglo population growing at a very slow rate,

---

5 - This presence has been thoroughly documented by anthropologist María Sprehn-Malagón and by co-authors Jorge Hernández-Fujigaki and Linda Robinson in their book Latinos in the Washington Metro Area, Mt. Pleasant, Arcadia Publishing Co, 2014; The "Expedition of Juan de Oñate: April 30 1598", Madrid Sotuer, D.L. 1997. And above all, theradio series "Forgotten Spaniards" on esradio. libertaddigital.com and also athttp://www.elespiadigital.com/index.php/informes/8662-de-tristan-de-luna-a-menendez-de-aviles

the contribution of immigrants will be fundamental to assure sustainable economic growth in the United States during the next twenty years. The study states that "The non-Hispanic labor force will not be large enough to compensate for their [the Hispanics] departure." It points out, moreover, that if the Gordian knot they have tied in Washington on the subject of immigration is ever untied, the economy of the United States could grow even more than current forecasts indicate, thanks to the involvement of immigrants, especially Hispanics, who must confront Hispanophobia and the anti-immigration phobia that exists in certain quarters, exemplified by U.S President Donald Trump with his insulting, false and irresponsible racist statements regarding Hispanic immigrants, specifically Mexicans—statements which led to his exclusion from NBC and **Univisión** during the electoral campaign, and his positions have had other negative consequences. Thus far he has not corrected any of them nor has he been duly reproached until recently. His views were followed by statements made by one of his defenders, the equally Hispanophobic Ann Coulter. But all this, instead of intimidating, only strengthens Hispanics' determination to prove the worth of their presence, their history and culture in the United States, stemming about the pride they feel for their identity, in preserving their dignity and affirming their contributions to the fundamental composition of their country—these United States, as promoted by—among other institutions—the **National Hispanic Foundation for the Arts**. Mr. Trump is only mimicking bygone discriminatory shouting like that of the paradoxically named Quakers of Pennsylvania who in 1729 referred to recently-arrived Scottish and Irish immigrants as "a gang of criminals in the making." (It should be noted that the Quakers are a religious group that call themselves "Society of Friends" who oppose all kinds of violence and war) In 1990 statistics revealed the percentages of active participation in the manual labor force of immigrant groups as follows: Mexico 69.7%: Colombia, 73.7%; Nicaragua, 74.7%; Guatemala, 75.7%; El Salvador, 76.3%, surpassing the average for United States citizens in general at 65.3% and that of immigrants groups from other countries such as Canada at 52.1%; Japan, 54.2% and Great Britain, 57.3%.

Almost prophetically, a fact as pointed out by José Antonio Crespo-Francés, the great documentarian of Hispanic influences on the development of the United States[6], in 1775, the Continental Congress, based on a proposal

6 - It is impossible to list all his books and articles on this subject which I have had the pleasure of reading over many years in attachments to emails he sent me or in links that he copied to me and from which I have been taking notes. I have only quoted a partial list of his books and essays: *El legado de Juan de Oñate*, (The legacy of Juan de Oñate), *Los últimos días del Adelantado*. (The last days of the advanced man), Sevilla: Arboleda, 2003, *Don Pedro Menéndez de Áviles: deuda histórica con un soldado ignorado de Felipe II*, (Don Pedro Menéndez de Áviles: an historic debt owed to a soldier ignored by Phillip II), Madrid J. A. Crespo-Francés, 2000. *Juan de Oñate y el Paso del Río Grande: el Camino Real de Tierra Adentro* (Juan de Oñate and the Río Grande Pass: the inland's royal road)

by Thomas Jefferson, interestingly, opposed the use of the sterling pound as the nation's currency and adopted the "Spanish Dollar" (*dólar*), as the country's basic monetary unit. The dollar sign signalizing our currency ($) was taken from columns of the Spanish imperial coat of arms under the motto "*Plus Ultra*". It is of note that today, the signatures appearing on U.S. dollar bills are those of Hispanic women who were United States Treasurers during the years appearing on that paper currency, namely: Romana Acosta Bañuelos (1971-1974), Katherine Dávalos Ortega (1983-1989), Catalina Vázquez Villapando (1989-1993), Rosario Marín (2001-2003), Anna Escobedo Cabral (2004-2009) and Rosa Gumataotao Rios (2009-2015).

Now, once more we will go back in time to José Antonio Crespo-Francés and his devoted task of documenting—with abundant brilliant "points of interest"—in several studies we have cited, referring to the Hispanic presence in all of the different stages of the development of the United States, with a brief survey of this treasured history which makes Hispanics so proud of their heritage beyond what has been called "the aesthetics of colonial violence."[7]

I am referring to actual facts such as the first Hispanic and European marriages, which took place in what would become United States territory, or events like the first celebration of Christmas in the history of the country in 1539 near Tallahassee, the present-day capital of Florida, at which time Hernando de Soto was appointed the first governor of that territory; the establishment of the country's first church in 1560 by Fray Francisco de Pareja at the spot where St. Augustine was later founded (September 8, 1565), by captain general Pedro Menéndez de Áviles— the oldest settlement in the United States—the first Thanksgiving mass having been observed there. Later, the founding of New Mexico (then part of present-day Texas) in 1598 by Juan de Oñate who was a New-World Hispanic from Zacatecas, Mexico, and the first Thanksgiving in the Southwest was celebrated in New Mexico. My Hispanic poet friend Robert L. Girón, born in Nebraska in 1952, recounts this in a poem included in the anthology *Al pie de la Casa Blanca. Poetas hispanos de Washington, DC* (At the Foot of the White House. Hispanic poets of Washington,DC), which I edited with Carlos Parada. In one of his poems he evokes that arrival and that Thanksgiving mass celebrated on April 30, 1598. The poem, "The First Thanksgiving" was written in English, which I

(1598-1998). Edited by Mercedes Junquera, Ministry of Defense, 1998. *La expedición de Juan de Oñate* (The Juan de Oñate expedition)," April 30, 1598. Madrid. Sotuer D. L. 1997, and above all, his series *Españoles olvidados* (forgotten Spaniards) on esradio.libertaddigital.com. and in http://www.elespiadigital.com/index.php/informes/8662-de-tristan-de-luna-a-menendez-de-aviles.
7 - Rabasa, José, (1993) *Aesthetics of Colonial Violence: The Massacre of Acoma* in Gaspar de Villagrá's *History of New Mexico* , College Literature 20 (3) 96-114).

translated into Spanish and contains the following annotation: "It has all been documented. Spain claimed territory in Florida 23 years before the Pilgrims landed in Plymouth. In 1598, the first Thanksgiving in Texas was celebrated the banks of the Rio Grande river." And the first unnamed theatrical work was performed in El Paso, now part of Texas, in 1598. (This information was uncovered by researcher Jorge Huerta). Another play was written in 1599 entitled *"Moros y Cristianos"* (Moors and Christians) by Captain Marcos Farfán de los Godos and Captain Gaspar de Villagrá, both of whom were members of Oñate's War Council.Villagrá was the first solicitor-lawyer in the territory in addition to being the author of a chronicle of the Oñate expedition —the first North American epic entitled *"Historia de la Nuevo México"*("A History of New Mexico,")—a work we will describe in more detail in later chapters.

Juan de Oñate is attributed with another first. In 1598 he founded the second oldest city in the nation, *San Gabriel de los Españoles* (St. Gabriel of the Spaniards), now called Chamita, NM, and in 1605 he founded the oldest capital city of any State,—*Santa Fe* (Holy Faith) NM. In 1602 the first trial was held in San Agustín (St. Augustine, FL), recognized as the oldest city in the U.S. In 1769 Fray (Friar) Junípero Serra was responsible for another historic Hispanic contribution to the future United States by founding the mission of San Diego de Alcalá—the first of 21 similar missions created in California prior to his death in 1784.

There is also some noteworthy information regarding Hispanic contributions to the American Revolution which were crucial to its outcome. We quote from the words of José Antonio Crespo-Francés: "In 1777, Spain offered French general La Fayette the use the Basque Country port of *Pasajes* at Guipúzcoa in northern Spain, as well as the use of the frigate *Victoria*, since France had refused to authorize him to join forces with George Washington's troops. Spain tried to intercede with England on behalf of the American colonies by urging her to grant them their independence. But England turned down this request and in 1779, Spain declared war on England. The English government told Spain that if it would abstain from joining the conflict in their American colony in support of the rebels, it would return the territories of Gibraltar and Florida and would grant her the right to fish in the waters of Newfoundland; Spain, however, rejected this offer. Spanish King Carlos III then offered to give the fledgling American patriot government five million 'hard pesos' and this became its first official currency. This was Spain's initial contribution to the Colonies' war of independence from England." Half of this money would come from the King's nephew, the King of France, through the commercial company known as *Rodríguez Hortález & Co.* During the same year that Spain declared war on Great Britain, Bernardo Gálvez, the Hispanic governor of Louisiana, defeated English forces and seized Baton Rouge and Saumure. Two years later, in 1781, after the Battle of Yorktown, he occupied Mobile and Pensacola after their capitulation, taking Admiral Chester and General Campbell as prisoners as well as 10,000 of their troops, thereby substantially weakening England's military push against Washington's troops."[8]

Following the Colonial Revolution, during the early formation of the United States, several events occurred with important implications for its future development. In 1781 the governor of Spanish Cuba, under orders received from Spain, began organizing in Havana .a collection of donations of silver and gold from among the populace to help General Washington. This effort was assisted by a Spanish agent by the name of Francisco Saavedra Sangronis, about whom José Antonio Crespo-Francés wrote, "From the people in Cuba he was able to collect 1.5 million pesos plus weapons, uniforms, clothes and troops, the latter setting sail aboard twelve boats just prior to the decisive battle of Yorktown which ended the Revolutionary War. After that famous battle, England attempted to reorganize its forces in the Bahamas, but a Spanish fleet there defeated that of British Admiral Maxwell and occupied one of the Bahama Islands.

As a culmination of Spain's contribution to the founding of the United States of America, mention should also be made of the many advantages found by American settlers in the nineteenth century when they began their westward push across the country. There they found roads, came across towns and cities, found guides, saw fields already planted in grains and other agricultural crops, saw large numbers of cattle, horses, pigs and all manner of domestic animals, as well as vineyards, fruit trees, rice fields, etc. Of these, we take special note of horses which the Spaniards brought into the Southwest of the continent, thus significantly changing the lives of the native prairie dwellers to whom this animal was entirely unknown and they obtained whatever horses they wanted by bartering or by attacking the Spaniards or other indigenous tribes who had already acquired these animals—mainly Pawnees and Comanches. They also captured wild horses, as the Spaniards had the habit of allowing pregnant mares to graze freely. And in the vast plains where there were often severe storms and where putting up fences was extremely difficult, so many horses roamed freely and were called *mestenos* by the Spaniards, from which the word "*mustang*" is derived. When white settlers started their move westward many Indian tribes had already been Hispanicized and Christianized. Without this Hispanic influence the "Westward ho" phenomena of the 19th century would have been much more difficult for the new emigrants, much more drawn-out, bloodier, and therefore very different from the situation faced

---

8 - http://hispanismo.org/historia-y-antropologia/17655-la-contribucion-hispanica-al-desarrollo-de-los-estados-unidos-de-america.html

by the mostly white settlers in that part of the country where they came across the mortal remains of Fray Junípero Serra, in Carmel, California."[9]

On this excursion of discovery, I want to share two additional significant pieces of information, without making any comparisons and simply because they refer to a phenomenon of this period that becomes ever wide-ranging and moves in many unsuspected and mostly unknown directions such as, for example, the fact that the famous Civil War Admiral David Farragut was a descendant of a Spaniard by the name of Jordi Farragut (known as George Farragut) from Minorca, Spain. After arriving in North America in 1766, he joined the forces of the American Revolution as a lieutenant in the South Carolina Navy and later in the continental Navy. And the oldest standing synagogue in the United States (the Touro Synagogue) in the colony of Newport in Rhode Island, was underwritten by an 18th century Iberian Jewish convert by the name of Duarte (or Aarón) López. After his arrival in the United States he turned to his religious roots and donated this synagogue to the Yeshuat Israel Congregation which has been in use there since as early as 1658, later welcoming immigrant members from the Caribbean at which time it became known as the Mordechai Campanal Synagogue. In 1677, Moisés Israel Pacheco and others bought land to create a Jewish cemetery in that community. The names of two of the other founding members—also Spanish-Iberians—were Simón Méndez and Abrahán Burgos.

Data such as this serves to illustrate the rich multifaceted Hispanic threads in the tapestry of these United States which will be documented throughout these pages without any pretense of being complete or definitive since, from its very outset, this is an evolving and developing nation whose reality and full story—over these last 500 years—would fill countless volumes. My purpose in writing this book is to honor this country's Hispanic-American heritage, to enlighten, to stimulate readers, potential researchers and initiators to make the Hispanic presence known, in the hope that it may be appreciated, appropriately integrated into the meaning of this country in its past, present and future formation, in order to update history books, correct misperceptions and the Spanish language and Hispanic culture be seen as integral to this process, their presence be made known, and museums be built alongside others to display another of the cultures that make up this great nation.

---

9 - http://hispanismo.org/historia-y-antropologia/17655-la-contribucion-hispanica-al-desarrollo-de-los-estados-unidos-de-america.html

## Clarifications on the terminology used in this book.[10]

The author's intention is not to come up with dogmatic explanations, but rather to validate predilections and preferences on issues (like all good ones) that arouse passions with feelings about the varied connotations of the perennial search for identity. In the pages of this book, I always refer to Spanish and Hispanic culture, rather than Castilian and Latino culture he tries to explain his positions through interpretations which he hopes will illuminate polemics and justify choices in the context of the Hispanic threads running through the tapestry that is the United States of America by taking the position of José Martí when he referred to the *hispanoamericanos de Norteamérica* (the "Hispanic-Americans of North America) and not the English-speakers of North America.

To paraphrase Albert Camus, if language is one's homeland, I would adhere to the universality of Spanish as expressed by Pablo Neruda in in his poem **Confieso que he vivido** (I confess, I have lived): He wrote: "What a good language, mine; what a good language, inherited from the grim *conquistadores*... the language. In the end, we lost... in the end, we won... They hauled the gold away and left us with gold ... They took it all and left it all... They left us with the words."

But why do I refer to the 'Spanish language' and not 'Castilian'? It is my choice, my preference gleaned from the vicissitudes of politics and history. While many consider these two terms as synonymous and some insist that we refer to the language as Castilian, well, in my home, in my school, in the country of my childhood, it was always called Spanish—the language handed down to us by the country we would refer to as *"our motherland"*— the language of Spain as a nation—a nation that also contains other languages like Galician, Catalan and Basque. An anonymous voice once stated: "The language we use to communicate our values is Spanish. It is thus called not because throughout Spain there is only one language common to all its inhabitants, since there are several others, but rather because in most of Spain it is the language that is most used." Gregorio Mayans y Siscar of Valencia noted in 1737 in his book **Orígenes de la lengua española** (origins of the Spanish Language): "The term 'Spanish language' I understand to mean the language that all Spaniards speak when we want to perfectly understand one another."

And that is the language they bequeathed to all Hispanics, and it is the one they used as they discovered and conquered the New World—from

---

10     With some modifications I include herein a translation of an article appearing in the newspaper *Long Island al Día* in its August 4, 2012 edition: ¿Hispano, Latino, Español o Castellano? (Hispanic, Latino, Spanish or Spaniard?)

Alaska to Patagonia; but not only did they use the language of Castile, but also that of León and Aragón. Parenthetically, the gaucho Spanish (of Argentina and Uruguay) has many Andalusian features and it is not difficult when talking to, say, a Canary Islander to see the similarities of his speech with that of Cubans or Venezuelans, based on the expressions used, the manner of speaking and the accent.

So, in my internal dialogue, by avoiding controversy and ambiguity, I choose to refer to the language Hispanics use in this country as U.S. Spanish— Spanish with an international and Pan-American aura that unites Hispanics beyond hybridizing, beyond dialects, beyond cultural influences, beyond manners of speaking and beyond regional socio-economic influences—all of which enrich it and distinguish it in a constant dynamic sociolinguistic evolution of inter-community dialogue.

I consider such preference to be appropriate based on several arguments (which, of course, can always be challenged). The term 'Spanish' is the preference of Spanish Language Academies and their Association (ASALE). In fact, the definition of *'español'* (i.e. Spanish) in the **Diccionario Panhispánico de Dudas** (Pan-Hispanic dictionary of doubts), is acknowledged by the Association of Spanish Language Academies, confirming the term as designating the common language of Spain and of many nations in the American continent, which is also spoken as a main tongue in other parts of the world; but it accepts both designations (Castilian and Spanish) as valid.

Now a days the debate over which of these two is more appropriate has ended. The term **Spanish** has become the more suitable one because it lacks ambiguity, as it refers to the language spoken today by more than four hundred million people. It is also the designation that is used internationally (including *espagnol*, *Spanisch*, *spagnolo*, etc.). So, even though 'Castilian' is synonymous with 'Spanish', it is preferable to reserve the former term to refer to the Romance dialect born in the Kingdom of Castile during the Middle Ages, or to the dialect spoken today in that region. In Spain, the word *castellano* (Castilian) is also used when referring to the common language of the Spanish nation in relation to the other official languages of its respective autonomous territories such as Catalan, Galician and Basque.

However, there are other voices, such as that of Andrés Bello, the renowned Venezuelan linguist and writer, who has a different opinion, expressed in his main work **Gramática de la lengua castellana** (Grammar of the Castilian language), who explains in preliminary notes (3b); "It is designated the Castilian language (less appropriately, Spanish) which is spoken in Castile and which, along with the Castilian coat of arms and laws, journeyed to America, and is now the common language of the Spanish-American nations". I do not share this point of view.

In the following countries this common language is identified as **castellano** (Castilian): Bolivia, Colombia, Chile, Ecuador, El Salvador, Paraguay, Peru, Venezuela and Spain. But now, however, after the enactment of the Constitution of 1978, in the following countries the language is referred to as **español**(Spanish): They are Cuba, Guatemala, Honduras, Nicaragua, Panama, Costa Rica, Equatorial Guinea, the Dominican Republic, Argentina, Puerto Rico and Mexico, even though not officially declared as such. In the United States official documents use the term 'Spanish' (*español*), when referring to the language and not 'Castilian'.

In general, countries, governmental and educational institutions as well as language academies, refer to this language which is common to Spain and Latin America (including the U.S.), as 'Spanish', preferring to apply the term 'Castilian', as stated earlier, to the native romantic dialect of the Kingdoms of Castile, León and Aragón during the Middle ages, or as currently spoken in those regions of Spain, as was pointed out in a preceding paragraph.

Therefore I stand firm on my preference for the term 'Spanish' in referring to the language that connects all Spanish-speakers with their history, cultures, outstanding literature, as the one that unites them and with which they identify continent-wide and in other continents.

After the above-stated, a logical, quick and seemingly easy conclusion would be, "If I speak Spanish then I am Hispanic." Or, conversely, "Why do they call me 'Latino'? I don't speak Latin." In this debate, emotions come into play based on people's experiences in practically all civilizations with their varied histories of conquest and re-conquest, some not as calamitous as others.

The academic world has dispassionately used the classifications created by certain literary critics, which are arbitrary as are all such classifications—these in particular, (without delving any deeper into the controversial nomenclature), when referring to writers as 'Hispanic' if they are of Hispanic origin, live in the United States and have chosen to write in Spanish, and as 'Latinos' if they are Hispanic in origin but prefer to write in English. I make such a case in a study published prior to the previously-mentioned anthology. It is entitled *Al pie de la Casa Blanca. Poetas hispanos de Washington, DC* (At the foot of the White House. Hispanic poets in Washington, DC), without favoring one term over the other, and being aware of repercussions and socio-political maneuvering, I uphold the term

'Spanish' and not 'Latino", because of the imperialist French origin of the word 'Latino'—a term which is often-preferred and perhaps more popular and, paradoxically, is used by some with pride and by others in a derogatory way.

By way of illustration, I quote from a recently-published report by the Pew Hispanic Center on the subject of identity which reports that 51 percent of individual Hispanics identify themselves by referring to their countries of origin and 24 percent use either the term 'Hispanic' or 'Latino'. But when it comes to choosing between these two terms, respondents choose the former by a margin of 2 to 1. (However, I have noticed a growing popularity and preference for the term 'Latino' in literature, academia and among certain media and political groups).

Even with a distinguished poet like Sandra Cisneros with her poem *Yo soy Latina* (I am Latin)and others who uncritically endorse the term 'Latino', which they presume refers to their identity, I still prefer 'Hispanic' because, despite the traumatic episode of the Conquest and acknowledging that historic misadventure, I disagree with those who try to eliminate the reality of Hispanic identity by replacing it with 'Latino'. (Whose 'Latinness'?—that of the Romans? the French?). Indeed the concept of Latino arises from the phrase 'Latin America' created in the nineteenth century by French sociologist Michel Chevalier (1806-1879) who was an advocate of French imperialism in the American continent. He was followed in 1861 by L. M. Tisserand, who called *"L'Amerique Latine"* the territories which were formally known as South America or the West Indies. This term—'Latin America'—created by Chevalier and used by Tisserand sought to justify French imperialistic aims, which materialized with the intervention of Napoleon III in Mexico (1861 -1867) and the intrusion of Emperor Maximilian. Although this foreign Emperor in Mexico turned out to be more liberal than expected and supported the rescue and promotion of native cultures, the adoption of the term 'Latino' was a ruse used by French imperialists to justify a kind of Latin "brotherhood" identity with the subjects they were trying to conquer—a curious kind of verbal justification of their efforts to make additional conquests.

In the United States I have noticed a derogatory tone when referring to someone as "Latino" or Latin as opposed to the pride Hispanics feel about their history, culture and language with all their deficiencies, which is the reason why I identify myself as Hispanic, and use this term in identifying those who in some way because of their language, history or culture, have been molded in an Hispanic context, whether they be of European extraction, of mixed race, Amerindians, African Americans, or of other backgrounds. Incidentally, it should be pointed out that Mexican, Central

American and South American indigenous immigrant populations reject being grouped as "Latinos". I concur with the opinion of Duard Bradshaw, the Panamanian president of the Hispanic National Bar Association who writes: "I'm going to tell you why I like the word *Hispano*. If we say *Latino*, we are excluding the Iberian Peninsula and Spanish nationals. The Iberian Peninsula is where we [Hispanics] come from; we all contain some of those threads that originate in Spain."

Above all, I prefer the term *Hispano* because it makes us more of a community, a socio-political force and a demographic presence with broad, unconventional connotations. Additionally, it enhances our ability to distinguish a large and growing U.S. population that is beginning to be respected for its ability to build on a rich history and culture of which Hispanics are proud and can be acknowledged by the white or Anglo majority, not simply based on the broad distinction between white northern Europeans versus the denizens of the Latin countries to their south.

To conclude these musings on my personal preferences regarding the matter of nomenclature, I agree with conclusions arrived at by Jorge J.E. García as stated in his book *Hispanic/Latino Identity ~ A Philophical Perspective*[11]. After analyzing these terms and concepts "Hispanic" and "Latino" from four broad and different approaches, that is, empirical, political-sociological, logical and pragmatic, he highlights his strategic preference for the term "Hispanic" as the identifier of this group because it is anchored in a network of historical connections which has been a constant for centuries including up to the present. Additionally he identifies Hispanics as a group, differentiating them very proudly and in a positive way beyond regional or national divisions without any need to either practice or encourage discrimination. Throughout this book, the reader will deepen his/her own preference and so I feel no need to apologize for writing passionately and sharing my simple assumptions and preferences regarding what I believe identifies Hispanics while, at the same time, showing sensitivity to those who choose alternative designations based on their sentimental rationale. In any case, without defending any nationalistic, political or institutional interest, nothing detracts from the **Hispanic Threads in the Tapestry of the United States** since everything else is nuance.

**Increasingly, we will see the Hispanic threads that are woven into the tapestry called the United States.**

Finally, we conclude this introduction with some data of interest by putting reliable recent numbers to these **Hispanic threads in the tapestry that is the United States**. It has been predicted that by the year 2050 the United

---

11 - Malden, MA: Blackwell Publishers, 2000

States—currently the second most populous Spanish-speaking country in the world—will become the most populous. Currently, 9 out of 10 people in the U.S. who are parents or plan to be parents want their children to learn Spanish in addition to English. 73.9% of Hispanics over 5 years of age speak mostly Spanish at home. The purchasing power of the current 54 to 57 million Hispanics in the country has increased exponentially. There are 11 million registered Hispanic voters. Optimism regarding the future use of the Spanish language and identification with Hispanic culture is based on figures showing this projection: At the time of this writing, 60% of U.S. Hispanics are under 35 years of age, 75% are under age 45, and their average age is 28 (for the entire U.S. population it is 37). A new perspective of a nation that prides itself on being a "melting pot" in which *Hispanidad*—as we will see in Chapter IV—is a key component of its national character as captured in the visionary appreciations of the iconic American poet, Walt Whitman.

# CHAPTER I

## THE INCIDENCE OF THE SPANISH LANGUAGE IN THE UNITED STATES

EL CAPITAN GASPAR DE VILLAGRA. DE EDD. 55. AÑOS.

GASPAR DE VILLAGRA

If Hispanics hope to proclaim an "Hispanic United States", one of their efforts and objectives must be to have pride in their ancestry and heritage. When talking on this subject I begin by referring to the incidence of the Spanish language in and of the United States as a basic component of the nation and part of a multifaceted effort to protect and value the language, Hispanic culture and its place in the country's history that identifies them as a community and enrichens all of us as a nation. For this I use some of the updated information detailed in the pioneering document *La Enciclopedia del Español de los Estados Unidos*[12] (The Encyclopedia of the Spanish Language of the United States), to which I had the honor of collaborating with three essays

## History

To understand the true incidence of the Spanish Language in the United States it is important to remember and be aware of the Hispanic aspect of the history the country going as far back as the 16th century—long before the arrival of the Pilgrims. While this early presence is based on occasional forays, like Ponce de León's incursions into Florida in 1512-13, which marks the beginning of Hispanic history in this land, I often dwell on the fact that white Anglo historians—even the most recent ones—in writing their histories of the United States, have tried to ignore and continue to ignore the Hispanic presence. Even in the case of Howard Zinn in his best-selling "*A People's history of the United States*"[13] in which Spanish settlements go unacknowledged and he only highlights

---

12 - Humberto López Morales (coordinator), *La Enciclopedia del Español en los Estados Unidos*, (Encyclopedia of Spanish in the U.S.) Madrid, Instituto Cervantes, Santillana 2008. (13) New York. Harper Perennial Modern Classics, 2005.
13 - New York: Harper Perennial Modern Classics, 2005.

the negative aspects of the conquerors Colon, Cortez and Pizarro whose incursions did not directly affect the United States. It should be noted that as early as 1513, there were Spanish incursions into southern Florida and northward up to what would later be known as New England, and into the west as far as Texas. In the west, they went from California as far as Alaska and made forays from the Gulf Coast to distant areas in what is now Iowa, the Dakotas and Nebraska.

These expeditions resulted in Hispanic settlements in many places which today are part of U.S. territory. In 1526, Lucas Vásquez de Ayllón founded the colony of San Miguel de Gualdape (erroneously referred to by some as Guadalupe) in the Carolinas. Two years later, in 1528, Pánfilo de Narváez disembarked near Tampa and explored the Floridian peninsula. Later, in 1539, Fray (Friar) Marcos de Niza accompanied by his black slave, Estebanillo, began an exploratory expedition into what is now New Mexico and Arizona. In that same year, 1539, Hernando de Soto was appointed the first Governor of Florida and from that year on until 1543 he explored not only Florida, but also territories in present-day Georgia, Arkansas, Mississippi, Alabama, Louisiana, and northeast Texas. He discovered the Mississippi River and was buried near its banks upon his death. In 1540 Francisco Vázquez de Coronado and Fray Marcos de Niza reached what has been called the imaginary Seven Cities with roofs of gold—a description which some scholars attribute to these explorers who, so described it because of the tremendous visual impact of first seeing and discovering, the Grand Canyon. Three years later, in 1543, Juan Rodríguez Carrillo explored the Oregon coastline, and his pilot, Ferrelo, reached the 44th parallel in what is present-day Washington State. In 1559-1561, Menéndez Aviles and Tristan de Luna Arellano lay claim to Florida—an historic fact also acknowledged by the dominant culture as duly noted in the Florida Historical Society's 1928 edition of "The Luna Papers"published that same year by Herbert Ingram Priestly. In 1561 the Axacan Jesuit missions were founded in Virginia and in 1565 Franciscan missions were established in Georgia, the same year that Menéndez de Áviles founded St. Augustine Florida, and in 1570 the Chesapeake missions. In 1598, during one of Oñate's exploratory campaigns, the town of San Juan was foundedin New Mexico; it was relocated years later and re-baptized Santa Fe (Holy Faith). The El Paso mission was founded in 1682 as well as another one in 1690 in east Texas. All this foundational activity continued into the 18th century. In 1718, the famous San Antonio mission was founded in Texas and, years later, in 1763 the entire territory of Louisiana was under the Spanish crown. Starting at that time, the colonization of California began with a firm footing led by Portola and Fray Junípero Sierra. This Hispanic political presence changed colors after 1810, and in 1821 the Cession Treaty was implemented whereby Florida became a part of the young United States, and the last Spanish Governor of California made his exit. Outside the continent, the sad—and still not totally resolved—Puerto Rican episode of 1898 took place. In spite of these events, the Hispanic imprint on the evolution of the U.S. is clearly visible in its history, culture and language, even though efforts have been made to ignore or erase it, and it is a presence that is today being rescued, and is thriving. Hispanics take pride in their contribution in a truly dynamic way, as acknowledged and proclaimed by Paz Soldán and Alberto Fuguet: "One cannot speak of Latin America without including the United States."[14]

As we will see in more detail in in Chapter 3, one of the founding fathers of the United States, the visionary Thomas Jefferson, spoke of the importance of Spanish in 1787 when he wrote the following to his nephew, Peter Carr, *"Bestow great attention on Spanish and endeavor to acquire an accurate knowledge of it. Our future connections with Spain and Spanish America will render the language a valuable acquisition. The ancient history of that part of America, too, is written in that language."*

## Demographics

Today the population of Hispanic origin in the United States totals 54.1 million people, making up over 17% of the total population of the country, according to the 2013 census. (The Center for Disease Control [CDC]and some others put the figure at 57 million). There are 16 states that have a million or more Hispanic citizens: (Arizona, California, Colorado, Florida, Georgia, Illinois, Massachusetts, Nevada, New Jersey, New Mexico, New York, North Carolina, Pennsylvania, Texas, Virginia and Washington) and 21 in which Hispanics constitute the largest minority (therefore, to the above-named states we now add Connecticut, Idaho, Iowa, Kansas, Nebraska, New Hampshire, Oregon, Rhode Island, Utah, Vermont, and Wyoming). Hispanics have become the largest group of immigrants in the country, ahead of the African-American and Asian populations. One of every four children born in the United States is of Hispanic origin and all the indices show this trend to be growing. It is of note that between July 1[th], 2005 and July 1[th] 2006 Hispanics

---

14      *Se habla español: voces latinas en USA* (Spanish is spoken: Latin voices in the U.S.), Alfaguara, 2001, p. 19.

accounted for almost half (1.4 million) of the total population growth figure of 2.9 million. Today it is estimated to be the fastest growing group in the country (accounting for 78% of all births). It is estimated that each year some 800,000 young Hispanics turn 18. As noted earlier, the youth among the Hispanic population, the high birth rate and a growing presence in the educational and employment systems, outline a future in which speakers of the Spanish language will assume a crucial role: By the year 2050 the US Hispanic population is expected to exceed 132 million, and according to the Census Bureau estimates will make up 30% of the total population of the United States. The current distribution of the Hispanic population in the United States is approximately 43% in the West, 33% in the South, 15% in the Northeast and 9% in the Midwest, with Mexicans[15] being the leading group, followed by Puerto Ricans, Cubans and, in recent decades, Dominicans, Salvadorans and other Central and South American countries; Spaniards are a growing minority in this population. It should be noted that in 2011 although more than half of this population speaks English fluently, about 40 million U.S. residents 5 years of age or older used Spanish at home.(That is, 76% of the Hispanic population age 5 or older), with this figure increasing 117% since 1990 when only 17.3 million were doing this. This means that those who speak Spanish at home amount to at least 12.9 % of U.S. residents 5 years of age or older; other factors may increase this percentage.

In a Pew Hispanic Center 2011 publication, the following table showed the statistical data of the U.S. States showing the highest percentage of Hispanic population growth between the years 2000 and 2010: South Carolina (148%), Alabama (145%), Tennessee (134% ), Kentucky (122%), Arkansas (114%), North Carolina (111%), Maryland (106%), Mississippi (106%), South Dakota (103%), Delaware (96%), Georgia (96%), Virginia (92%). According to this Pew Hispanic Center publication, the following States had the largest Hispanic populations, (shown in millions) for the year 2011: California (14,014), Texas (9,461), Florida (4,224), New York (3,417), Illinois ( 2,029), Arizona (1,895), New Jersey (1,555), Colorado (1039). New Mexico (953), Georgia (854), North Carolina (800), Washington (756). The following is a list of the States showing the percentage of their Hispanic populations: New Mexico (46.3%), Texas (37.6%), California (37.6%), Arizona (29.6), Nevada (26 , 5%), Florida (22.5%), Colorado (20.7%), New Jersey (17.7%), New York (17.6%), Illinois (15.8%), Connecticut (13 , 4%), Utah (13%).

This significant demographic presence, in addition to the growing interest in learning Spanish and having it taught in schools, places Spanish as the

---

15 - In written Spanish, Mexico and Mexican can also be spelled *Méjico* and *mejicano* (no initial capital letter).

second most spoken language in the United States. As it is spoken in the United States, Spanish has the linguistic, grammatical and lexicographical components of all its countries of origin, as well as Creole, indigenous and Anglo (Spanglish) influences plus that of the source language (Castilian, Andalusian, Canarian) with a dialectology replete with nuances and differentiable, demonstrable sociolinguistic characteristics of a popular, home-grown well-spoken language variations of hereditary Spanish. The United States and is the second-largest Spanish-speaking country in the world, with more speakers than Spain, Colombia and Argentina. In Arizona, California, New Mexico and Texas (and I should add the metropolitan area of the U.S. Capital, Washington DC.), one of every four or five people speaks Spanish. In this regard I cite an anecdote from my family album:

> In 1984, I received a call from the Director of the Spring Hill elementary school where my son, Xavier, was a student (then 5 years old; today, a doctor in Biophysics) because he had gotten into a fight with another student. Upon questioning him at home, this was our exchange: "Yes, Dad I fought with another kid because he called me a *Mexican* and I told him no, that I was a *Virginian*. But he insisted on calling me a *Mexican*. Thus I got angry and punched him and they took me to the principal's office."Then he turned to me with an expression on his face that I still remember, asking me, "But, Dad, what is a*Mexican?*" I concluded at that moment that we in Virginia also speak Spanish. Jefferson demands it of us.

## Culture, language, identity, literature and other arts

The Spanish language and Hispanic-U.S. (or U.S. Hispanic) culture is thriving in its diverse forms of expression—i.e. literature, music, arts, theater, cinema, with a history going back to the Sixteenth Century colonial period, even though, I repeat, we dislike the so called "aesthetics of colonial violence." Allow me here to use the genre of poetry, with which I am more familiar, to illustrate this Hispanic presence in the country's language, history, culture, and identity.I must refer the reader to chapter V which expands on literature—especially poetry—written in Spanish in the United States from 1549 to the present, impossible to summarize here but we will take a bird's eye view of the six poetic groups that make it up, namely,Colonial, Mexican-American, continental Puerto Rican, the Cuban-American poetry of the Spanish exiles, South American, Central American, Spanish Caribbean, and current movements, and we will add references to works in the narrative genre and in prose, such as novels and other literary genres, including essays and theater.

As you will see, the historical richness and the universal literary value of the Spanish language in the United States, will be demonstrated. The same detailed analysis has been made in *La Enciclopedia del Español en los Estados Unidos* (The Encyclopedia of Spanish in the United States) previously cited with genres of fiction and essays by Mexicans, Central Americans, Cubans, Dominicans, South Americans and Spaniards); drama (Chicano theater, Puerto Rican, Cuban, Hispanic theaters in general), mentioning publications, plays and shows produced by all Hispanic sectors, so numerous that they preclude detailed mention in this limited space, although we will attempt to present this in Chapter V. Here is a sampling here of some names: Tomás Eloy Martínez, Gioconda Belli, Isabel Allende, among the internationally recognized authors who decided to write in Spanish from the United States and Hispanic Pulitzer prizewinner Oscar Hijuelos and Junot Díaz who wrote their novels in English, although with clear Hispanic flavor, which I expand upon in the last chapter. More books are appearing specifically about the idiosyncrasies of the Spanish language as used in the United States, such as John M. Lipski's *El español de América* (Spanish in the Americas[16], that of Carmen Silva-Corvalán, *Sociolingüística y pragmática del español* (Spanish-language Sociolinguistics and Pragmatics[17], and Ángel López García-Molina's *El español de Estados Unidos y el problema de la norma lingüística* (The Spanish language in the United States and the problem of linguistic norms[18], *El español en los Estados Unidos: E Pluribus Unum? Enfoques Multidisciplinarios* (Spanish in the United States: E Pluribus Unum? Multi-disciplinary approaches) – A collection of Linguistic Studies by Domnita Dumitrescu.[19]Even one with a somewhat nasty title except for the irony *Smart Spanish for t ... s (tontos tachados)*[branded, fools]*Americanos*[20]by Eleanor Hamer and Fernando Diez de Urdanivia, which reminded me the experience of my poet laureate friend Robert Pinsky whom I reincarnated in Spanish when I compiled his selected poems in the bilingual edition of *Ginza Samba*[21]including his poem entitled (in Spanish)*"El burro es un animal"*(the donkey is an animal)in which he recounts angrily, with sarcasm and poetic passion a school experience: "We, the boys' Class Fools couldn't enroll in French, so instead we learned the difference between the verbs *ser*and *estar* (to be)... /. Is it a long story? The language of Cervantes and Gongora was /right for us, fools that we are. There are two kinds of *to be*."(Pp.138-141).

---

16 - Madrid: Cátedra, 1996.
17 - Washington, DC, Georgetown University Press, 2001.
18 - New York: North American Academy of the Spanish Language, 2014.
19 - New York: North American Academy of the Spanish Language, 2013.New York.
20 - Skyhorse Publishing, 2012.
21 - Madrid / Mexico: *Vaso Roto Ediciones*, 2014.

It is also important to point out that in the publishing industry in the United States, one showing sustained growth is the production of books written in Spanish which in recent years has had an unprecedented increase in volume.Sales of books in Spanish total over $350 million. This figure exceeds Bible sales and competes with the sale of electronic books in English. This increase in the reading of Spanish material in the United States puts it in second place in the importing of books from Spain in the Americas, according to statistics gathered in 2008.To this we must add the abundance of both popular and literary magazines and/or specialized publications in Spanish and the increasing activity of cultural institutions in the United States that carry out their activities in Spanish. For more details on this and the other so-called "industries" I refer to the Working Paper entitled *Los latinos y las industrias culturales en español en Estados Unidos*(Latinos and cultural activities in Spanish in the United States) by Jéssica Retis and Ángel Badillo, published in January 2015 by the Elcano Royal Institute.[22]

**In the field of music** one always hears of the Latin Grammy Awards held annually in Los Angeles and the success that artists such as Alejandro Sanz, Selena, Shakira, Ricky Martin, Julio and Enrique Iglesias, Juan Luis Guerra and Carlos Santana, have achieved in United States—which also include such well-known figures as Antonio Machin, Celia Cruz, etc., to which we add the "Latino/Hispanic boom" that took place in Hollywood in the late twentieth and early twenty-first century. Also there is a strong Hispanic presence in the areas of dance, performances and classical music with a notable presence in the last decade of the twentieth and the early twenty-first century. Suffice it to point out figures like tenor opera singer Plácido Domingo, who was conductor and artistic director of the Los Angeles Opera and director of the Washington Philharmonic Orchestra and the National Opera beginning in 1986.Then there is Gustavo Dudamel of Venezuela who, according to National Geographic magazine, has rejuvenated classical music. There are dancers and directors of dance companies such as the Russian-Hispanic Maya Plisetskaya, the Argentine U.S. resident, Paloma Herrera of the American Ballet Theatre; Julio Bocca, Jose Limón, Ángel Corella; Antonio Carmena and Gonzalo García (New York Ballet); Jaime García Castilla; Rubén Martin and Clara Blanco (San Francisco Ballet); Yuri Yanowski (Boston Ballet); Sergio Torrado who interpreted Rothbart in the movie "Black Swan" (Pennsylvania Ballet) and many others (names that repeat themselves as a refrain). It is no longer necessary to talk of the fame of many actors and directors of Hispanic origin in the U.S. film industry (for example, Benicio del Toro, Salma Hayek, Pe-

22 - In:http://www.realinstitutoelcano.org/wps/wcm/connect/cca34480471bd3ab9079ba12dd3b-68de/DT01-2015-Retis-Badillo-latinos-industrias-culturales-en-espanol-en-EEUU.pdf?MOD=A-JPERES&CACHEID=cca34 480471bd3ab9079ba12dd3b68de

dro Almodóvar, etc. . .), but rather to note how "Spanish is becoming an important part of medium and high budget productions," as my friend Joaquín Badajoz points out in an article referring to the bigger picture which he wrote with Roberto Fandiño entitled, "Spanish Cinema in the United States."[23] We will expand a little on this topic at the end of this excursion.

**Other impacted areas: non-governmental institutions, government and legislation, education, the media and participation in the commercial sector.**

**Non-governmental institutions, government and legislation:** Among the non-governmental institutions I am referring to are religions and churches, which in addition to their historical role, have been and remain the main channel for integrating immigrants into the social, cultural and political life of the United States. They have created centers for religious activity, using Spanish in their ceremonies such as Mass and other services as a liturgical language, in songs, and in all other activities in serving their parishioners and congregations. Also in the fields of health, medicine, and hospital care, Spanish is widespread, having the support of numerous Hispanic associations. My two daughters-in-law have learned Spanish— one of them through her gynecological practice in hospitals in Virginia and Washington DC and the other in her work as a professor. Also services available to citizens provide for Spanish translation and interpreting to assist people, without discrimination. There are 64 Federal agencies or organizations that offer such assistance in Spanish, each with their own particular title, running the gamut from the Courts, the Department of State to the Food and Drug Administration (FDA). All can be found on the Internet. In terms of the law it is of note, as pointed out by Leonel Antonio de la Cuesta, that "Federal legislation, in some cases, allows for the foreign language publication of certain documents as well as information relating to the different activities of said organizations, but this is not done systematically ... (hence) ... in the constitutional legislation of the Federated States, thirty proclaim English as their official language and twenty do not address this issue, Hawaii being the only state that officially promotes bilingualism. Spanish is *de facto* the second most-spoken language in the United States ... (even though) for it to be proclaimed as such or for it to become co-official in relevant legal texts is JUST a future possibility."[24] We should clarify that it is commonly assumed that New Mexico is a declared

---

23 - "Spanish-language Cinema in the United States," in "The Encyclopedia of Spanish in the United States", pp. 867-911.

24 - "The Spanish Language and US law" in "The Encyclopedia of Spanish in the United States", p. 548

bilingual state given that Spanish and English are its "official" languages. But in reality its original 1912 Constitution decreed a bilingual government without reference to an official language (or languages). Its Constitution declared that during the following twenty years, all laws adopted by the Legislature must be made known in both languages. Today many legal documents are required to be issued in both English and Spanish. Bill Clinton once said that he hoped he would be the last U.S.President who did not know Spanish.

With regard to the **teaching** of the Spanish language, the following considerations and data should be borne in mind. Linguistic studies attempting to evaluate the quantity and quality of the teaching of Spanish in the United States reveal the need to address the concern of unifying the language's usage. This needs to be addressed in order to consider the future of the Spanish language in relation to its dissemination, quality and presence in the public sector. Paradoxically, in this regard, analyses reveal an often-times restricted use of Spanish, limited to families and neighborhoods. On the one hand, there is resistance to it in the labor force and in educational and cultural circles. On the other, there is a marked growth of interest in the language and in promoting its use in all these areas in spite of bans and campaigns against it. There are two items of note deserving special attention: 1) the classification of Spanish as a foreign language (to the detriment of bilingual education), and 2) its privileged position in secondary education compared to the study of other languages. The debate over bilingual education in the United States took center stage in the second half of the Twentieth Century with the increasing number of immigrants, the struggle for civil rights, and pressure from certain Spanish-speaking populations.

The dominance of a monolingual policy in defense of "one language for one country" faces the problem of integrating students who do not know English and the current need for multilingualism, as well as the need for communication within and with communities where the Hispanic presence is predominant. Therefore, in response to the position of English first we could, in any case, look to transitional bilingual education oriented toward its acquisition (see the Bilingual Education Act of 1968) and at the same time offer an array of courses for learning Spanish, to confirm what I told them in 1968 when I served on the White House Committee for the Development of the Hispanic community and they insisted that I should-speak English, I countered, "Better still, you should learn Spanish." Now, those members who are still living, when they see me tell me, "Luis, you were right!"

Indeed, learning Spanish speaks to a reality, as it is the most studied foreign language in the United States. Statistics reveal that in lower secondary schools, it accounts for 78% of class enrollments, followed distantly by French (28.8%) and German (5.4%). Spanish continues to be the preferred foreign language in United States universities. The number of students far exceeds that of other languages. In 2006 there were more than 820,000 students of Spanish in universities, compared with just over 200,000 for French and 90,000 for German. In total, including all the institutions for public and private education, there are about 6 million Spanish-language students. Interest in the language continues to grow with an estimated increase of 60% over the next few years. This growing interest is reflected in the number of centers where Spanish is taught in the United States. In addition to significant university centers for the study of Spanish and Latin American literature and the number of distinguished Hispanic scholars in the United States, I highlight here some of the institutions that promote Spanish in the U.S., beginning with the North American Academy of the Spanish Language , then The Cervantes Institute, The Hispanic language Association, The Hispanic Society, The Spanish Institute, the Spanish Cultural Center of Miami, The National Hispanic Cultural Center in Albuquerque, The Observatory of the Spanish language and Hispanic Cultures in the United States at Harvard University, The Association of Hispanic Graduates and Doctors in the United States (ALDEEU), The Circle of Ibero-American Writers and Poets (CEPI), the United States Hispanic Cultural Foundation, The International Hispanic Association of Poets and Writers (AIPEH), The Hispanic-American Association of Teachers of Spanish and Portuguese (AATSP), The Modern Language Association (MLA), The Hispanic Division of the Library of Congress, among other organizations.

The following statistics show the educational level of Hispanics in the United States: According to figures from 2009, 62% of Hispanics 25 years or older have gotten a secondary education, while 14% (more than 4 million) have a Bachelor's degree or higher of whom about one million have advanced Masters Doctorates or other professional degrees. In 2008, 12% of college students and 20% of all primary and secondary school students were Hispanic. Between 2009 and 2010, Hispanic enrollments at the university level amounted to 349,000 students compared to an increase of 88,000 for African Americans and 43,000 for Asians while there were 320,000 fewer non-Hispanic white enrollments. These figures reflect the reality and can be seen as goals to reach for.

**The mass media:**The media and cultural activities best reflect the impact of Hispanics and the Spanish language in the United States, as was pointed out in the introduction: -There is a steady increase in the use of Spanish in the press, in national and international radio stations and their expanding networks. Then there is the influence and social impact of TV channels and the use of the Internet; the proliferation of a cultural industry that includes the production of narratives and essays as well as magazines and literary publications, cinema, theater, music, etc. Currently one can listen to a large number of Spanish-language radio stations and watch Spanish TV programs anywhere in the United States and can find newspapers in Spanish in every corner of the country. This quantitative growth is linked to improvement in the quality of these publications—a process parallel to the increase in income and knowledge of the Hispanic population. Some examples are the daily *La Opinión* of Los Angeles, with a circulation of 124,000 copies and areading public of 520,000, or New York's *La Prensa*, with a reading public of approximately 240,000 and we could also add El *Diario las Américas, El Nuevo Herald, Hoy, El Tiempo Latino,The Washington Hispanic*, etc. 600 Hispanic publications produce 20 million editions which are distributed daily in the United States with a potential reading audience of 40 million.

The growing magnitude of Spanish television is even more impressive. In the United States, the leading channel broadcasting in Spanish is **Univision**—the fifth largest TV chain in the nation, just behind NBC, ABC, CBS and FOX. *Telemundo* is the second most important TV channel broadcasting in Spanish, which for marketing reasons is under the NBC umbrella, while other English-speaking media organizations have Spanish-language subsidiaries, as it's the case of CNN and its chain of news channels in all the Hispanic countries including Mega TV, Direct TV, *Mundo Fox, UniMás,* and Brin Sports. In this context, the advertising market increasingly invests in promoting their products in Spanish, because, as noted, 50% of Hispanics pay more attention to ads appearing in the Spanish language. As for social networks, according to the Cervantes Institute, Spanish is the third most frequently used language on the Internet and the second most used on Facebook, Twitter and Wikipedia.

**In the economy**: While not all economic activity is conducted in Spanish, I simply want to share some data to bring the reader up to date (as of the end of 2016) on the state of the Hispanic market, its purchasing power and that of Hispanic enterprises and how in the last decade these businesses saw an increase of more than 80%—with regard to both the number of companies as well as their earnings. This has direct implications in the use of Spanish in promotional campaigns, customer service, community relations, employment and social programs affecting the Hispanic community. Interesting data includes the buying power of the U.S. Hispanic population which reached $870 billion in 2008 and was projected to reach $1.3 trillion in 2015. There are nown early two and a half million businesses owned by Hispanics—an increase of almost 45% more than in 2002 and this number is expected to reach 4.3 million in six years, at a projected growth rate of 41.8%. Income generated by these companies exceeded the $345.2

billion in 2007—a 55.5% increase compared to 2002, and is expected to reach $539 billion in six years—a 39% increase. To appreciate the magnitude of this growth we should note that the amount was only $29 billion just ten years ago. There are more than 80,000 Hispanic CEO's; 51,000 physicians and surgeons; 49,000 university professors, 39,000 lawyers and 2,800 journalists, reporters, correspondents—numbers which Hispanics expect to see increase. I shall illustrate the significance of a Hispanic presence in the executive, professional and business environment, both now and in the future, with an anecdote taken from the family album:

> On a family skiing trip to West Virginia, at the bottom of the ski slope, as I was giving instructions in Spanish to my children (then ages 10, 5 and 4), a tall, blond young man, about 30, looks at me and said, "Stupid!". I confronted him immediately, my children clinging to my leg, imploring me *"Papi no hagas un escándalo"* ("Daddy don't make a commotion,") I said to him, "Excuse me, sir"... you called me 'stupid' and I would like to know how you reached that conclusion. Shall we compare our university degrees, etc.?" To which he simply responded, "Speak English."Then I let him know that I speak Spanish by choice so that my children can inherit a wealth of culture and have a worldview, etc. that he can't even imagine. Then, I asked him if he had ever traveled outside West Virginia and told him that my children, by knowing Spanish as well as English (their native language), they are able to understand Portuguese, Italian and Latin making it easier for them to learn French and other languages. He didn't argue back but simply repeated: "Speak English." Ever since that incident my children proudly stand by the richness of their Hispanic language and culture... My oldest son, after receiving his Master's degree in Business Administration at Virginia Tech University and recalling that childhood West Virginia skiing trip incident and inspired by a poem entitled "Communion",received an award from the University for his essay entitled, "The importance of bilingualism and bi-culturalism in international marketing for the American entrepreneur."This was a significant occasion from two points of view: that an American businessman should feel proud of his bilingualism and bicultural orientation and expound on these concepts as a recipe for the future, and that a university such as that one—located in southern Virginia and promoting technology—would pay tribute to and honor him.

In terms of a civic participation, there are two indicators. In the 2008 presidential elections, 9.7 million Hispanics voted—(50% of those eligible) and 2 million more than those who voted in the 2004 elections (a 47% increase). In President Obama's re-election in 2012, the Hispanic vote made a differenceas it had twelve years earlier (in 2000) in Al Gore's costly loss in Florida due to the Cuban-American bloc, and the election went to George W. Bush. More than 1.1 million Hispanics are, or have been, members of the United States Armed Forces, a significant number compared to the total, which in 2011 was 1,477,896 active members plus a reserve of 1,458,500. An important factor is language which synthesizes Hispanics' complex but recognizable identity, motivating them to vote and serve the homeland from their worldview perspective and the values they cherish, including personal relationships, a sense of community, the importance of the family and faithfulness to their inherited cultural and social ethics.

## Pride and the future

The Spanish language is like a homeland—a basic part of what defines Hispanic identity and anchors them to a rich history and culture in their home countries, in the United States and throughout the Americas —from Alaska to Patagonia— as well as in Europe and Asia. Once again, Pablo Neruda speaks out on their behalf: "The language...they (the Spanish *conquistadores*) took away the gold and gave us gold..."—their language is a treasure that enriches Hispanics as individuals and as a community.

The future for the Hispanic community is promising and at the same time a constant challenge in the face of disparate interests. Now, without digressing and because I live in the United States I would like to proclaim the proven benefits of bilingualism (as I would if I had lived in any other country where diverse cultures co-exist) by retaining and using both Spanish and English. In the formation of one's personality (i.e., his/her individual and social identity) being bilingual makes one more sensitive, more human, more open and multi-dimensional; it bestows added resources, frees one from ethnocentrism, broadens one's worldview, promotes self-esteem, appreciation of other cultures, increases cognitive capacity and unquestionably makes learning other languages easier. With regard to work and competition in the global economy and commerce, my daughter, who is a doctor specializing in epidemiology at a prominent University Children's Hospital, once received a proposal from El Salvador's Ministry of Public Health. When she presented it to her supervisor, he asked her to translate the Spanish document into English. In her haste, she entrusted this task to the easy technology of Internet translation, which left her dumbfounded because the translated document header showed the official request coming from The "Ministry of Public God Bless You!" which my daughter clarified to mean "The Ministry of Public Health" (*Ministerio de **Salud** Pública)* The word ¡*Salud!* is also an idiomatic expression for "God bless you". So, when looking at this really bad cybernetic mistranslation she was immediately able to clarify it.

The vitality of Spanish in the United States, even in its bilingual hybridity, is evident. Hispanics feel increasingly proud of their language and culture and they are re-discovering their history. And Anglos, too, are learning to appreciate historical happenings prior to the Mayflower and are learning the Spanish language in ever-larger numbers; this, in spite of campaigns against it such as "English only" movements, to promote it as the United States' official language with the intention of eliminating all others. As far back as 1980, the popular magazine *Times* tirred up Americans with its proclamation that the 1980's would be "The Hispanic Decade." In July 2000, the Albuquerque Sunday Journal published a special article under the title "Hip to Hispanic -MANY LATINOS SAY THE REST OF THE NATION IS JUST CATCHING UP TO WHAT THEY ALWAYS KNEW: THEIR CULTURE IS COOL". In countering the xenophobic comments like those of the once influential American politician Newt Gingrich, who said that "Spanish is the language of the ghetto" and the ignorant and racist article by Samuel Huntington talking about "the Hispanic threat to the American dream," I tell my friends that for people such as these, there is no remedy. They will have to get used to the history-based and sociopolitical reality of the increasingly significant Hispanic presence in the United States (in its history, language and culture), in light of Hispanic demographic growth (49% of the total population increase in 2006) due to birth rates and immigration. So, I urge people to accept these things and to learn Spanish as one of the United States' living national languages and I tell them that the country will survive these linguistic idiosyncrasies in spite of campaigns to eliminate the Spanish language ("erasure strategy") which is immune to being eliminated by the dominant language but not to the impurities resulting from sociolinguistic cohabitation.

In support of these points of view, I propose—without departing from the theme of this chapter—that we opt for an intelligent bilingualism because such an approach provides us with an opening and freedom of choice, as commented on by Prof. David de los Reyes: "...in using and benefitting from the incredible but real McLuhanian galaxy of the contemporary media universe... thanks to speech that awakens worlds and imprints astonishment—the most human of emotions."[25] Also because bilingualism, once acquired, allows us to move from the concept of "forever a foreigner" to "forever a citizen" in an ideal world in which the "*we*" and the "*them*" as a structure for creating dissociation, is gradually overcome, based on our multi-faceted experiences as are other such categorizations which have

---

25 - "The Spanish language and US law" in "The Encyclopedia of Spanish in the United States", p. 548.

only divided us and singled people out and it will become a force for unity: (men, women, Hispanics, Anglos, whites, blacks, Orientals, Occidentals, etc.), as Hugo de St. Victor, a 12th Century mystical monk dreamed, as quoted by Edward W. Said in his work *Culture and Imperialism*:

> "It is, therefore, a source of great virtue for the practiced mind to learn, bit by bit, first to change about invisible and transitory things, so that afterwards it may be able to leave them behind altogether. The man who finds his homeland sweet is still a tender beginner; he to whom every soil is as his native one is already strong; but is perfect he to whom the entire world is as a foreign land."[26] (Or perhaps we could update this by say ingmotherland" with diversity being a factor leading to wealth, not of poverty, in the ecosystem we all share).

Even though one may never stop feeling what I expressed in my poem "Communion", which has been a subject of study in schools and universities,[27] the full text and history of which are included in the next chapter, consisting of verses that viscerally poured out from me long before I heard the following question posed by my Cuban poet friend Herbert Padilla:

*"How can one continue to live*

*with two languages,*

*two homes,*

*two nostalgias,*

*two temptations,*

*two melancholies".*

**There are no definitive conclusions.** Everyone comes to his own conclusions according to his feelings, his life, his individual and community circumstances, his experiences, beliefs, struggles and responsibilities, as well as his achievements and contributions. In my particular case, in addition to my militancy on behalf of Hispanics in my support of them, in helping them to rescue and fully live their history and culture and the use of the Spanish language by which they can joyfully express their presence and their contributions to the United States of which they are an integral part, I must conclude that genuine bilingualism and biculturalism in

26 - Edward W. Said, "Culture and Imperialism", Vintage Books, New York: 1994, p. 335.

27 - See, for example, the doctoral thesis by Elisa Hopkins, Pennsylvania State University, "Sharing multicultural poetry with elementary education students: A teacher inquiry into developing critical consciousness", 2007.

which Spanish is retained alongside English, has been extremely positive throughout my life, my experiences and expectations, both personally and professionally. I am proud of my Hispanic culture and language with which I have been blessed in my roots and I feel that Hispanics, with an effort and willingness as U.S. citizens to use the language, promote it, defend it, teach it, can help the majority population to value it and come to regard it as a treasure in its own context and essence, and as a U.S. citizen I firmly believe that the Spanish language will continue to flourish throughout time and space as one of the United States' very own languages.

# CHAPTER II

## BILINGUALISM AND IDENTITY[28]

28 - Adaptation of the keynote lecture delivered in February 2008 during the "Fourth Educational Seminar" organized by the Hispano-Canadian Teachers Association (APH-C), at the University of Toronto and the response speech to one honoring City Hall delivered at Metro Hall, Toronto, during the Twentieth Word and Image Festival which took place in September and October 2011, sponsored by York University and other institutions.

JOSE MARTÍ

Digging deeper into the subject I sketched out at the end of the previous chapter and dreaming now not as an academic but as a poet, I would have preferred to limit myself to reciting the following poem from China which I translated from the English version, as a romantic view of the issue of identity and duality:

*Chuang Tzu dreamed he was a butterfly,*

*delighting in floating on the breeze*

*with no thought to who he was.*


*When Chuang Tzu awoke, he found himself troubled:*

*Am I the man who dreamed he was a butterfly?*

*Or am I a butterfly,*

*that dreamed I was a man?*

*Perhaps my life is merely a flicker in a butterfly's dream!*

Perhaps, however, more painfully, rebellious and militant and more suitable to the Hispanic reality of life in a predominantly Anglo culture, the issue of Hispano-American identity is persistent in the poem "Communion"which I first composed in English then translated it into Spanish. Curiously enough it was then translated back into English by writer Lori Carlson of Columbia University who changed the title to "Learning English."Over 500,000 copies of this poem can be found in print, 30,000 on CDs, and 20,000 on DVDs. In my original version, before its interesting mutations it was called

COMUNIÓN:

*Life*

*to understand me*

*you must know Spanish*

*feel it in the blood of your soul.*


*If I speak another language*

*and use different words*

*to express the same feelings*

*I do not know if in fact*

*I will still be*

*the same* person.[29]

Herein arise the issues of language, bilingualism, biculturalism and identity, which I will discuss based on three generations of a personal bilingual family experience in the U.S. and will refer to research into the historic, cultural and literary Hispanic presence in the United States.

In this chapter I will highlight the richness, value and difficulties of bilingualism with regard to identity; that is, identification (sameness) and differentiation, in the context of association by spatial integration (individualization), temporal integration (sameness) and social integration (belonging), according to Leon Grinberg's categorization system[30] or to the anthropological models summarized by Robbins: *the identity health model, the identity interaction model* and *the identity world-view model.*[31] We must also take into account the concepts of "imposed" identity, "assumed" identity, and "negotiable" identity according to categorizations developed by Pavlenko and Blackledge.[32]

When I address bilingualism I do so only in the general context of U.S. English as the predominant language and Spanish as the language of a growing Hispanic (a politically unifying label to replace "Latino") minority. I am referring to Spanish—a language that has aroused the most antago-

---

29 - In *Bridges to Literature*, McDougal Littell, New York: 2002, 2008; Cool Salsa, Bilingual Poems on Growing Latino in the United States, ed. Lori M. Carlson, Henry Holt and Company, New York, 1994.

30 - Leon Grinberg, *Teoría de la identificación* (theory of identification), Madrid: *Tecnipublicaciones*, 1985.

31 - R.H. Robbins, "Identity, culture and behavior", *Handbook of Social and Cultural Anthropology*, Chicago, Honingman Ed., Rand McNally and Co., 1973.

32 - Pavlenko, Aneta and Adrian Blackledge, "Introduction: New Theoretical Approaches to the Study of Negotiation of Identities in Multilingual Contexts." Pavlenko, Aneta and Adrian Blackledge, eds. *Negotiation of Identities in Multilingual Contexts*. Clevedon: Multilingual Matters: 2004, pp. 1-33.

nism in the U.S., both among those who don't speak it, as well as those who do, not only because it competes with English but because it is the vehicle of a foreign cultural identity and because of its tendency of being overtaken by what is called "Spanglish" and suffers from other subtle infiltrations such as the Anglicisms that have invading its grammar, syntax, vocabulary and thinking.[33] As mentioned earlier, I am referring to the language—the 'gold'—of Pablo Neruda's confession, and to Spanish (as opposed to Castilian), because it is the language Hispanics learned at school which unites them beyond all of the language's dialects, regional transformations, provincialisms, national influences and cases of linguistic co-existence (as with Guaraní and Spanish in Paraguay), with sociolinguistic, socio-economic, and geopolitical nuances in this "melting pot" taht is the Spanish-speaking population in the United States.

## Language, bilingualism and identity

Language—a fact of human life—is a universal and ethnically singular phenomenon, active and vital individually and collectively (as well as something arbitrary—which is pertinent to the topic under discussion), embodying and defining one's identity, allowing it to be lived out dynamically, envisioning itself and constantly adapting. It is, therefore, an instrument for appropriating inherited individual and collective experience and is, at the same time, a form of discovery that safeguards and projects that experience in the social arena. It is an inclusive process of identity that helps us to know ourselves and others in satisfactory, happy and comprehensive ways because of what it signifies and communicates. It is language as experience and as an expression of cultural identity, one's worldview and a system of values amounting to a structure and a social institution. No doubt we can agree that the sociolinguistic approach is not the only one by which we can address the subject of identity and related issues, but we are definitely talking about linguistic heritage. In the specific case of Hispanic Americans it is an experience of supranational interaction, pan-Hispano-Americanism when using a language shared by Spanish-speaking Americans who were born, as Octavio Paz put it, in a universal moment for Spain,[34] In *Laberintos de la soledad* (Labyrinths of solitude) he wrote:

"We must use the language [. . .] of Góngora and Quevedo, Cervantes and St. John of the Cross to express a very different world... For us writing

---

33 - Therefore some, like John Lipski, speak of *La Lengua Española en los Estados Unidos*: *avanza a la vez que retrocede* (the Spanish Language in the United States: advancing while at the same time losing ground).*Revista Española de Lingüística* (Linguistics Journal of Spain) 2004, No. 33, pp. 231-260.

34 - In *Las peras del olmo* (pears of the elm), Mexico, National Autonomous University of Mexico: 1965, p.11.

[and we could add "teaching" here] means breaking down the Spanish language and recreating it in such a way that it becomes [say] Mexican, without ceasing to be Spanish. Our fidelity to the language thus implies fidelity to our people and fidelity to a tradition that is not totally ours but only through an act of intellectual violence."[35]

And in this way, Hispanics are rooted as writers, advocates, teachers, heirs and beneficiaries of a language that identifies us as bearers of an abstract Hispano-Americanism—in the works of such great personalities as Domingo Faustino Sarmiento, José Marti, Rubén Darío, Alfonso Reyes, Pablo Neruda, Octavio Paz and many others who have taken on the task of being the expression, source and focus of a truly Hispanic culture, often in the face of uprooting and disintegrative local realities, to paraphrase the words of Andrés Gallardo.[36] And to paraphrase Mauricio Ostria, we could argue that the [Spanish] language and literature have "truly been one of the most effective tools in the creation of a fused continental consciousness. And, clearly, literary creativity, representing moments of reflection by which a sufficiently mature culture envisions itself, constitutes a kind of knowledge of the world and of self-recognition in that world and is, therefore, a way of perceiving one's cultural identity."[37]

That is why U.S. Hispanics, in spite of speaking English more than 75% of the time, at least in the first, second and even the third generation, are reluctant to give up Spanish, not only as a means of communication, but as a way of clinging to identity, which has been documented in, among other cases, that of the people of Puerto Rico in considering its historical, psychological, social, political, and educational implications, including such matters as access to private and public services (healthcare and others) in both positive and negative terms, as discussed below.

If we analyze the **definition, history and philosophy of language**, through Plato's eyes we will see the importance and difficulty of conscientiously naming things (i.e. with reasoning)—a reflection of ideas ("logos" in Greek, meaning both "word" and "reason"). In Plato's *Cratylus* and in the Sumerian-Hebrew culture, to name something is to possess it (which explains why God is not named). The one who creates a name is responsible for determining things; he/she is the legislator of that which exists. In *Genesis* when God talks, He creates; therefore we could continue with

---

35 - Mexico, *Fondo de Cultura Económica*: 1983, p. 147.
36 - Octavio Paz, *Identidad y lenguaje* (identity and language) inter-disciplinary Latin American Studies Center at http://209.85.165.104/search?q=cache:tJ6ASR2XixMJ:www.fh.userena.cl/ciel/octavio_paz_identidad_y_lengua-je.html+%22como+Domingo+Faustino%22%2BRub%C3%A9n+dar%C3%ADo&hl=en&ct=clnk&cd=10&gl=us
37 - *Lo uno y lo diverso en la literatura hispanoamericana*, in *Estudios Filológicos* (the one and the diverse in Hispanic-American literature), Philological Studies, 1989, No. 24, p. 99.

Aristotle and his concept of the political importance of human beings as sociolinguistic realities.Hobbes is enthusiastic in stating that language is man's most useful and humane invention, but he also suffers from Cartesian doubts and the influences of Kantian idealism, as well as Rousseau's savagery and he refers to Hegel and his "Phenomenology of Spirit."He also dwells on the significance of language, asserting that, dialectically, it expresses the self, the individual and universality, and he concludes that through language both presence and permanence are acquired. Then there is Sausurre who talks about the antinomy between language and speech; then there is Chomsky and others. The following quote from Ulibarri synthesizes the complexities:

> *"In the beginning was the Word. And the word was made flesh. It was so in the beginning and it is so today. The language, the Word, carries within it the history, the culture, the traditions, the very life of a people, the flesh. Language is people. We cannot conceive of a people without a language, or a language without a people. The two are one and the same. To know one is to know the other."[38]*

To document the long and challenging history of Hispanic-American Spanish and Anglo English in the United States, it should be borne in mind that the Spanish spoken in territories that are now part of the United States precedes the founding of the nation and the arrival of the English language, as noted in the introduction. In addition, historical events exacerbate the difficulties andcomplicate the coexistence and rivalry between these two languages and cultures in the United States: In 1836-1848 the secession of Texas and the Mexican-U.S. War took place. In 1849, there was the Angloforay into California in search of gold in which the invaders consider Spanish speakers already living there as "enemies." In 1898 the Spanish-U.S. War led to the "independence" of Puerto Rico and Cuba from Spain, but then they forcefully came into the sphere of United States' political influence. From 1910-1920 the Mexican Revolution brought about massive migrations into the United States. In 1912 New Mexico was founded as a State. From 1918 to 1930 the *Braceros* program brought poor Mexicans to the U.S. as laborers. Xenophobia increased during World War II against Mexicans living in the United States. In 1948, with Operation Bootstrap there was an influx of Puerto Ricans. In 1959 and 1960, a mass immigration of Cubans took place following the Cuban Revolution, although Cuban influence (such as in literature) have always been present in New York, Florida and elsewhere. César Chávez defended Hispanic civil rights in the 1960's. In the 70's, South American refugees arrived, fleeing dic-

---

38 - Ulibarri 1972, quoted by Carlos J. Ovando y Collier V. in his book *Bilingual and ESL Classrooms. Teaching in Multicultural Contexts.* New York, McGraw-Hill: 1985, p. 64.

tatorships and socio-political conflicts in their countries (Argentina, Chile and Uruguay). In the 1980'sthere was a significant migratory wave of Central Americans (Nicaraguans and Salvadorans) for the aforesaid reasons. Additionally, in the 1990's, the Dominican population in the U.S. was on the rise. All these events which brought about the growth of the Hispanic population in the U.S., created great opportunities but also aroused strong resentment in the dominant culture which traditionally and historically was already predisposed to bias against the Hispanic culture and language as can be seen in earlier confrontations and U.S. interventions in the Spanish Caribbean (Puerto Rico and Cuba), Central America (Nicaragua and Panama) and covertly in South America (the Chilean military coup against Salvador Allende), and Argentina'swar with Great Britain over the Falkland Islands, with the U.S. opposing Hispanic-American nations and favoring the British, often with conflicting positions. Within the U.S. there was an attitude of antagonism and of "tokenism"—i.e. the nominal admitting of a limited number of religious and racial minorities in the work force, education, organizations etc., (seemingly just to comply with the law and/or to placate public opinion) with regard to Hispanic-Americans, which were seen in cultural clashes or amounting to a "clash of civilizations" according to the thinking of Samuel Huntington.

Of the **psychological aspects** of the relationship between language (bilingualism) and identity in the Hispanic-American-English context, I wish to emphasize that while there is a relational identity it is not a relativistic one. The concepts, existence and behavior of the self (the individual) and otherness (the other[s], time, space and the environment), are configured, humanly confirmed and affirmed in a dynamic process of both uniqueness and differences.

In paraphrasing Brown[39], we said earlier that language is a way of life; it is at the very root of our being, interacting simultaneously with our thoughts and feelings in a concrete, specific and diverse way. An attack on a person's native language (say, Spanish) by those in authority (such as at a school or at the workplace), by prohibiting its use, deprives, humiliates, hurts, disconcerts, and causes feelings of low self-esteem. Such actions amount to an attack on one's inner self, one's way of life, one's person and one's origins. Studies have shown, moreover, that people who are fully bilingual have a sense of high self-esteem. In an extreme context, it should be noted that most of the victims of hate crimes in the U.S. are of Hispanic origin. I am referring to violent attacks on their very identity that enables them to be at peace with themselves individually and within their communities. Misperceptions make them vulnerable at their very

---

39 - D. Brown, *Principles of Language Learning and Teaching*, New Jersey: Prentice Hall Regents: 1994, p. 38.

core, causing them to feel psychologically overpowered due to feelings of suspicion that lead to insecurity and distrust. This phenomenon does not occur in a vacuum; it is hardened by history, education, deep-rooted prejudice, manipulation and ignorance on the part of the dominant culture in trying to maintain its hegemony, resulting in devastating psychological consequences for those belonging to discriminated minorities in denying them their linguistic and cultural identities, as documented by Sharon F. Lambert in 1987, and others.

The **sociological** implications of the triad of language, bilingualism and identity are numerous and complex. Language, in its role as an identifier of individualization, differentiation and belonging is certainly a factor in the process of social interaction, but also in all implied conflict and in the process of creating identities in interactions between those competing to identify and understand existing circumstances. We call to mind Dewey's statement that the words "communication"and "community"have the same etymological root as the word "common". We have previously addressed the relational function of language as a creator of identity. We must also bear in mind the concept of language as a mediator and determinant of community, of collective imagination, of being and of social consciousness, dealing with conflicts and their resolution through commitment, labeling, setting rules and standards of behavior. Additionally, the dialogical and dynamic character of social experience and language influence the configuration of society and changes within it through a process of adaptation and innovation. It has been shown that a bilingual (or multilingual) person has the leeway and ability to adapt and to change the content and register of language codes, according to the social circumstances under which he/she lives, with the possibility of adopting a positive view with respect to whatever identities may be involved—much more so than for a person who is monolingual and has negative feelings toward other identities, as we shall illustrate in more detail in the next segment.

In this discussion, I wish to emphasize some issues in the **political context** of language, bilingualism and identity. To frame the discussion, let's look at a poem written nearly two centuries ago by New Mexican poet José María Alarid in which she refers to a subject that is constantly repeated in this scuffle between cultures, i.e. the matter of language:

*Beautiful Spanish language*

*So, they want to ban you?*

*I don't think there's any reason*

*Why you should cease to exist.*

We have already referred to and will further expand on the controversy between the acceptance of bilingualism and bilingual education as a political reality versus the "English only" movements based on a monolingual and ethnocentric devotion aimed at closing down other national languages within this country. As a point of interest, it should be noted that on occasion police have been called in to enforce "English only" programs at the exclusion of bilingualism and bilingual education. But there would be no need to enforce such policies if one of bilingualism and bilingual education were to be adopted. Language is not only a means of identity, of defining an individual and a vehicle for societal interaction and intercommunication, but, from the outset, it is an important tool for administering public policy, for controlling and transmitting the signs and symbols of ideologies and shaping national identity. It is an instrument of power and influence because it is an identifier and determiner, establishes hierarchies and values,provides symbolism and meaning—and writes history. To paraphrase Hannah Arendth, she once stated that language is not necessarily a search after truth, but rather it wants to create a sense of the past in order to explain and motivate both the present and the future, and to create cohesion among a particular population group. Paulo Freire, a Brazilian educator-with whom I had the pleasure of participating in a round table discussion in 1970, had us reflecting on educational policies by making us aware of how it is possible, through language, to build a new society capable of overcoming systemic social injustice, that this can be achieved by the content of that language.[40]In the geopolitical context of  U.S. "monolingualism"or "linguicism"of the "English only"position, it is like all other negative "isms" (racism, classicism etc.); it is nothing more than an ideological structure to legitimize, create and perpetuate an unjust division of dominance based on language to "impose" an identity and to, for example, to create categories such as "high" and "low" Spanish, "the language of the ghetto,"in the ignorant, racist words of Newt Gingrich, (a formerly influential U.S. politician) who with his bedfellows promote xenophobic homogeneousness, especially with regard to the Hispanic cultures.

In this context, control of the **media**, plays an important role. The presence of an Hispanic media in the U.S.market (TV, radio, newspapers and magazines), resists voices such as that of the aforementioned Mr. Gingrich and constitute a political force that seeks to maintain cultural identity through sounds, images, movement, and music by disseminating the Spanish language, even though at times its responsibility with regard to the language does suffer. The book *Hablando bien se entiende la gente* (*By speaking well people understand each other*) and many other initiatives

---

40 - Pablo Freire, *Pedagogy of the Oppressed*, New York, Continuum: 1970. *The politics of education*. South Hadley, MA, Bergin and Garvey: 1985.

promoted by colleagues at the North American Academy of the Spanish Language, on Yahoo, TV programs and other media, constantly strive to provide guidelines to avoid some of the "Spanglish horrors" committed by Spanish speakers daily in the United States. To illustrate the difficulties of Spanish-English coexistence, an ironic poem was penned by a 19th century California poet published under the pseudonym "V", as follows:

*Conocí aquí en California*

*A una paisana muy bella*

*Con dieciocho primaveras.*

*Mas como estaba educada*

*En la americana escuela,*

*Inglesaba algunas frases*

*Que olían a gringo a la legua.*

*Con frecuencia se le oía*

*Llamar al cesto basqueta,*

*Cuenta las cuadras por bloques,*

*A un cerco decirle fensa*

*Al café llamarlo cofe*

*A los mercados marqueta*

*Al bodegón grosería*

This leads to some preliminary reflections on the role of education and educational institutions with regard to the matter of language, bilingualism and formation of identities (in a process of personal development, socialization and acculturation, in light of inherited, assumed and negotiated identities.) The emphasis on bilingualism in educational settings involves committed professionals with amenable and "decolonized"methodologies (see Smith)[41] and to paraphrase Paul Freire,[42]have to show humble and liberating courage and dedication to help overcome the forces of imperialistic oppression in matters of identity and culture. Scholarly sociolinguistic research and communications studies have demonstrated that students' cognitive abilities greatly benefit when the full range of their talents and language communication skills are used.[43]Bilingual education, as defined

---

41 - L.T. Smith, "Decolonizing methodologies", London: Zed Books Ltd .: 1999.
42 - Pablo Freire, *Pedagogy of the oppressed*. New York, Continuum: 1970.
43 - Tharp & Gallimore 1988.

by Jim Cummings is not, as some have tried to argue, a "plot" or conspiracy by Hispanic activists, but rather a series of measures implemented in different countries around the world to provide effective learning opportunities for speakers of both minority and majority languages.[44]We should add that this concept is based not only on the acquisition of a language in addition to one's own but that schools, in a modest way, should contribute concepts and provide information, as well as instill attitudes, offer a worldview and teach students' their responsibilities as members of a global community of diversity. In summary, theorists Cummins,[45]Hammers & Blanc[46] have stated that it is necessary to abandon dominant educational models oriented to merely "transmitting" knowledge of a language but adopt a model that will enable students to value their linguistic and cultural talents through active participation in the community, thereby obtaining significantly greater linguistic and cultural growth and solidifying democratic coexistence, enhanced by the richness of diversity.

## Bilingualism and identity within the United States: Where are we headed?

The vitality of Spanish in its different variations according to regions, countries, cultural background and migratory patterns, has contributed to the growth and expansion of language in the United States, and is an identifying factor of social change in communities throughout the nation. As Suzanne Romaine states in her book **Bilingualism**[47]"at the semantic level, a bilingual person can convey meaning better in one of these two languages, especially with regard to certain issues or in certain contexts." (p.13) bilingualism . . . is a "resource to be cultivated and not a problem to be overcome." (p.7) Cultural studies and critical theory have emphasized the importance of bilingualism in creating positive identity—as well as self-esteem—through language, race, gender and class.

Fortunately, in their personal and professional **context and reality**, the majority of U.S. Hispanics also speak English which enables them to be in the work force and cultivate good relations as individuals, as family units in society as a whole, as well as maintaining connections beyond the country's borders. In spite of the attitude of those who oppose bilingualism and bilingual education, fluency in two languages contributes to greater individual skills. This is the conclusion reached by the U.S. General Accounting Office in an independent study carried out in 1987, which contradicts then

---

44 - Jim Cummins, *Bilingual and ESL Classrooms*, Ovando/Collier: June 1997: prologue, p.x.

45 - Jim Cummins, *Empowering minority students*, Harvard Educational Review, No. 56: pp. 18-36.

46 - *Bilinguality and Bilingualism*, Cambridge, Cambridge University Press: 200.

47 - Oxford: Wiley-Blackwell; 2nd. Edition, 1995.

Secretary of Education William Bennett's efforts to impose an "English only" policy as the way forward for this country. However, it is a matter of adding to life, not subtracting from it.

Hispanics face **challenges and struggles** in their efforts to defend their linguistic and cultural identity in the spirit of bilingualism. Facing armed guards trying to impose English as the only language and expression of culture, Hispanics will be there with pastors and will pray, but they will not stop standing up for what they believe is right and necessary for the country. We have already referenced many historical and cultural conflicts between the U.S. and the Hispanic-American world. We have seen that, in general, the courts have sided on behalf of those who oppose bilingualism, especially in the workplace, dismissing the defense's position that language is intrinsically linked to one's origin and identity; and they have ruled that the use of a language other than English is detrimental to the morale of those who only speak English (monolinguals) and that only this language should be spoken as a means to ensure harmony and a proper running of the work place. So, "English only"—the standard ideology of homogeneity—becomes the norm whereas linguistic and cultural diversity is looked on as the deviant position. One should dream in English and the Anglo population clings to this language more as a reaction to what they perceive as a Hispanic linguistic and cultural threat. Initiatives to legislate banning the Spanish language in schools, the workplace and in public services have had momentary success but have been declared unconstitutional in States where this has been attempted. Furthermore, this entire position is based on the promulgation of myths and characterizations of a "lack of American (i.e. U.S.) values" by those who speak other languages. Samuel Huntington in his above-mentioned article warns worriedly that if Hispanics don't start using English, the U.S. will suffer an erosion of values and lose individual rights, the rule of law and a work ethic, as well as the ability and duty to create a better world within the canons of Anglo-Saxon Protestantism. All this, in this extremely biased position, would be replaced by "Hispanic tendencies" described as a lack of ambition and trust, a deficient work ethic, a lack of a desire to be educated, a distrust of the world outside the family circle, an acceptance of poverty as a way of life based on the concept of the division of earth (a place of suffering) and heaven (the prize) based on the teachings of the Catholic religion. Note that the "values" of English only and "monoculturalism" are considered positive while the characterization of other languages and cultures is verbalized negatively as "lacking" in this or that trait, feeding on the myth that those who speak other languages (especially Hispanics) are unruly, rude, cause trouble, have bad habits and are violent and vulgar. I prefer to be optimistic and believe that such attitudes are just the "the swan's last song". I am pleased to note that the special privileges accorded to monolingual Anglos are being reviewed and even challenged by legislatures, courts and in out-of-court settlements. Increasingly the need to learn Spanish is becoming understood and promulgated in the United States—to such an extent that former President Bill Clinton should himself express his hope, as we mentioned earlier, of being the last U.S. President who doesn't know Spanish. In short, we are faced with either accepting prejudice or we must acknowledging that promoting a linguistic monoculture does not help the country nor is it in line with democratic ideals and an acceptance of rich diversity.

Against this background, I think that **the responsibilities** of U.S. Hispanic citizens, educators, writers, custodians and promotors of the Spanish language and Hispanic culture, in a bicultural and bilingual context are, as I said in a speech in Toronto's 2007 *Festival of the Word and Image, Latino-Canadian Footprints*, to which I was invited by CCIE[48]: I spoke (1) of the need to express ourselves with commitment, sometimes in rebellion and always with nostalgia in order to overcome oblivion, to keep memories alive, even lacking in words, the heart of a population that makes up Hispanic America—the Spanish speakers living in the United States and Canada, (2) to **proudly contribute to the rescuing** of their history, culture, art, theater, music and language, within the dominant culture which—to its own detriment and privation—sometimes tends to ignore the Hispanic minority, sometimes belittling it (contrary what the wise and visionary Thomas Jefferson advised his nephew Peter Carr in 1787 in a letter previously cited): "Apply yourself to the study of the Spanish language with all the assiduity you can." At other times and by other people the language has been repudiated (as in the unfortunate previously-cited case of xenophobic former congressman and presidential candidate Newt Gingrich) when he called Spanish "the language of the ghetto" and when Samuel Huntington spoke of "the Spanish threat to the American dream,"—statements that deserve censure and rejection, not only by U,S. Hispanic-Americans but by all civilized and thoughtful American citizens, (3) to **make known** to the world the historic and vibrant Hispanic presence, which is the purpose of this book and that of many others: to **teach these things** with dedication, care, pride and passion (expressed through language); to formally teach respect with an awareness that respect contributes to the formation of a better citizenry, to the enrichment of one's cultural heritage and identity and to the configuration of an open society adapted to the requirements of an integrated world living in peace and ever-progressing. (4) to **celebrate and cultivate** this history, these cultural and artistic expressions, this rich and growing Hispanic life in North America, which many organizations and individuals are already doing; (5) **to seek connections and harmony** by reaching out, joining hands, accepting an increasing Hispanic presence

---

48 - *Celebración Cultural del Idioma Español* (cultural celebration of the Spanish language).

and representation, so that their voices may be increasingly heard and appreciated. (6) **To struggle** so that our country, the United States, can adopt an attitude which is more European, recognizing the right to use the Spanish language in this country, without restrictions since it is the language of the nation's largest minority second to that of English speakers.

Hispanics firmly believe in a promising future while always facing constant challenges by opposition groups. The proven benefits of bilingualism in the formation of personality (one's individual and social identity) which makes one more sensitive, more human, more open, multidimensional, with added resources, freed from ethnocentrism, having broad-mindedness in one's view of the world, possessing self-esteem, having an appreciation of other cultures, possessing cognitive ability and a facility for learning additional languages—all these are undeniable benefits, including being able to compete in a global economy.

The increasing use of the Spanish language in the United States in its bilingual hybrid state **is(es)** evident and **is (está)** proven. (These are the two Spanish verbs for **to be** [**ser** and **estar**] which fascinate my friend Robert Pinsky, the United States poet laureate). Bilingualism opens the possibility of prosperity, opens one's horizons and provides freedom of choice as stated in the previous chapter quoting Prof. David de los Reyes. The positive benefits of bilingualism as practiced by the North American country of Canada, can be seen in terms of its national identity, civic nation building and opportunities for its citizenry (as documented by Stacy Churchill in her study *Language education, Canadian civic identity and the identities of Canadians*)[49] and should serve as an important and edifying example to consider by the huge country on its southern border (the U.S.) with similar realities but in certain sectors of which ethnocentrically clings to the concept of English only. Although I have described the typical U.S. citizens as Anglo or Anglo Saxon as a monolingual (i.e. English only) devotee, things are changing and more and more people understand that we must be prepared for the reality of a post-monolingual nation.

### Once again, there are no conclusions, only projections.

Again, I reiterate what I brought up in the previous chapter, but now more forcefully, that there will be increasing support for this position. For me, in my personal, social and professional life bilingualism and biculturalism have been tremendously positive and, through my own experiences, I have been able to validate conclusions reached by Holm & Holm

---

49 - See http://www.coe.int/t/dg4/linguistic/Source/ChurchillEN.pdf.

(1990) and mentioned by Jon Reyner in his article *Bilingual Education for Healthy Students, Healthy Communities.*[50] I can say the same of my own children, whose native language is English. I play with my grandchildren, all nine of them, ages one to thirteen. They call me *abuelo* (grandfather) and talk to me in Spanish. One of them, a five-year-old, proudly intones "*Hola amigos!*" (Hello, friends!). Therefore, I can only leave them to walk the pathway that each one will tread, citing a poem by Antonio Machado, transformed into a chant which today, once more, is a song we sing:

*Todo pasa y todo queda*

*pero lo nuestro es pasar*

*pasar haciendo camino,*

*camino al andar...*

*caminante no hay camino*

*se hace camino al andar.*


**Translation:**

*(Everything goes and everything stays*

*but our fate is to pass*

*to pass making a path as we go on*

*making a path as we walk the path...*

*wayfarer, there is no path*

*a path is made by walking.)*

---

50 - July/August 2006 issue of the Journal of the National Language Learner Association for Bilingual Education, pp. 8-9.

# CHAPTER III

## FROM THE FOUNDING FATHER:

## THOMAS JEFFERSON AND THE SPANISH LANGUAGE

## HIS PRAXIS, VISION AND POLITICAL PHILOSOPHY

THOMAS JEFFERSON

Another of my significant discoveries of a fundamental part of the Hispanic United States is the person of Thomas Jefferson—one of the founders of our country. We will see why in the following detailed documentation of his vision, practice and conviction. Figures like Thomas Jefferson, Mahatma Gandhi and Cervantes are geniuses who belong to all of humanity, even if they have shone within a particular geography, epoch and space. They transcend both space and time; they are prophets, leaders, universal patriots, immortal beings. Their multifaceted genius means that they can be valued from many points of view, without their necessarily being perfect in their different attributes. One must not confuse genius with perfection[51].

Thomas Jefferson (born in Shadwell, Virginia, 1743), has been called the wise man of Monticello—one of the most fascinating figures in history and sometimes referred to as the "creator" of the United States of America. He was a Renaissance man, a genius, whose full life incarnates paradoxes that have given rise to numerous interpretations and analyses which have been detailed by Alf J. Mapp, Jr., in his masterlyfull synthesis of Jefferson's contributions (both positive and negative) entitled *Thomas Jefferson: A Strange Case of Mistaken Identity*[52] *and Thomas Jefferson: Passionate Pilgrim.*[53]He was the mentor for the founding articles of U.S. democracy which has existed without interruption for more than 200 years. He asserted freedom of expression, freedom of religion and other human rights, demonstrating exceptional qualities and vision in his praxis and political philosophy in general, but most notably in a little known facet which I wish to document here: namely his learning of, relationship to,

---

51 - I wish to clarify that in this chapter I have used and complement information found in the volumes entitled The Road to Monticello, The Life and Mind of Thomas Jefferson, by Kevin J. Hayes (Oxford University Press: 2008), and The Life and Selected Writings of Thomas Jefferson, edited by Adrienne Koch and William Peden, (New York, The Modern Library: 1998), as well as other documents and biographies of Thomas Jefferson which I have consulted. Mostly I have been personally responsible for the Spanish translations of all the texts appearing in the English originals of the bibliographical material cited throughout this work.
52 - Lanham, Madison Books: 1987.
53 - Lanham, Madison Books: 1993.

defense and promotion of the Spanish language, a fact which Hispanics and supporters of multiculturalism can identify with, Jefferson—genius that he was—and possessor of a multiplicity of talents, abilities, and extraordinary attainments, offers almost infinite possibilities for finding areas of identification with him. I identify with him and celebrate his admirable characteristics which are of great relevance in the historical legacy of none other than the author of the United States Declaration of Independence and the architect of the fundamental principles that make up the constitutional basis of this country. By his way of being he establisheda personal and statesman-like example that stands out at this time when attitudes still persist based on xenophobic and short-sighted antagonisms between the Angloa nd Hispanic cultures such as those expressed by the previously mentioned Samuel Huntington and Newt Gingrich—proponents of "English only" and other extreme positions.

Without ignoring or underestimating his familiarity with other languages and their written literature, our main concentration and emphasis in this historiographical essay is to amass concrete and historical data throughout Thomas Jefferson's multifaceted life as a landowner, student, professional, thinker, inventor, diplomat, political leader and founder of universities for the purpose of illustrating in a convincing way the fascinating and visionary life of this exceptional individual and universal champion of social and political thought.

Reviewing a bit of history, Thomas Jefferson has been described as a philosopher of liberty and an apostle of the Age of Reason. He drafted the Declaration of Independence in 1776, in which he captured the ideas of, among others, John Locke, justified the rebellion in the Colony because of the transgressions of King George III against the established rights of citizens according to the unwritten constitution of Great Britain, which may have been based on the ideas of the Spanish Jesuit Juan de Mariana (*De Rege et Regis Institutione*), whose book **Historia de España** appears in the Jefferson Library catalog, as noted by bibliographer E. Millicent Sowerby. His defense of democracy, equality, the right of the people to govern themselves and man's natural right "to life, liberty and the pursuit of happiness"[54] indicated these ideals, although not always present in the later history of the United States. It is important to note that although Thomas Jefferson idealized the small independent farmer, he himself belonged to the aristocracy of the big landowners of the South—a position he attained after much schooling and receiving a law degree. His intellectual curiosity attracted him to the philosophy of the Enlightenment and to liberal ideas given his exceptional literary erudition.

---

54 - Words written by Jefferson for the Declaration of Independence. See the analysis by Dr. John C. Munday Jr. in his article "Life, Liberty, and the Pursuit of Happiness" at http://www.avantrex.com/essay/freetalk.html.

When Thomas Jefferson lost the presidential election in 1796 to the Federalist John Adams, due to a constitutional provision that was later repealed, he became Vice President, as the second most voted-for candidate (1797-1801). Finally, he won the presidential election in 1800 and 1804 and became the third President of the United States, serving for two consecutive terms, from 1801 to 1809.

I include the following quote from the first paragraph of his inaugural address as he assumed the presidency in the hope that it can be repeated and practiced by the political leaders of all nations on this planet:

*"Equal and exact justice to all men, of whatever state or persuasion, religious or political; peace, commerce, and honest friendship with all nations, entangling alliances with none; the support of the State governments in all their rights, as the most competent administrations for our domestic concerns;...the preservation of the General Government in its whole constitutional vigor, as the sheet anchor of our peace at home and safety abroad..."*[55]

The most important achievements of his two mandates was the consolidation and delegation of functions among the constitutional powers, according to which the federal government was to be in charge of matters of defense and foreign policy, giving the individual States broad autonomy in domestic policy. Thus he once again put into practice his philosophical convictions regarding the need to limit powers as a safeguard to freedom.

### Thomas Jefferson and the Spanish language

His erudition and genius are seen here by the way in which he anticipated the times and valued the history of Hispanics in the United States, as well as his appreciation for, knowledge of and interest in promoting the Spanish language by acknowledging its cultural and geopolitical importance. Being convinced of the relevance of languages in general in understanding, becoming familiar with and sensitive to the various national idiosyncrasies[56], Jefferson practiced what he preached by learning at least six languages with varying degrees of fluency in them. A polyglot and avid reader of original versions and translations of the Greco-Latin classics (the Odyssey, the Iliada, Aeneida), Arabic literature, French and English literary and philosophical creations (including Scottish and Welsh authors), his interest and

---

55 - Taken from the "First Inaugural Address" in the book Thomas Jefferson, Writings, editor Marril D. Peterson (New York: Library of America, 1984), pp. 492-496.

56 - ". . . I have long considered the filiation of languages the best proof we can ever obtain of the filiation of nations." To John S. Vater, 599. (M., 1812.) 4459 ("Cyclopedia", p. 474).

familiarity with the Spanish language, although at first rudimentary, dates from well before 1784, based on comments made in 1775 in a meeting with John Duane, who in turn told John Adams, as follows: "He [Jefferson] has learned French, Italian, Spanish and wants to learn German."[57] This is an achievement that would be quite in line with his concept about the importance of early language learning (among which Jefferson mentions Spanish).[58] This language learning very likely took place during his university years. I agree with biographer B.L. Rayner that Jefferson learned Spanish while studying at William and Mary College in Williamsburg, Virginia where he graduated with highest honors. This was confirmed by Jefferson himself in a letter he wrote to Joseph Delaplaine, dated April 12, 1817.[59]

This implies that this learning took place much more than a decade before his well-known trip in July, 1784 to Ceres, France to fulfill his position and mission as minister plenipotentiary in Paris. During the 19-day crossing, described by John Quincy Adams in his memoirs[60], (based on notes written after having dinner with Jefferson in 1804), he would have been learning (or, rather, working on perfecting) his knowledge of Spanish by referring to a Spanish grammar book and a copy of *Don Quixote* given to him on loan by Mr. Cabot. The following is John Quincy Adams'textual annotation in his diary: "As to Spanish, it was so easy that he had learned itwith the help of a *Don Quixote* lent him by Mr. Cabot, and a grammar, in the course of a passage to Europe, on which he was but nineteen days at sea. But Mr. Jefferson tells large stories..." In fact, when Jefferson returned and thanked Cabot for the two borrowed volumes of *Don Quixote*, he wrote the following: "I deliver to Mr. Tracy to be returned to you the copy of Don Quixote that you were so obliging as to lend me: for which I return you many thanks. The winds have been so propitious as to let me get through one volume only; yet this has so far done away the difficulties of the language as that I shall be able to pursue it on shore with pleasure. I have found it a very advantageous disposal of time..."[61]

It is also highly significant how Jefferson worked assiduously to inculcate—with the typical passion of his personality—his stance and vision about the Spanish language to his immediate family and circle of influence. A letter

57 - John Adams, Diary and Autobiography of John Adams, editors. L. H. Butterfield et al., 4 vols. (Cambridge, Mass.: Belknap Press of Harvard University Press, 1961) 2: 218.

58 - "In general, I am of opinion, that till the age of about sixteen, we are best employed on languages: Latin, Greek, French, and Spanish . . . I think Greek the least useful ". - To J. W. Eppes, 192. ("Cyclopedia" P., 1787).

59 - Life: 1998, p. 621.

60 - John Quincy Adams, Memoirs of John Quincy Adams (Philadelphia: J. B. Lippencott & Co., 1874), 1: 317.

61 - Letter from Jefferson to Mr. Cabot, July 24, 1784, *Papers*, 27: 739-740.

dated October 15, 1785 to J. Bannister Jr. includes a reference to the learning of the Spanish language as a required subject, in response to the question "What are the objects of a useful American education?"[62]

Nothing more or nothing less than *Don Quixote*—the quintessential novel of the Castilian language and of universal canon—constituted the basic text for learning the Spanish language, not only by Jefferson personally, but also his daughters. Thus in 1783, to this end, he gave a copy of the book to his eldest daughter Martha Jefferson Randolph, and it was the text that another of his youngest daughters, Mary Jefferson Eppes, used for studying the Spanish language. In a letter to his aunt, Elizabeth Eppes, with whom his daughter Mary resided, he wrote: "I have insisted on her reading ten pages a day of her Spanish **Don Quixote**, and getting a lesson in her Spanish grammar." [63]And her progress in learning Spanish was a subject that Jefferson constantly followed up on in his letters to his daughter Mary.

Regarding this remarkable insistence and interest on the part of Jefferson that his family and friends learn Spanish, in my presentations[64]I have often referred to the above mentioned letter that Thomas Jefferson sent from Paris to his nephew Peter Carr on August 10, 1787 in which he writes: "Spanish. Bestow great attention on this, and endeavor to acquire an accurate knowledge of it. Our future connections with Spain and Spanish America will render that language a valuable acquisition. The ancient history of that part of America, too, is written in that language. I am sending you a dictionary."[65] He had already encouraged him before, writing from Paris on August 19, 1785, in the following words, after referring him to the Baretti English-Spanish Dictionary and sending him a Grammar book and other books in written Spanish: "Our future connection with Spain renders Spanish the most necessary of the modern languages, after the French. When you become a public man, you will have opportunities to use it, and the circumstance of having such a language could give you a preferential situation over other candidates."[66]And with renewed concern he reminded him again in 1788: "Apply yourself to the study of the Spanish language with all the assiduity you can. It and English covering nearly the whole face of America, they should be well known to every inhabitant, who means to look beyond the confines of his farm."[67]

---

62 - Life: 1998, p. 358.
63 - Letter from Jefferson to Elizabeth Eppes, March 7, 1790.
64 - "The Incidence of Spanish in the United States" at www.lawrencebookfair. com/images/Ambroggio. pdf.
65 - *Life*: 1998, p. 398.
66 - Life: 1998, p. 350.
67 - To Peter Carr, 409. ("Cyclopedia", P., 1788. ).

It was a subject on which he dwelt with great insistence as evidenced by the following letter dated July 6, 1787 to his future son-in-law Thomas Mann Randolph, speaking about his education in general: "… Spanish is most important to an American. Our connection with Spain is already important and will become more so daily. Furthermore, , the earliest part of American history is written chiefly in Spanish."[68]

In line with this attitude, the quantity and quality of works in Spanish that Jefferson read and collected throughout his life as part of his praxis is remarkable and worth examining. During his above-mentioned sojourn in Paris, Jefferson bought two separate editions—one in in French and the other in Spanish of *Las Aventuras de Telémaco* (*The Adventures of Telemachus*) by Fénelon in order to continue to further his mastery of Spanish. Furthermore, his enthusiasm for Spanish and its literature, as well as his curiosity to read about the history of the initial Spanish explorations in the territories of the Americas led him, while in Europe, to acquire numerous books that enabled him to expand his knowledge of Spanish and its literature. Among them he acquired the *Obras Poéticas* (Poetic Works)of Don Vicente García de la Huerta—a contemporary neoclassical Spanish playwright known for the political tone of his poems and tragedies; all nine volumes of the poetic anthology *Parnaso-Español*, compiled in 1768 by Juan José López Sedano, as well as a collection of romances by several authors, including texts by Francisco de Quevedo and Sancho de Moncada, entitled *Romances de Germanía*, originally published in 1609 by Juan Hidalgo and, finally, *Las Eróticas*—classical lyrical poetry by Esteban Manuel Villegas (1774 edition), which also contains Spanish translations of Horace and a Spanish version of a book by Boethius entitled *De consolatione Philosophiae*, which Jefferson himself later used as a means of consoling himself prior to the departure of his friends the Cosways, but especially Mary Cosway to whom he was attracted and with whom he had a deeply congenial friendship. Imitating the dialogue between the head and the heart narrated in Boethius' book, he unburdened himself of his intimate thoughts and feelings regarding his relationship with her. This book, according to Julian Boyd contains "one of the most remarkable love letters in the English language."[69]

Also, following Jefferson's interest in knowing the Hispanic history of the American Continent as narrated by the most outstanding writers of the day, in the summer of 1786 he requested and received from William Carmichael —the *Chargé d'Affaires*at the United States Embassy in Spain—two outstanding "Inca" books by Garcilaso de la Vega entitled **La Florida del**

---

68 - Life: 1998, p. 394. An exchange of letters between Jefferson and Thomas Mann Randolph, July 6, 1787 (also found in *Papers*, 11: 558) and March 8, 1790 (*Papers*, 16: 214).
69 - In his edition of *Papers* 10:453.

*Inca y Comentarios reales*(*Florida of the Inca and Royal Commentaries*), very likely this Peruvian chronicler and historian's greatest work, which has been called the point of departure for Spanish-American literature. He also obtained a masterly work by Fray Juan de Torquemada entitled *Los veintiún libros rituales i Monarchia Indiana, con el origen y guerras de los Indios Occidentales, de sus poblazones, descubrimientos, conquista, conversión y otras cosas maravillosas de la mesma tierra,* better known by its abbreviated title of *The Indian Monarchy and the Natural and Moral History of the Indies.* All this, as he explained to James Madison was to satisfy his "intense desire to collect the original Hispanic writers of American history,"[70] an interest he cultivated including the reading of English translations of works such as one by Francesco Saverio Clavigero: *The History of Mexico* which, according to Jefferson, "deserves more respect than any other work on this subject."[71]

But these are not the only Spanish-language books that Jefferson read as indicated by anecdotes from different stages of his life. For example, Captain Nathaniel Cutting recorded in his registry of daily events that he witnessed Jefferson, after breakfast, reading to his daughter Mary from *La Historia de la Conquista de México* (*The History of the Conquest of Mexico*) by Don Antonio de Solis y Rivadeneyra—an engaging work written by royal decree and originally published in 1684,its full Spanish title being *LaHistoria de la conquista de México, población y progresos de la América septentrional, conocida con el nombre de Nueva España* (history of the conquest of Mexico, population and progress of North America, known as New Spain), which intersperses narratives of the conquerors with descriptions of native customs and rites, as do works written in Spanish in the United States by Gaspar de Villagrá in his *Historia de la Nueva México 1610* (History of New Mexico, 1610) and by Fray Alonso Gregorio de Escobedo in his *La Florida,* written in 1587. Cunning, in his diary also records the tenderness with which Jefferson helped his 11-year-old daughter, Mary, in her scholastic studies of the Spanish language, general history and geography.[72]

In February, 1790, when preparing for a trip to New York, Jefferson packed as reading material, the book entitled **Historia general de las Indias y conquista de México** (General history of the Indies and the conquest of Mexico) by Francisco López de Gómara, a Spanish chronicler who served as a chaplain and assistant to Hernán Cortes. At the time he continued sending letters to his daughter Mary insisting that she persevere in her Spanish studies. She responded by informing him of her progress

---

70 - Letter to James Madison dated August 2, 1787, "Papers", 11: 667-668.
71 - Letter to Joseph Willard dated March 24, 1789, "Papers", 14: 697-698.
72 - "Extract from the Diary of Nathaliel Cutting", "Papers", 15: 497-498.

in reading an original of *Don Quixote*, and on finishing it, she told him of her intention to read *La vida de Lazarillo de Tormes y de sus fortunas y adversidades* (The life of Lazarillo de Tormes, his fortunes and misfortunes)—a work which at the time of the Inquisition was considered heretical but which in Spain marked the beginning of the genre of picaresque novels. Then, when his eldest daughter Martha gave birth to a girl (Anne Cary Randolph), Jefferson, with a grandfather's humor, wrote a letter to his daughter Mary on February 16, 1791, which said: "I hope you pay close attention to your niece and henceforth provide her with harpsichord and Spanish lessons, etc."[73]

In the year 1790, Jefferson received a gift from William Short —who obviously knew his friend's tastes— consisting of a recent edition of *Don  Quixote* published by the Spanish Royal Academy, founded in 1713 and legally constituted in 1714 by Felipe V. This bit of information moved me for two reasons: first, because I have the honor of being a member of the Academy and, secondly, because it correlates to the mission and objectives of the American Academy of the Spanish Language, whose Delegation I preside over in Washington, which Jefferson would no doubt enthusiastically support today.

During his stay in France, in addition to nourishing their sensorial presence and because of his admiration for them (he was of those who acknowledged the idea "I think, therefore I am"), he acquired portraits of Columbus, Americo Vespucio, Cortés and Magellan, and when people like Margaret Bayard Smith visited his residence in Monticello, he proudly showed them these portraits as well as his library containing his precious volumes, including the *Historia de la Nueva España* by Hernán Cortés as well as his collection of Cortés' letters from Mexico and other documents and notes by Francisco Antonio Lorenzama the Bishop of Mexico, according to notes by Mrs. Smith in her diary.[74]

While it is impossible to detail all of the incidents regarding the Spanish language in Jefferson's life and in his relationships with his children, grandchildren, relatives, friends and other participants in his conversations including those who received his attentions or letters, all of the above paints an ample picture of what we set out to document regarding his appreciation of the language in terms of his knowledge of it, its use and appreciation, his vision and valuation of it as an element of his political philosophy.

Even in his retirement when he began to think about reducing, selling, or donating his collection of books, we have been able to verify his deep and

---

73 - "Papers", 19: 282.

74 - Margaret Bayard Smith, The First Forty Years of Washington Society, editor: Gaillard Hunt, New York, Charles Scribner's Sons, 1906, pp. 66-79.

continued interest in Spanish. Until the end, among other masterworks, he retained a copy of *Don Quixote* in his library as well as one for his personal use; and after founding the University of Virginia, in one of the items that he was proud to add to his library, he ordered the purchase, among others, of a work by Francisco Álvarez entitled *Noticia del establecimiento y población de las colonias inglesas en la América Septentrional*; subtitled *"religion, orden de gobierno, leyes y costumbres de sus naturales y habitantes, calidades de su clima, terreno, frutos, plantas y animales, y estado de su industria, artes, comercio y navegación"* (news of the establishment and populating of English colonies in North America; *subtitled* "religion, order of government, laws and customs of the natives and inhabitants, qualities of their climate, terrain, fruit, plants and animals, and state of their industry, arts, commerce and navigation,") published in 1778.

## Jefferson, the Library of Congress and the Hispanic Division

The looting and destruction of the Library of Congress by British troops in August, 1814, and the three thousand volumes that made it up was a disgusting and revolting act that saddened and infuriated many, including Jefferson, that genial lover of books. Prior to this tragic event, Jefferson had supported the Library of Congress from the executive branch and, more importantly, as President, he appointed a person to be in charge, designated the Librarian of Congress, and persuaded legislators to buy books from Benjamin Franklin's Library, among others. This destructive act motivated Jefferson to decide to sell his own library without delay to form the basis of restored Library of Congress which he considered not so much a personal honor, but rather as another way of supporting the nation's legacy. In a draft resolution submitted by Robert Goldsborough on October 7, 1814 for the consideration of both chambers of the legislature to authorize the purchase of the library of the former President Jefferson, there were debates and objections of all kinds, including the voices of those who preferred an exclusive library to contain only items strictly related to the field of Law. Among them were those promoting an exclusivist English-only Anglo-Saxon ethnocentrism. Charles Ingersoll, the representative from Pennsylvania, commented: "The discussion and votes of the House of Representatives in connection with the purchase of the Jefferson Library betrayed the English prejudices of some, the narrow parsimony of others, and the prejudices of nearly all."[75] More specifically, much of the contents of the Jefferson Library was objected to, and the fact that "a large proportion of his books were written in foreign languages."[76]

---

75 - Charles J. Ingersoll, History of the Second War between the United States of America and Great Britain, 2 vols. (Philadelphia: Lippincott, Grambo, 1852), 2: 271-272.
76 - New Hampshire Sentinel, November 5, 1814.

Finally, wiser heads who appreciated (or at least did not look down on) multidisciplinary references, education and competence, diversity, and the cultural and linguistic richness of the country reflected in its life, the library and Jefferson's vision prevailed. On January 30, 1815, legislation authorizing the funds was approved at the amount of approximately $4.00 per volume (which was the amount Jefferson had proposed)—a monetary estimate that certainly did not reflect the intrinsic value of the collection. Approximately 6,700 of Jefferson's volumes were shipped from Monticello. On May 8, 1815, he wrote to Samuel Harrison Smith: "Today the tenth and last cart was loaded with books . . . It is the most select collection of books in the United States, and I hope it will not fail to have a general effect on the literature of our country."[77]

The key above-cited Spanish-language literary works, histories and culturally-related material as well as other volumes, including extant copies of *Don Quixote* in the Jefferson Library, gave birth to the Hispanic Division of the Library of Congress[78] which contains one of the most complete collections of books in Spanish in the entire world and its headquarters—such are the coincidences of life—are in one of the most beautiful historic buildings in Washington DC—the main Library of Congress—which is deservedly and justly called "The Jefferson Building." Everlasting thanks are due from all of us to this genius who once said,"I cannot live without books." To which this humble admirer would add "without books in Spanish."

**Death and legacy**

Thomas Jefferson died on July 4, 1826, at his home in Monticello, Virginia, on the 59[th]anniversary of the Nation's Independence, the Declaration of which he had drafted, leaving the following epitaph he himself composed which reveals his predilections among his many lifetime achievements. The epitaph is significant both for what it contains and what it omits. Curiously, he does not mention his presidency; instead he highlights his contributions to ideas, education and academia. In fact his *Manual of Parliamentary Procedures* influenced not only the legislative branch of the United States government, but also many other legislatures around the world,

---

77 - Ticknor, "Life, Letters and Journals", I: p. 36.
78 - For example, in addition to "Don Quixote", the following original works by Cervantes were part of the Jefferson collection purchased by the Library: *Los Seis libros de Galatea* (the six books of Galatea) (1784), *Trabajos de Persiles y Sigismunda* (works of Persiles and Sigismund - 1781), *Novelas Exemplares* (exemplary novels ), *Viage al Parnasso* (travel to Parnasso -1784), among the hundreds of Spanish-language books included in the collection, as Reynaldo Aguirre notes in his volume Works by Miguel de Cervantes Saavedra in the Library of Congress, Washington DC: Hispanic Division, Library of Congress, 1994.

and even during his life had been translated into French (1814), German (1819) and Spanish in 1826.

**HERE WAS BURIED THOMAS JEFFERSON**

**AUTHOR OF THE DECLARATION OF AMERICAN INDEPENDENCE**

**OF THE STATUTE OF VIRGINIA FOR RELIGIOUS FREEDOM & FATHER**

**OF THE UNIVERSITY OF VIRGINIA**

**Born April 2, 1743**

**Died July 4, 1826**[79]

Jefferson's legacy is endless, vast, a cause of astonishment at the many innovations we have documented here. Although he sometimes intimates that he is not entirely convinced that there is life after death, Jefferson lives and will continue to live in the immortality of his authentic genius, through his historic and ideological contributions, his *avant-garde* passion for life centered on his sentiments, his vision and his geopolitical philosophy which—among many other of his prodigies—led him to appreciate and promote the Spanish language in all its dimensions. This is a fact which—in addition to all his patriotic achievements and commendations—has caused him to be recognized as an extraordinary example, a hero and a role model for those (whether Hispanic or not) who yearn for the rescue and appreciation of the history and culture encompassing the Spanish language in the United States, which has been present and vibrant within this nation's territory since 1513, being one of the several cultural and linguistic groups that make up this country. Also there are those of us who wisely and with vision choose the model of a multilingual culture in the United States, including the 50 million Spanish-speaking Americans whose numbers are estimated to reach one 132 million by the year 2050—a population which is proud of its culture and Hispanic-American history and which is striving to maintain, rescue and cultivate the Spanish language as a basis for Pan-Americanism because it is the second most spoken language in the United States—a country which Thomas Jefferson wisely helped to create with his visionary principles and achievements.

---

79 - Date added upon his death.

# CHAPTER IV

## An Emblematic Literary Voice:
## The Hispanic Element in U. S. Nationality
## According to Walt Whitman.
## His Hispanic Resonance

WALT WHITMAN

Although it may seem strange, the "Cosmos"—the old bearded man of Manhattan, Walt Whitman, is another of my great discoveries in the context of the Hispanic United States—an integral part of Hispanic America. I open this foray into the Whitmanian world by citing the words of Pedro Mir of the Dominican Republic who poeticized:

*No, Walt Whitman, here are the poets of today,*

*the workers of today,*

*the pioneers of today,*

*the* campesinos*of today,*

*firm and standing tall to vindicate you!*

But I want to go deeper because in the dusty immortality of life which the son of Manhattan sang in his epic poetry with overtly naïve lyricism, that eternal "now"which in this chapter is mine and of any of us, I will quote great Hispanic voices like that of Rubén Dario in his admiration for democracy and humanism, the reverent affinity and heartfelt sincerity of José Martí attributing to Whitman even more virtues than his real ones, the conceited and altered imitation of Chocano, the vehement and impudent protest of Pablo de Rokha, as well as Langston Hughes' non-invitation. We will see how Walt Whitman is in each one of us: We embrace him and do so with enthusiasm in his complexity as the inspired prophet of natural and human liberation, master of emanations, semi-divine and an indestructible vagabond, in spite of his own demands, and for his great admiration of the Hispanic element in this American nation. With Pablo Neruda's indebtedness we sense the egalitarian in his "impure" poetry; with Jorge Luis Borges, the mystical; with Octavio Paz, the contradictory liberal; with Rubén Dario, the "great old man, like a handsome patriarch, serene and holy." So, with my friend Fernando Alegría (and his now classical volume entitled *Walt Whitman in Spanish America*)[80] I surrender to the multifaceted genius

80 - Mexico: *Colección Studium*, 1954.

who in *Leaves of Grass*, especially in *"Song of Myself"* conjures up for us the paradoxes and ironies of his idealization, his devotion to liberalization and anti-domination, to his openness toward all immigrants, to myths and multiple readings, admiration of him and the mixed reactions his complex genius stimulates. This is the poet who in the nineteenth century said he was *the poet of the Body and the poet of the Soul, of old and young, of the foolish as much as the wise*; one of the Great Nation, the nation of many nations, the smallest the same, and the largest the same, the mate and companion of people, allas immortal and fathomless as he himself*, a free lover becoming incarnated with the *amplitude of time* and all humanity, who embodies *all presences outlaw'd or suffering* and who maintained that we are nothing if we *are not the riddle, and the untying of the riddle,* that we all *breath the common air that bathes the globe,* and who had the courage to prophetically self-evaluate in his contradictions with these famous lines: *Do I contradict myself? / Very well, then I contradict myself, / (I am large, I contain multitudes).*

**The Hispanic element in Whitman's poetic democracy and his conceptions of what constitutes American nationality.**

Using Whitman's language—that pleasurable and daring promiscuity of oneself in everyone and everyone in oneself, I wish to convey this aspect of his thinking, creation and writing, which also lives in me and inspires me to act on, with humble pride in documenting and highlighting the Hispanic presence and poetry in and of the United States. In addition to using Spanish words in his poems such as *Libertad* (liberty) or *camarado* [sic] (comrade) and expressing his appreciation for the contribution of Spanish to the English lexicographical treasure chest, I find it admirable that Whitman, despite his youthful and misguided support for the Mexican-American War (which caused Mauricio González Garza, in his *Manifiesto de Destino*(Manifest Destiny), to refer to him in the sub-title of his book as "racist, imperialist, and anti-Mexican," in response to an invitation to celebrate the 333[rd]anniversary of the founding of Santa Fe with forward-thinking and visionary statements at the end of the nineteenth century (1892), when speaking of the "Hispanic element of our nationality". He writes with wholehearted and convincing assertions that in the composite American identity of the future, the :"Hispanic character will supply some of the most needed components. No ethnicity shows a greater historic retrospect—greater in religiousness and loyalty, or for patriotism, courage, decorum, gravity and honor... As to the Hispanic stock of our Southwest, it is certain to me that we have not begun to appreciate the splendor and sterling value of this ethnic element. Who knows but that element, like the course of some subterranean river, dipping invisibly for a hundred or two years, is now to emerge in broadest flow and permanent action?"[81]This is a prophetic, apocalyptic aspect of Whitman's complex democratic discourse with myriad enumerations and varieties which have not yet been highlighted enough and have gone unnoticed or ignored by many of his scholars, critics and admirers around the world.

### Resonances of Whitman's poetic democracy in Spanish-American Poets

From this point on, I invite the reader to verify for him/herself how some outstanding Spanish-American writers responded in unison by Hispanicizing Walt Whitman's life, poetry and poetic vision.

His presence and utopiandemocraticvision, reflected in the works of Spanish-American poets in modernist, avant-garde and post-avant-garde expressions, has been likened to that of a spirit, a ghost, a leprechaun and—as Fernando Alegría put it—"to study Walt Whitman in Spanish-American poetryis like looking for the fingerprints of a ghost whose presence is felt everywhere but is nowhere to be seen. All types of critics quote his verses with dubious accuracy; poets of the most varied tendencies have been inspired by his message and have dedicatedly praised him in sonnets or have repeated his words in a kind of candid renunciation."

The first Hispanic American writer to concur with and highlight Whitman's relevance in the context of this historiographic journey was the precursor of modernism and a Whitman contemporary—**José Martí**—the Cuban revolutionary poet in his essay "*The Poet Walt Whitman*" which he wrote in New York and sent to be published in the Mexican newspaper *El Partido Liberal*(the liberal party) 1887, and later in the Buenos Aires newspaper *La Nación* (the nation) and it became the inspiration for Rubén Dario's "Ode to Whitman" in his poetic work *Azul*(blue). In that article, and others, which I will refer to later, Marti—who knew Whitman personally—admiringly writes of the cultural spaces of beauty and nature and of the poet's novelty and rebellion, resulting in his being admired and idealized in Spanish-America. Thus he writes in *La Opinión Nacional* (national opinión) on November 15, 1881, in an essay entitled *Carta de Nueva York* (letter from New York) appearing in *La Opinión Nacional* on November 26, 1881, which mentioned: ". . . verses, great and irregular like Walt Whitman's mountains "(OC, IX, p. 132). In addition to this we cite the following paragraphs from

---

81 - Whitman, Walt. Prose Works. Philadelphia: David McKay, 1892; Bartleby.com, 2000. /http:// www.bartleby.com/229/5004.html.

*La Opinión Nacional*, dated December 28, 1881: "Walt Whitman, the American poet, rebellious toward all forms, who sings in tender language full of the imagery of moons the things of the firmament, the wonders of nature, celebrates with spring-like nakedness. even sometimes with idiosyncratic daring the rough and carnal forces at work on the earth, painting red things exceedingly red, and languid things exceedingly languid . . ." In his "Letter to Bartolomé Mitre and Vedia" dated 19 December 1882 he writes,"There is a young novelist with French tendencies, Henry James. But there is this great, rebellious and vigorous poet, Walt Whitman."There is also an article entitled "Essential reform in the program of American universities –the study of living languages –the gradual ending of the study of dead languages", published in *La America*, in January 1884: "...there is no greater poet in the United States since the death of poor Sidney Lanier, than Walt Whitman, an admirable rebel, who breaks a branch in the forestand and finds poetry therein—more so than in the aged books and golden chains of the "academy," but Walt Whitman is a member of an academy, presides over it sits in its firmament."There are many other such references.

In Martí's most complete text "The Poet Walt Whitman" (1887)he writes: "He looked like a god last night, sitting on a red velvet chair, all white hair, beard on chest, eyebrows like a forest, holding a cane in his hand." This is what one of today's newspapers says about the poet Walt Whitman, a seventy-year-old man of whom the great critics, who are always in the minority, assign an extraordinary place in the literature of his country and his time. Only the sacred books of antiquity provide a comparable doctrine because of his prophetic language and robust poetry which this old poet-emitsin great and priestly apothegms like puffs of light, and his astounding-tome is off limits... He must be studied, because even though he may not be the poet of the best taste, he is the most intrepid, encompassing and yet freed from his time. In his small wooden abode which is on the verge of destitution, a mournfully little portrait of Victor Hugo glows in the window. Emerson, whose writings purify and exalt, threw his arm over his [Whitman's] shoulder and called him "friend". Tennyson, who is one of those who seethe the very root of things, sends the most tender of messages to the "great old man." The truth is that his poetry, though at first causing astonishment, leaves in the soul tormented by collective smallness, a delightful sensation of convalescence. He creates his own grammar and logic. He can read the eye of an ox and the sap in a leaf. "He is one who cleans up your house, and he is my brother! "His apparent irregularities, which baffle at first, then become—save for brief moments of portentous loss—that sublime order and composition by which the peaks on the distant horizon are made visible." He concludes: "Thus, by celebrating strength and daring, he invites onlookers to fearlessly stretch out their hands when passing by; he listens to the song of all things with outstretched palms,surprising and delightfully proclaiming colossal lushness; and in epic verses he talks of seeds, battles and oak trees, pointing out to the astonished ages the radiant beehives of men who disperse throughout the valleys and summits of America who with their bee-like wings brush against the fringes of vigilant freedom,herding the friendly centuries into the haven of eternal calm. Walt Whitmanawaits, while on simple tablecloths his friends serve him the first spring catch of fish sprinkling it with champagne—a happy hour when the material world abandons him, after revealing to the world a truthful man, sonorous and loving who, abandoned to the purifying air, germinates and stirs in its currents, 'set free, triumphant, now departed!'"

Even though Marti, in his admiration of Whitman, categorized him as heterosexual and Christian beyond what was factual, I maintain that his empathy with the son of Manhattan can be summed up in the brilliant assertion of a colleague of mine, Oscar Hijuelos who wrote: "José Martí fortified his patriotism with poetry," which also describes Walt Whitman in the sincerity of his poetics of a nationhood united in diversity beyond a merely romantic nationalism, echoes of which occasionally appear in Marti's *Simple Verses*.

The iconic invocation of the poem "**Walt Whitman**" by **Ruben Darío**— the recognized leader of the modernist movement in the history of Spanish-American literature—is included in the 1890 edition of **Azul**, and offers another reading of this American poet to whom, with clear reservations and challenges, pays homage in his prologue to *Prosas Profanas* (1917) as he does in his *Autobiografía* (1918) and imitates characteristic Whitmanian exuberance and detail in his "*Canto a la Argentina*" (Song to Argentina - 1916), and the repetition of "*os saludo*" (I greet you) "*Salut au monde!*" (Hello world!) and "*From the pampas*". Some commentators have affirmed (although I do not share their opinion) that Darío, prior to the publication of **Azul**, had not read Whitman's works nor was he fully aware of the content of his poetic revolution in terms of subject matter and form, but rather became acquainted with these by reading a French translation. I don't think this is true of Darío but of certain other poets and writers, and their reading of—among others—the works of León Bazalguette's sonnet entitled *Walt Whitman: L'homme et son oeuvre* (The man and his works - 1908). In his sonnet, Dario doesn't seem to celebrate Whitman but rather invokes him with incongruous labels such as "holy", "prophet", "priest" etc. (acknowledging him as an iconoclast, reformer, pioneer and individualist), contrasting the images of a "patriarch" and the "proud face of an emperor"—feelings which were inspired by the "iron country of the North" (i.e. the United States) about which he would later express his feelings in his well-known anti-imperialist poem "To Roosevelt" (1905). Nevertheless, Darío and Whitman both align themselves with humanism in their approach the topics of human emotions, love and the defiant notions of democracy, sensually without inhibitions, beyond realism and with diverse perspectives. Darío alludes to Whitman with rhetorical praise in the fifth verse of his sonnet, after referring to him as "beautiful" in the second one: "*His mirror-like infinite soul*", putting aside his predominant approach to Whitman with a metaphor of power that exudes such expressions as the following: "*something that reigns and overcomes with noble charm*", "*with the proud face of an emperor!*"

## Walt Whitman

*In his country of iron lives the great old man,*

*handsome like a patriarch, serene and holy.*

*In the Olympic wrinkle of his frown*

*he has something that reigns and overcomes with noble charm.*


*His mirror-like infinite soul;*

*his tired shoulders worthy of the mantle;*

*and with a harp made of aged oak*

*as a new prophet singing his song.*


*A priest who breathes a divine breeze,*

*announcing for the futurea better time.*

*To the sailor the eagle cries out: "Fly!""Row!",*


*and to the strapping worker "Produce!".*

*So goes that poet along his pathway*

*with the proud face of an emperor!*

**Federico García Lorca** includes in his *Poeta en Nueva York* (Poet in New York - 1930) an "*Ode to Walt Whitman*", which has been called a disconcerting, confusing, contradictory and definitely off limits "apocalyptic elegy". It was published in Mexico just once, in 1934, during Lorca's lifetime in a limited edition of fifty copies. It is curious to note that the author preferred not to refer to the poem in his public readings, thus, in a certain sense, he lived a double life, as did many other poets and well-known artists, such as Aleixandre. By his behavior Lorca validated the fact that until not long ago,

78

society was less bothered by the private practice of any kind of sexuality rather than bringing it out in the open. Cernuda, who faced his own homosexuality, stated that in his ode Lorca gives voice to "a feeling that was the very reason for his existence and work." Ian Gibson masterfully brings this out in his book *Lorca and the gay world*[82] as does Tomás Tuero's review in the magazine*Clarín*.[83] The "Ode to Walt Whitman" overflows with vehement contempt for what others see in him, and for what he fears he is. Tuero points out that Lorca was never able to be—and did not want to be—"openly homosexual", as he affirms in a letter about one of his works, although he certainly made use of surrealism's license to say things or leave them unsaid and to confess things openly without being discovered. In some way Lorca is able to twist "Calamus's" sensualist neck (to paraphrase the title and image of a memorable sonnet by the Mexican poet González Martinez). He does not celebrate virile camaraderie, the love of his friends or the miracle of the "electric body" (including the phallus); instead he denounces the miseries of exclusion, prostitution and secrecy. *Lorca's homosexuals: (murky with tears / fleshfor the whip)* no longer fall in with Whitman's jovial comrades. The poem, which is transcribed below in its entirety, seems to be a rarefied one since it isn't exactly what today would be called a vindication of a certain sexual minority or a repudiation of a social phobia—not even a gentle, ironic evocation of that male figure—that lovely old man who screeched *like a bird whose genitals had been pierced by a needle*. Rather it abruptly poetizes an indignant revulsion of the *cities'homosexuals*. Perhaps all the aggressiveness expressed in the poem: *aquellos esclavos de la mujer* (those slaves to women) will fall upon those he calls *the effeminate slaves of the boudoir bitches,/ exposed in public squares feverishly fanning*. The general tone of the poem seems to reflect irritation with the hypocrisy of certain more or less liberal or perverse American mannerisms; perhaps a superficial attitude, insincerely tolerant of a condition he lived with in secret with painful tension. The city homosexual is the enemy. *No quarter given! Be warned!* He detests them and composes a hilarious harangue, confronts them in a battle with no truce: *against you always, you who give the boys/ drops of foul death with bitter poison.* He goes into more detail in the poem so that no one is rescued by the inclusion of a list of the nicknames by which homosexuals are designated in the jargon of different places: the United States, Havana, Mexico City, Cadiz, Seville, Madrid, Alicante and Portugal: *Fearies, Pájaros* (birds), *Jotos. Sarasas, Apios*(celery), *Cancos, Floras* and *Adelaides*. He ends up ranting: *Homosexuals the world over, dovekillers!* Then, in a lower tone, invokes the old poet in the last stanza—almost resignedly or in defeat—as if coming to: *And you, beautiful Walt Whitman, you sleep*

---

82 - Planet Barcelona, 2009.
83 - http://www.revistaclarin.com/1118/la-vida-privada-%E2%80%A8de-garcia-lorca/.

on the banks of the Hudson...Sleep. Nothing remains. / dancing barriers shake the prairies/and America drowns in a flood of machinery and weeping. Thus, he seemed to express how lies, barriers and machines had destroyed the American dream. According to Ian Gibson and Tuerco, "Lorca sees a fundamental failure in the Whitmanian utopia; he sees the definitive founding of an empire of militia and consumption. He also sees its chaos and the impossibility of living his own life there. The attack on homosexuals is a paradoxical and an improper defense of his own privacy—a defense that can only take on the stigma of the forbidden: *That is why I do not raise my voice, old man Walt Whitman, against the child who writes/a girl's name on his pillow/nor against the boy who dresses up as a bride/in the darkness of his closet.* His opposition is clear: a transvestite but in the dimness of his closet and not openly in the *squares fanning feverishly*; the name of a girl, but *on the pillow*, not in front of the woman's *boudoir*." This is one of the approaches to this multifaceted Ode in which Lorca paradoxically both upholds and exhibits his own poetic identity.

## Ode to Walt Whitman

*By the East River and the Bronx*

*boys were singing, exposing their midriffs*

*with the wheel, with oil, leather and the hammer.*

*Ninety thousand miners getting silver from the rocks*

*and children drawing stairs and pictures.*


*But none of them could sleep,*

*none of them wanted to be the river,*

*none of them loved the broad leaves*

*or the shoreline's blue tongue.*


*By the East River and Queensboro*

*boys were battling industries*

*and the Jews were selling the rose of circumcision to the river faun,*

*and over bridges and rooftops, the sky poured out*

*herds of wind-driven bison.*

*But none of them paused,*

*none of them wanted to be a cloud,*

*none of them were looking for ferns*

*or the yellow wheel of a tambourine.*


*As soon as the moon rises*

*the pulleys will spin and topple the sky;*

*a border of needles will sever memory*

*and the coffins will bear away those who refuse to work.*


*New York slime,*

*New York slime and death.*

*What angel is hidden in your cheek?*

*What perfect voice will sing the truths of the wheat?*

*Who, the terrible dream of its stained anemones?*


*Not for a moment, Walt Whitman, lovely old man,*

*have I failed to see your beard full of butterflies,*

*nor your corduroy shoulders frayed by the moon,*

*nor your thighs pure as Apollo's,*

*nor your voice like a column of ash,*

*old man, beautiful like the mist,*

*you screeched like a bird*

*its sex pierced by a needle.*

*enemy of the satyr,*

*enemy of the vine,*

*and lover of bodies beneath the rough cloth...*

*Not for a moment, virile beauty,*

*who among mountains of coal, billboards, and railroads,*

*dreamed of becoming a river and sleeping like a river*

*with that comrade who would place on your breast*

*the small pain of an ignorant leopard.*


*Not for a moment, Adam of blood, macho,*

*man alone at sea, Walt Whitman, lovely old man,*

*because on penthouse roofs,*

*gathered at bars,*

*emerging in groups from the sewers,*

*trembling between the chauffeurs' legs ,*

*or spinning on dance floors wet with absinthe,*

*the faggots, Walt Whitman, dreamt of you.*


*He's one, too! That's right! And they land*

*on your luminous chaste beard:*

*blonds from the north, blacks from the sand,*

*crowds howling and gesturing,*

*like cats and like snakes,*

*the faggots, Walt Whitman, the faggots,*

*murky with tears, flesh for the whip,*

*the boot, or the biting of the tamers.*


*He's one, too! That's right! Stained fingers*

*point to the shore of your dream*

*when a friend eats your apple*

*with a slight taste of gasoline*

*and the sun sings in the navels*

*of the boys who play under bridges.*

*But you weren't looking for scratched eyes,*
*nor the darkest swamp where they immerse the children,*
*nor cold saliva,*
*nor the toad's slit open curved belly*
*that the faggots wear in cars and on terraces*
*while the moon lashes them on the terrified street corners.*

*You looked for a man naked like a river.*
*A bull and a dream who would join wheel with seaweed,*
*father of your agony, camellia of your death,*
*who would moan in the flames of your hidden equator.*

*Because it's appropriate if a man doesn't look for delight*
*in tomorrow's jungle of blood.*
*The sky has shores where life is avoided*
*and there are bodies that should not appear again at dawn.*

*Agony, agony, dream, ferment, and dream.*
*This is the world, my friend, agony, agony.*
*Bodies decompose beneath city clocks,*
*war passes by in tears with a million gray rats,*
*the rich give their mistresses*
*small illuminated dying things,*
*and life is neither noble, good, nor sacred.*

*Man is able, if he so wishes, to channelhis desire*
*through a vein of coral or naked blue.*
*Tomorrow affectionswill become stones, and Time*
*a sleeping breeze in the branches.*

*That's why I don't raise my voice, old Walt Whitman,*

*against the little boy who writes*

*the name of a girl on his pillow,*

*nor against the boy who dresses as a bride*

*in the darkness of his closet,*

*nor against the solitary men in casinos*

*who with revulsion drink prostitution's water,*

*nor against the man with dirty looks in their eyes*

*who love men and burn their lips in silence.*

*But yes against you, urban faggots,*

*inflamed flesh and unclean thoughts.*

*mothers of mud, harpies, sleepless enemies*

*of the Love that delivers crowns of joy.*


*Always against you, who give boys*

*drops of foul death with bitter poison.*

*Always against you,*

*Fairies of North America,*

*Pájaros of Havana,*

*Jotos of Mexico,*

*Sarasas of Cádiz,*

*Apios of Seville,*

*Cancos of Madrid,*

*Floras of Alicante,*

*Adelaidas of Portugal.*


*Faggots of the world, killers of doves!*

*Slaves of women, boudoir bitches.*

*Opening in public squares with their feverish fans*

*or ambushed in barren hemlock landscapes.*


*No quarter given! Death*

*radiates from your eyes*

*and gathers gray flowers at the mire's edge.*

*No quarter given! Be warned!*

*Let the confused, the pure,*

*the classical, the celebrated, the suppliants*

*close the doors of the bacchanal on you.*


*And you, lovely Walt Whitman, remain sleeping on the banks of the Hudson*

*with your beard toward the pole, hands open.*

*Soft clay or snow, your tongue calls out for*

*comrades to keep watch over your disembodied gazelle.*

*Sleep on, nothing remains.*

*Dancing barriers shake the prairies*

*and America drowns in a flood of machinery and weeping. .*

*I want the powerful gust from the deepest night*

*to blow away flowers and inscriptions from the archway where you sleep,*

*and for a black child to announce to gold-craving whites*

*that the empire the stalk of grain has arrived.*

Of all the contemporary Hispanic-American poets, **Pablo Neruda** is the most often compared to Whitman, especially after the publication of his *Canto General* (General Song ~1950), which led him to openly declare himself Whitman's heir. In that poem he explicitly calls Whitman one of the great North American literary figures: "Whitman, uncountable as grains of cereal along with Poe, Dreisser, Wolfe and others." Undoubtedly, Neruda considers Whitman's "lesson of life" to be the epitome of true American democracy, along with Abraham Lincoln, and on the same level. Soviet writer Illya Erehmburg, in his foreword to the Russian translation of the poems of Nicolás Guillén, makes a reference to the relationship of Neruda's poetry to that of Whitman: "The poetry of Pablo Neruda has nothing to do with so-called peoples' poetry; behind it is the temptation of the ages: Quevedo and Góngora, Butler and Rimbaud, Whitman and Mayakovsky."

Although, as Fernando Alegría points out, his first literary and ideological connection with Whitman is seen in his work *Residencia en la Tierra* (Residence on Earth ~1935), *España en el corazón* and *El Canto General* (Spain in the heart and the General Song) which are Neruda's most relevant books in the Whitmanian tradition, including his poetry*"without purity"*, with inconsistencies, self-sufficiency and encompassing American geographic, personal, temporal and eternal spaces, to which he surrenders, clings to, finds himself in, and sings of. In these verses, the Chilean Nobel Prize winner sings of the root factors in the people's social liberation and, in the analysis of Fernando Alegría and other critics of Neruda's work, he makes use of Whitman's poetic and political medium, his free verse, his enumerative realism, his proletarian and artisan vocabulary by expressing a spirit of universal fellowship.

Perhaps one of the most curious aspects of the poetic relationship between Neruda and Whitman, beyond the sensuality, autoerotism, the sense of companionship in their vision and aspirations, is the fascination that the presence and qualities of the sea held for both of them. As Fernando Alegría explains it, "On countless occasions they contemplate it with rapture, study it from a distance in its infinite rhythms, penetrate it to is depths by analyzing with astonishing patience the wonderful secrets of its animate and vegetative life, separating it from the universe as an abstraction that symbolizes the mysteries of life and death and, finally, reconstruct it poetically in images full of nostalgia, without neglecting—no, quite the contrary, accentuating—the pictorial beauty of its forms, its surface and its multicolored waters."

To which he adds: "Neruda identifies with America as much as Whitman does, but not in a pantheistic, but rather in a materialistic sense, echoing problems that he identifies directly in the environment. Most of his descriptions of landscapes in his *Canto General* are a lyrical framework of a political and social nature. Both poets meet across time despite theirpolitical, philosophicaland literary differences because both are inspired by an authentic love of people and life. The comprehensive expression of faith contained in *Leaves of Grass* has its equivalent in the world view of *Canto General*. Neruda and Whitman wish to see mankind free of the chains that impede its well-being and progress and, above all, they wish to see all men fraternizing in peace. Both make love of country a primordial subject of their poetry and both long to reach their fellow men with the message they feel so deeply about."

Of anecdotal interest, I would like to make mention of an impressive collection of works and studies on Whitman displayed prominently in Neruda's libraries at his homes in Isla Negra, Valparaiso, and his residence *La Casona* in Santiago, Chile. As he himself confessed he could not resist acquiring all the different editions of *Leaves of Grass* that he could find, including the first one, published in 1855. I also personally saw the portraits of Whitman—his "companion"—in each of his homes, sharing the seascape and the daily sunrise.

## Ode to Walt Whitman

*I can't recall*
*at what age,*
*or where,*
*whether in the vast humid South*
*or on the fearsome*
*coast, where the seagulls*
*cry out sharply,*
*I touched a hand and it was*
*that of Walt Whitman*
*I walked the earth*
*barefoot*
*I walked on the grass*
*on the firm dew*
*of Walt Whitman.*

*During*
*my entire*
*youth*
*that hand accompanied me,*
*that dew,*
*its firmness of patriarchal pine, its expanse*
*across the prairie,*
*and its mission of encompassing peace.*

*Not*
*disdaining*
*the gifts*
*of the earth,*

*nor the copious*
*curve of the column's*
*capital,*
*nor the initial*
*purple color of wisdom,*
*you*
*taught me*
*to be an American,*
*you raised*
*my eyes*
*to books,*
*to*
*the treasure*
*of the grains:*
*broad,*
*in the clarity*
*of the plans,*
*you made me to see*
*the high*
*tutelary*
*mountain. From*
*subterranean*
*echoes,*
*you gathered*
*everything*
*for me,*
*all that came forth*
*you harvested,*
*galloping in the alfalfa,*
*picking poppies for me,*
*visiting*
*the rivers,*
*coming into the kitchens*
*in the afternoon.*

*But not only*
*soil*
*was brought to light*
*by your spade:*
*you unearthed*
*man,*
*and the*
*humiliated*
*slave*
*there with you, balancing*
*the black dignity of his stature,*
*walked on, attaining*
*joy.*

*To the stoker*
*Down below,*
*in the stoke-hole,*
*you sent*
*a little basket*
*of strawberries.*
*to every corner of your town*
*a verse*
*of yours arrived on a visit,*
*and it was like a piece*
*of clean body,*
*the verse that arrived,*
*like*
*your own fisherman's beard*
*or the solemn treading of your acacia legs.*

*Your poet's and nurse's*
*silhouette*
*passed among the soldiers,*
*the night caretaker*
*who knows*
*the sound*

*of agony's breathings*
*and with the aurora you await*
*the silent return*
*of life.*

*Worthy baker!*
*Older cousin*
*of my roots,*
*crown*
*of the araucaria,*
*it's already*
*been*
*a hundred*
*years*
*since on that grass of yours*
*when it took root,*
*the wind*
*gusts*
*without your perceiving.*

*New*
*and cruel years in your fatherland:*
*persecutions,*
*tears,*
*prisons,*
*poison weapons*
*and raging wars,*
*have not mashed*
*the grass of your book,*
*the vital spring*
*of its freshness.*
*And, alas!*
*those*
*who killed Lincoln*
*now sleep on his bed,*

*they shot down*
*his seat*
*of fragrant wood*
*and in misfortune and*
*blood-spattered*
*raised a throne*

*But*
*your voice*
*sings in*
*the outlying*
*stations,*
*in*
*the*
*eventide*
*wharves*
*it sloshes*
*like*
*murky water*
*your word,*
*your people—*
*white*
*and black*
*a populaceof the poor,*
*simple people*
*like*
*all*
*people,*
*they do not forget*
*your bell:*
*they gather singing*
*under*
*the magnitude*
*of your expansive life:*
*walking with love among the people*

*caressing*

*the pure expansiveness*

*of brotherhood on earth.*

After that testimonial Ode, paradoxical in Neruda's expressing his admiration and criticism of Whitman, I will end these paragraphs by transcribing the opinion of Fernando Alegría according to which, Neruda in his *Canto General* wrote, "he felt certain within himself that he incarnated the people of Hispanic America. Such an impulse inspired Whitman to express in this one book the gospel of the United States—I mean his conviction that he was a living picture of the nation that was forming."

As Andrés Morales points out in an article entitled *"Walt Whitman in contemporary Chilean poetry"*, on which this segment is based, Whitman's influence on other Chilean poets such as **Gabriela Mistral**, **Huidobro** and **de Rokha** is unmistakable. These three poets have expressed their admiration for the works of this American poet and, furthermore, important segments of their own poetry clearly reflect that influence. It would seem that, in the early periods of each one of these Chilean poets, reading from the author of *Song of Myself* was essential. Academics have pointed out that this phenomenon is clearly evident even in the younger authors of today. In Gabriela Mistral's poems it is possible to find clear similarities in the conceptions of nature, biblical readings, the way in which the earth is perceived and, definitely, the concepts of Americanism shared by both of the above. Already at the time of the publication of Mistral's first book *Desolación* (in 1922), which, ironically, was published in the United States, she poetizes the Whitmanian plurality of self and refers, among other things, to "the intentions of clay." The extraordinary hymns in the *"America"* section of her book *Tala* (1938) are a strong testimony to the thematic union or her works with Whitman's. For example, in her poem *"Sol de Trópico"* (Tropical sun), the narrator's intention is to assimilate or merge with the American landscape. In **Vicente Huidobro's** "creationism", his poem *Adam* (1916) clearly reveals Whitmanian influence. This poet is then linked literally—though by contrast to Whitman—(*"Ah, ah, I am Altazor, the great poet . . . I am the one who has seen it all, who knows all the secrets without being Walt Whitman, for I've never had a beard as white as the pretty nurses and the frozen rivulets"*). In this poem he recreates the astonishment of the earth's "first inhabitant" encircled by nature and all the elements that encompass and dazzle him: the sea, the mountains, and this same poet transforms himself into that mythical Adam who through his words creates everything anew: nature and earth, existing within them in an echo of the expressions found in *Song of Myself*. The influence of Whitman's poetry on **Pablo de Rokha** is even more direct. While Huidobro will discard Adam's perspective to go on from there, echoing Emerson's impulses toward the postulates of creationism and created images, de Rokha will to the very end retain the influences of Whitman's works in *Los Gemidos* (Wailing, groans - 1922) and *Acero de Invierno* (Steel of Winter - 1961), expressing himself as the incarnation of humanity, with social, political and cosmic solidarity (including the line ". . . with a cow, Whitman's widow . . ."). As Fernando Lamberg pointed out, ". . . the intense voice of America, its vigor, its energy, are to be seen in Whitman, and reading his works was one of Pablo de Rokha's most profound intellectual experiences. . ." Then in the so-called generation of the 1980's, Whitman's figure reappears in the intense discourse surrounding political and social influence in relation to Chile's military coup in 1973. Through his poetry, **Raúl Zurita** emerges as Whitman's heir in his thematic emphasis on nature as the central referent of the desert and of the universe which he loves and interprets, as seen in his first two works *Purgatorio* (Purgatory - 1979) and *Anteparaíso* (1982) as well as in his later poems *El amor de Chile* (Love for Chile - 1987) and *La vida nueva* (New life - 1993), in which nature and indigenous peoples are the unmistakable protagonists of Zurita's refrain, as in his poem *"Las nuevas tribus"* (New tribes)—a paradigmatic example in which the poetic "I", with prophetic force as a part of nature, speaks of her and for her, thus linking himself to Whitman and his ritual of representing his voice as the voice of everyone—old, young, gifted, needy, aboriginal or otherwise, with a self-struggling to overcome the collective pain felt by "all of us".

Now moving on to Argentina, I should like to begin with my fellow province dweller, **Leopoldo Lugones** and his first book *Las montañas de oro* (Mountains of gold) published in 1897, with its cosmic "I", a Biblical quality and a revolutionary vision inspired by Whitmanian democratic dynamism and solidarity; however, over time Lugones would move from his earlier anarchism and socialismto stand for a somewhat controversial and even repudiated kind of conservatism. In one of his enumerations, he includes this stanza:

*Whitman intones a serenely noble chant.*

*Whitman is the glorious worker of oak.*

*He adores the life that bursts from every planting,*

*the great love that tills works female flanks;*

*and all that is force, creation, the universe,*

*sits heavy on the vertebrae of his poem.*

Better known is **Borges**' recurrent relationship to Whitman, in an exchange of lofty tones. His first contact with his works occurred in Geneva at the age of fifteen or sixteen when Borges found him in a German translation. And while in Seville in 1919 he published his first poem *Un himno al mar* (a hymn to the sea), in which he said *he did all he could to be Walt Whitman*. Fifty years later, he made a new translation of *Song of Myself* because of the indignation he felt at León Felipe's previous one. (This is a supposition, but he never contradicted it) As we shall see, in addition to articles such as *"The Other Whitman"* (I, pp. 206-208)[84] Borges frequently dedicated to Whitman certain precise, brief critical passages, revealing his long maturation process which is synthesized and definitely accurate. As Nicolás Magaril summarized in his essay *"Walt Whitman: A Strange Creature,"* Borges, basically, with characteristic frankness, in just a few lines corrects remarkable, more or less harmful misconceptions on which he bases many of the bio bibliographic myths that always fascinated him: namely, the discrepancy between the *modest author* of his literary works and their *semi-divine* protagonist. Borges stated that *Whitman fashioned a strange creature we didn't quite understand and gave it the name 'Walt Whitman'.* In the end, he dedicated a sonnet to him entitled *Camden, 1892*, in which he returns to the well-known scene of the old man in Camden, poor yet glorious, who moments before dying, piously takes on the writing of the poem of his life. In Magaril's summary of that poem, it's a Sunday; Whitman has read the newspaper and has browsed a colleague's book, then looks at his face in the mirror, and thinks that face is himself: *I am almost not, but my verses rhyme / life and its splendor. I was Walt Whitman.* This last phrase, spoken by the poet, somehow culminates that vast cycle which begins with the previously mentioned *Walt Whitman, a kosmos, of Manhatan the son.* And this renews, in a simple but slightly melodramatic sketch, the mirror-like unfolding of their lives and their works (those of Whitman and Borges), reconciled at last.

**Camden, 1892**

*The smell of coffee and newspapers.*

*Sunday and its tedium. Morning*

*and on the glimpsed page that vain*

*publication of allegorical verses*


*of a happy colleague. The old man*

*lies prostrate and pale in his decent*

---

84 - The quotes and pages cited are to be found in his four volumes of Complete Works edited in Barcelona by Emecé Publishers, Volume I-III (1989), Volume IV (1996).

94

*humble habitation. Idly*

*he sees his face in the weary mirror,*


*And thinks, no longer surprised, that that face*

*is he himself. The distracted hand touches*

*The turbid whiskers and ravaged mouth.*


*The end is not far off. His voice proclaims:*

*Almost I am not, but my verses rhyme*

*life and its splendor. I was Walt Whitman.*

*(II, p. 291)*

Borges was always fascinated by the multiplicity of "I's" in Whitman's works and in his own game of "the other and himself", "Me and Borges." He writes: "My conjecture of a triple Whitman, the hero of his epic, which he does not intend to senselessly erase or to somehow diminish the wonder of his pages. Rather he intends to exalt himself, to contrive a two- and three-level character in the end—a never-ending one—which could have been the ambition of a merely ingenious man of letters, and to bring this intention to a happy end is Whitman's unequalled exploit."Whitman is present not only in Borges' poems or essays specifically dedicated to him, but also in the verses of different poems such as in "*Lines that I could have written and lost around 1922*" from *Fervor de Buenos Aires* (Fervor of BA), in which he writes "Walt Whitman, whose name is the universe", or in expressing thanks to "the divine one" in *Otro poema de los dones* (Another poem of merits) from *The other one, the same* byWhitman and St. Francis of Assisi who already wrote the poem", or when in the poem "On his blindness" (p. 347) from *The Tigers'Gold* he writes:"not by Walt Whitman, that Adam  he mentions / the creatures under the moon," ... " or in *Himno*(hymn)  from the book of poems entitled *La cifra* (Number): "Whitman sings in Manhattan" (III, p. 307), in which Borges poetizes that Whitman "took the ... infinite / resolution to become all men / and to write a book that stands for everyone" —an idea that he repeats in his poetic prose entitled *Someone dreams* from the same book of poems and it other works. Also Whitman appears in Borges' poetic notes. For example, when he clarifies the poem *Aquel* (that one), in the book of poemsLa Cifra (Number): "This composition, like almost all the others, exaggerates in its chaotic enumeration. Of this figure, on which Walt Whitman so happily lavished its virtues, all I can say is that it gives the appearance of chaos and disorder and in its inmost essence must be a cosmos, an order".

In the Caribbean, after José Martí, the poem *Contracanto* (countersong) by Dominican poet Pedro Mir materializes with more clarity his feelings for and about Whitman. Mir's poem is one that, among those mentioned here, more formally resembles Whitman's work. Like Whitman, it celebrates man and his universe and thus creates a new identity—that of a democratic *we;* that is, a collective identity, the transformation of the self-centered "me" into an altruistic "we". Hence the subtitle: *Song to ourselves*. Both Mir and Whitman, like Neruda in his *Canto General* (General song), assume the role of official spokesmen for their fellow citizens; both become prophets of the future in the course of their respective refrains. Furthermore, Mir's poem, as in other contemporary allusions to Whitman, reflect, as we said when analyzing Darío's poem, the attitude of many Latin American writers towards the United States and its interventionist politics, which to some of them was a betrayal of Whitman's utopian democratic dream. Nevertheless, the poem has the rich complexity of many other original connotations that allude to mankind, nature and socio-political ideals:

**Countersong to Walt Whitman**

Pedro Mir's *Countersong* to a famous poem of Walt Whitman's published in 1855 under the title *Song of myself* which begins: *"I, Walt Whitman, a cosmos, a son of Manhattan ..."*

*I,*

  a son of the Caribbean,

*Antillean to be exact.*

*The raw product of a simple*

*Puerto Rican girl*

*and a Cuban worker,*

*born indeed poor,*

*on Quisqueyan soil.*

*Overflowing with voices,*

*full of wide open pupils*

*throughout the islands,*

*I have come to speak to Walt Whitman,*

*a cosmos,*

*of Manhattan the son.*

*People will ask,*

*Who are you?*

*I understand.*

*Let no one ask me*

*who Walt Whitman is.*

*They would go and cry into his white beard.*

*But nevertheless,*

*I will say again who Walt Whitman is,*

*a cosmos,*

*a son of Manhattan.*


*I*

*There once was a virgin wilderness.*

*Trees and land without deeds or fences.*

*There once was a perfect wilderness.*

*Many years ago. Long before the ancestors of our ancestors.*

*The plains with the play of galloping buffalo.*

*The endless coastlines playing with pearls.*

*The rocks released diamonds from their wombs.*

*And the hills with the frolic of goats and gazelles …*

*…The breeze would swirl through clearings in the woods,*

*heavy with the bold play of deer and birch trees*

*filling the pores of evening with seed*

*And it was a virgin land full of surprises.*

*Wherever a clump of earth touched a seed*

*suddenly there grew a sweet-smelling forest.*

*At times it was assaulted by a frenzy of pollen*

*squeezing out the poplars, the pines, the fir trees,*

*and pouring out the night and landscapes in clusters.*

*And there were caverns and woods and prairies*

*teeming with brooks and clouds and animals.*

2

*(Oh, Walt Whitman of luminous beard ...!)*

*He was the wide open Far West and Mississippi and*

*Rocky Mountains and the Kentucky Valley*

*and the forests of Maine and the Vermont hills*

*and the plain of the coasts and more ...*

*and only*

*the delusions of the man and his head were missing.*

*Only the words were missing*

*my own*

*to penetrate the mines and caves*

*and fall into the furrow and kiss the North Star*

*And every man*

*wearing on his chest,*

*under his arm, in his look and on his shoulders,*

*his mighty self,*

*his permanence*

*within himself,*

*to unleash it over that unbridled territory.*

3

*Nobody had better ask me*

*who Walt Whitman is.*

*I would go cry into his white beard.*

*I am going to say again who Walt Whitman is,*

*a cosmos,*

*of Manhattan the son.*


*4*

*There was once an unblemished pure territory.*

*The only word missing was*

*mine*

*to penetrate its dark regime.*

*But nevertheless,*

*The self that was going to say it was there*

*but was caught*

*like a fish*

*in its ribbed net.*

*It was there*

*but inner, stern and confined*

*loved and defoliated its yellow stems.*

*Outside was the firm system of Law.*

*The jealous one was there*

*regulator of behavior.*

*The law of cotton, the Law.*

*The Law of Cotton, the Law of sleep,*

*The English law, hard and definitive.*

*and only*

*a fleeting self emerged twixt two eyelids,*

*the fulfillment of the Law was illuminated.*

*And so,*

*everyone annulled his dismissed self*

*among the moss, the shadow, the poppy*
*and the ox.*


5
*And one day*
*(Oh, Walt Whitman of unsuspecting beard ...!)*
*at the foot of the word*
*"me"*
*the word Democracy shone forth.*
*It was a leap.*
*Suddenly the most remote "me"*
*found its secret value*
*Freedom of Vocation. Freedom of Conscience.*
*Freedom of Speech. Freedom of Action.*
*Freedom of adventure, project and fantasy.*
*Freedom to fail, to love, and choice of surname.*
*Freedom with no going back,no pinnacles or nettles.*
*Freedom to love me and to look me in the eye.*
*Freedom of the sweet assemblage that I have*
*within my heart*
*with you and with all of infinite humanity that rolls along*
*throughout*
*all the ages, years, lands, countries,*
*creeds, horizons ... and was the necessary*
*means of joy.*
*The hills unleashed stars and fireflies.*
*The grapes were drunk on wine and were perennial.*
*In the entire territory*
*the great gateway of opportunity opened up*

and everyone had access to the word
"mine".


6

Oh, Walt Whitman, of sensitive beard;
it was as a net in the wind!
It throbbed and filled with the ardent figures
of sweethearts and youth, of rough men and farmers,
of country boys walking to the stream,
of rowdies wearing spurs and smiling maidens,
of the hurried marches of countless beings,
of tresses or hats …
And you were listened to
road after road,
striking their heartstrings
word after word.
O Walt Whitman of guileless beard,
I have come through the years to your red blazing attire!


7

The men advanced with their
robust and sweaty masculine destiny
They piloted the boats
and the days. On their way they fought the Indians
and their women. In the evenings they told their stories
and spoke of their cities. They hung their shirts in the wind
and on the roads. In the valley there were stagecoaches
and cities. They hung their shirts in the wind
and there was the smell of breasts preceding the ax

*and sometimes they went astray in the darkness*

*of the maidens' wombs...*

*That territory was growing upward*

*and downward.*

*Skyscrapers*

*and mines*

*were moving away from the earth,*

*connectedyet distant.*

*The strongest, the most enlightened, the most*

*capable of disrupting a road, they went forward.*

*Others were left behind. But the march*

*went forward without pause, without looking back.*

*Self-confidencewas necessary.*

*It was necessary*

*faith.*

*And softly the song was forged:*

*me the cowboy and me the adventurer*

*And I Alvin, I William with my name and my lucky*

*Deck of cards,*

*and me the preacher with my baritone voice*

*and me the maiden with my face*

*And me the whore with my curves*

*And me the merchant, captain of my silver*

*and me*

*the human being*

*in pursuit of fortune for me, above me,*

*behind me.*

*And with the whole world at my feet, subordinate to my voice,*

*carried on my back*

and at the height of the mountain range "me"

And the thorns of the plain "me"

And the glow of the plowshares "me"

And the banks of the streams "me" and the heart of the amethyst "me"

and I

Walt Whitman

a cosmos,

a son of Manhattan ...!


8

The secret wonder of a story being born ...!

With that far-reaching cry

a giant nation was built,

Made up of stories and smaller nations

which then were as the world

Between two great seas ...

And then

it has filled up with gulfs, islets and whales

slaves, Argonauts and Eskimos ...

On the wild seas

the Yankee clipper began to sail,

on land structures of steel were raised,

poems and codes and marbles were inscribed

and that nation won its fiery battles

and its glorious dates and its total heroes

that they still had even on their lips

the fragrance

and the nectar

of the fragrant earth with which they made their bread

their journey and their luggage ...

And that was a great nation of pathways and choices.

And of self

—the turning of all the mirrors

toward a single image—

found its prodigious primitive message

in an immense, pure, unblemished territory

thatlamented the absence of the word

"mine".


9

For

what has a great, undeniable poet been

but a crystal-clear pool

where a people discovers its perfect

likeness?

What has it been

but an inundated park

where all men recognize each other

through speech?

And what

but the chord of a boundless guitar

whereon the people's fingersstrum

their simple, their own, their strong and

true, immeasurable song?

For that's why you, abundant Walt Whitman, who saw and

ranted

just the right word for singing of your people,

who in the middle of the night said

*"me"*

*and the fisherman understood himself in his tent*

*and the hunter heard himself in the midst of his firing gun*

*and the woodcutter recognized himself in his axe*

*and the farmer in his yellow reflection on*

*the water*

*and the maiden in her town-to-be*

*growing and maturing*

*under her skirt*

*and the prostitute in her source of delight*

*and the miner of darkness in his walking beneath the homeland …*

*When the tall preacher, bowing his*

*head*

*held between his two long hands said*

*"me"*

*The entire town hears itself in you yourself*

*when it heard the word*

*"me", Walt Whitman, a cosmos,*

*a son of Manhattan …!*

*Because you were the people, you were me,*

*and I was Democracy, the surname of the people,*

*and I too was Walt Whitman, a cosmos,*

*a son of Manhattan!*


*10*

*No one knew that unruly night,*

*a cold face, a primitive coelenterate,*

*was found on a coin. What dry*

*face*

*suddenly seemed a metallic and*

*sonorous circle.*

*What dry face saw circulating from hand to*

*hand and that dry mouth suddenly said*

*"me".*

*And it began to fit together, to fulfil itself and to multiply*

*in all currencies.*

*In coinsof gold, copper, nickel,*

*in handcoins of virgin veins*

*of farmers and shepherds, of goats and*

*bricklayers.*

*No one knew who disappeared first.*

*But another hand was seen buying*

*conscience.*

*And from the bottoms of rivers and ravines, of*

*themarrow*

*of the bushes, of the mountain ranges' peaks,*

*passing by streams of sweat and blood,*

*then came the Banks, the Trusts,*

*the monopolies,*

*the Corporations .... And, when nobody*

*knew*

*they went there to show the face of the girl and the heart*

*of the adventurer and the mischief of the cowboy and the*

*longings*

*of the pioneer ... and all that immense*

*territory*

*began to circulate through the banks' coffers, the*

Corporations' books

the skyscraper offices,

machine calculators ...

and then:

he was seen one morning nearing the great door of

opportunity

and then nobody else had access to my word

and no one else has understood the word "me".


11

Ask the night about that and the wine and the dawn ...

Beyond the hills of Vermont, the coastal

plains

across the wide Far West and Rocky Mountains,

through the Kentucky Valley and the forests of Maine.

Pass by the furniture and automobile factories,

the docks,

the mines, apartment houses, the

heavenly

elevators,

the brothels, the artists' instruments;

look for a dark piano, wind the strings,

the hammers, the keyboard, break the silent harp

and throw it on the last rails of the early morning ...

Pointlessly.

You will not find the clean accent of the word

"me".

Destroy a phone and a disc of bakelite,

pull the wires off a nighttime loudspeaker,

take from the sun the soul of a Stradivarius
violin ...
Pointlessly.
You will not find the clean accent of the word
"me"
(Oh, Walt Whitman of shabby beard!)
What of gloomy faces, tiedtongues,
defeated livers and routed arteries ...!
You will never find
but never
the spotless accent
of the word
"me".


12
Now,
Listen to me carefully
if someone wants to againmeet
the old word
"me"
go to the street of gold, go to Wall Street.
Do not ask for Mr. Babbitt. He will tell you.
—I, Babbitt, a cosmos,
a son of Manhattan.
He will tell you
—Bring me the West Indies.
on different speedy calibers, on
machinegun belts,
from the tanks caterpillar treads

*bring me the West Indies.*
*And in the midst of a silent aroma*
*there comes the island of Santo Domingo*
*—Bring me Central America.*
*And in the midst of a dreadful aroma*
*there comes silent Nicaragua*
*—Bring me South America*
*And in the midst of a pathetic aroma*
*there comes Venezuelalimping.*
*And in the midst of a Bogotá sky*
*Colombia is falling.*
*Ecuador is falling.*
*Brazilis falling.*
*Puerto Rico is falling.*
*In the midst of saline volume*
*Chileis falling...*
*They're all coming. They're all falling.*
*Cuba brings its wrath wrapped in a shaking*
*of pageantry.*
*Mexico brings its aversion wrapped in a single glance*
*at the border*
*And Haiti, Uruguay and Paraguay, are all falling.*
*And Guatemala, El Salvador and Panama, are falling.*
*They're all coming. They're falling*
*Do not ask for Mr. Babbit, I have already told you.*
*—Bring me all those peoples in sugar, in*
*nitrate,*
*in tin, in oil, in bananas,*
*in syrup.*

*bring me all those people.*

*Do not ask for Mr. Babbitt, I have already told you.*

*They're all coming, they're falling.*

*13*

*If you want to find the hard*

*modern accent*

*of the word*

*"me"*

*Go to Santo Domingo.*

*Pass through Nicaragua. Ask in*

*Honduras.*

*Listen to Peru, Bolivia, Argentina.*

*Wherever you go, you will find a sonorous captain*

*a "me"*

*A luminous leader, a "me" a cosmos,*

*A providential man*

*a"me", a cosmos, a son of his*

*homeland.*

*And in the midst of the blistering night of*

*America*

*you will hear, beyond maturity and*

*fragrance intermingled with deaf moans,*

*with blasphemy and*

*shouting,*

*with sobs and clenched fists, with streaming tears and long*

*lines and long curses*

*a self, Walt Whitman, a cosmos,*

*a son of Manhattan.*

*An old song converted into forceful*
*argument*
*between the factories' gears, in the*
*citystreets. A "me", a cosmos in the*
*guardrails,*
*And on the wagons and in the plant's*
*mills.*
*An old song turned into an argument for blood and*
*for misery*
*a"me", a Walt Whitman, a cosmos,*
*a son of Manhattan ...!*


*14*

*Because*
*What has caused the people's happiness*
*but continuous change, eternal*
*movement,*
*an infinite fire that burns and then*
*dies out?*
*What has been*
*but an unstoppable stream,*
*yesterday a mirror of hills and palm groves,*
*today a white cloud?*
*And what*
*but an inexorable struggle*
*which today is led by a handful of the greedy*
*and tomorrow by charming fists,*
*fragrant and frenetic in the*
*myriad people?*

*That's why you, numberless Walt Whitman,*

*who in the middle of the night said "me"*

*and the sonorous smithyfound himself in the fire*

*and the blacksmith and the stoker*

*and the lighthouse caretaker of celestial look*

*and the smelter worker and the woodcutter*

*and the celestial girl percolating the dawn*

*and the pioneer and the fireman*

*and the coachman and the adventurer and the muleteer ...*

*You,*

*who in the middle of the night said*

*I, Walt Whitman, a cosmos,*

*a son of Manhattan*

*and a whole town found itself on your*

*tongue*

*and threw itself into building its dwelling*

*today,*

*and has lost that dwelling,*

*today,*

*with a handful of smiling and*

*cocky greedy ones,*

*today*

*who have changed the infinite fire that*

*burns and then dies*

*today...*

*today a tattered Walt Whitman*

*does not recognize you,*

*because your sign is kept in the*

*banks'*

*coffers,*

*because your voice is in the islands*

*protected by*

*reefs*

*of bayonets and daggers,*

*because your voice floods the decrees and the center of*

*Charity*

*and lottery games,*

*because today*

*when a rosy magnate,*

*in the middle of the cosmic night,*

*unreasonably utters*

*"me"*

*beneath his throat you hear the noise of*

*the*

*bloodied*

*sheltered crowd explode*

*that grimly says*

*"you"*

*and spits blood onto the gears,*

*onto the borders and the umbrellas...*

*Oh, Walt Whitman of endless beard!*


*15*

*And now it is no longer the word*

*"me"*

*the accomplished word*

*the password to activate the world.*

*And now*

*now it is the word*

*"we".*

*And now,*

*now has come the time for the Countersong.*

*We the railroad workers,*

*we the students,*

*we the miners,*

*we the peasants,*

*we the wretched of the earth,*

*the denizens of the world,*

*the heroes of everyday work,*

*with our love and our fists,*

*enamored of hope.*

*We the white-skinned,*

*the black-skinned, the yellow-skinned,*

*the Indians, the copper-skinned,*

*the Moors and the dark-skinned,*

*the red-skinned and olive-skinned,*

*the blonds and platinum blonds,*

*united by work,*

*by misery, by silence,*

*by the cry of a solitary man*

*who in the middle of the night,*

*with an absolute whip,*

*with a meager wage,*

*with a golden dagger and*

*an iron face,*

*wildly cries out*

*"me"*

*and hears the crystal-clear echo*

*of a shower of blood*

*that relentlessly feeds from us*

*we ourselves surrounded by docks*

*receding in the distance*

*we ourselves*

*below the skyline of the factories*

*we ourselves*

*and in the flower, in the pictures, in the tunnels*

*we ourselves*

*in the tall structure on the way to orbit*

*we ourselves*

*on the way to marble halls*

*we ourselves*

*on the way to prisons*

*we ourselves ...*

*16*

*And one day,*

*In the midst of the most astonishing thing in history,*

*passing through walls and fences*

*trough laughter and victory,*

*lighting in the eyescandles of joy*

*and in the tunnels and in the rubble,*

*Oh Walt Whitman of our definitive*

*beard!*

*We for us, about us*

*and in front of us ...*

*We will gather fists and seedbeds from all*

*the villages*

*and in a race of shoulders and arms reunited*

*we will quicklyplant them*

*in the streets of Chile, Ecuador, and*

*Colombia,*

*Peru and Paraguay*

*El Salvador and Brazil,*

*in the suburbs of Buenos Aires and*

*Havana*

*and there in Macorís del Mar, a small town*

*of mine*

*deep corner of lost waters in the*

*Caribbean,*

*where the blood sounds*

*like propellers breaking in the*

*river ...*

*Oh Walt Whitman of proletarian stamp!*

*On the streets of Honduras and Uruguay.*

*In the fields of Haiti and on the roads of Venezuela.*

*Inland in Guatemala with its young stalk.*

*In Costa Rica and Panama*

*In Bolivia, in Jamaica and wherever,*

*wherever a working man*

*represses his smile, suppresses his expression,*

*the silent throat spits*

*at the face of the rifle and on the salaries*

*Oh, Walt Whitman!*

*Whitening the heart of our days*

in front of us,

us and us and us.


*17*

*Why did you want to listen to a poet?*

*I am speaking to one and to others.*

*To those of you who came to isolate him from his people,*

*to separate him from his blood and his land,*

*to flood his road.*

*Those of you who drafted him into the army.*

*The Those of you who defiled his luminous beard and put a gun*

*on his shoulders carrying maidens and pioneers.*

*Those of you who do not want Walt Whitman, the democrat,*

*but a different Whitman—atomic and savage.*

*Those of you who want to outfit him with boots*

*and crush heads of nations.*

*To grind into blood the temples of little girls.*

*To smash into atoms the old man's flesh.*

*Those of you who take the tongue of Walt Whitman*

*as a sign of shrapnel,*

*as a flag of fire.*

*No, Walt Whitman, here are the poets of today*

*standing up to justify you!*

*"Poets present! ... Arise! because you must justify me!"*

*Here we are, Walt Whitman, to justify you.*

*Here we are for*

*your sake*

*demanding peace.*

*The peace you may need*

*to exhort the world with your song.*

*Here we are*

*saving your Vermonthills,*

*your woods in Maine, the sap and fragrance of your land,*

*your spurred rowdies, your*

*smiling maidens,*

*your rough country boys walking to the stream.*

*Saving them, Walt Whitman, from the*

*traffickers*

*who take your language for the language of*

*war.*

*No, Walt Whitman, here are the poets of*

*today,*

*the workers of today, the pioneers of today, the peasants*

*of today,*

*firm and standing up to justify you!*

*O Walt Whitman of upright beard!*

*Here we are beardless,*

*with no arms, with no ears,*

*with no strength on our lips,*

*looking around,*

*ruddy and persecuted,*

*with eyes*

*dilated throughout the islands,*

*full of courage, of knots of arrogance*

118

*which throughout the nations loosen,*

*with your sign and your language, Walt Whitman,*

*here we are*

*standing up*

*to justify you,*

*our constant Manhattan companion!*

In the Caribbean others also reflect Whitmanian influences as is the case of Cuban poet José Lezama Lima in his analysis entitled *La expresión americana* (The American expression - 1993), in which he refers to Whitman and emphasizes his integrationist romanticism as does, more recently, José Kozer in the neo-baroque context of his poem "*Animus*".

In this review, we must also include a critical analysis by Mexican novelist and poet **Octavio Paz** of what he refers to as the essence of Whitman's poetry. In his book of essays entitled *El Arco y la lira* (The bow and the lyre) - Whitman, poet of America, he states "Walt Whitman is the only great modern poet who does not seem to experience dissatisfaction with the world—not even loneliness. His monologue is like an immense choir. No doubt there are in him at least two personalities—the public poet and the private person who conceals his true erotic inclinations. But his mask— that of the poet of democracy—is more than just that; it is his true face. Despite certain recent interpretations, his poetic and historic dreams coincide perfectly. There is no mismatch between his beliefs and his social reality. And this is more important—I mean broader and more significant—than his psychological circumstances. However, the singularity of Whitman's poetry in the modern world can only be explained in terms of another, even greater one: that which encompasses it: the poetry of America." In fact, Octavio Pazargues even more forcefully that "Whitman—with full confidence and innocence—can sing of democracy on the march because his utopian America is intermingled with and indistinguishable from American reality. Whitman's poetry is a great prophetic dream, but it is a dream within a dream, a prophecy within an even greater one that nourishes it. America dreams of herself in Whitman's poetry because she herself is a dream and she dreams of herself as a concrete, almost physical, reality with her people, her rivers, her cities and her mountains. All this enormous mass of reality moves quickly, almost unthinkingly and, in fact, lacks historical weight. He is incarnating the future. The reality Whitman sings of is Utopian. By that I don't mean it is unreal or that it only exists as an idea, but that its essence—that which moves it—justifies and gives meaning to its evolution, gives gravity to its movements. It is the future—a dream within a dream. His poetry is realistic only for this reason: His dream is about reality itself—something which has no substance other than an invention and a dream about itself. America dreams of herself in Whitman because she herself was a dream, an abstract creation, in light of what others previously and now poeticize as "the American nightmare"—a different kind of dream. However, even though Octavio Paz might want to deny Whitman's direct influence, he is current in his Pan-American ideology, in his focus on identity issues, on the reinvention of America and his transcendentalist and sensual dedication to Mother Earth.

Although we have quoted only a few poets, I would like to mention that there are **many others** in Spanish and Hispanic American literature who reflect a linkage to Whitman in their conceptions of poetic democracy. To briefly cite a few: **Miguel de Unamuno** shares with Whitman his views on immortality, continuous innovation, the independence of summaries. **Antonio Machado** and some others reflect the characteristics of enumeration and a Whitmanian atmosphere. **Rafael Alberdi** declares himself a comrade in arms. Whitman's influence on the cosmic pantheistic lyricism of **Jorge Guillén's** *Cántico* (Canticle) has been noted. The creations of some of the initiators of "social poetry", such as that of Uruguayan poet **Carlos Sabat Ercasty**-who paraphrases Whitman in his *Poemas del hombre* (Poems of man) and elsewhere in his poetic writings which deal with the concept of identity within an interminable cosmic plan; and in his poems *Pantheos* (1917), *Verbo de América; discurso a los jóvenes* (Verb of America; talking to the youth - 1940), *El espíritu de la Democracia*, (Democratic spirit - 1944). Furthermore, Whitman's influence on many other poets is well-known, such as the poetry of **Ernesto Cardenal**, who in his prologue to his *Anthology of American poetry,*[85] which he published together with **José Coronel Urtrecho**, expresses enthusiasm for the optimistic picture painted in Whitman's democracy as a communion of all mankind, of man with nature and the cosmos. Hence its inclusion, for example, in an *Anthology Free Poetry* published in 1981 by Nicaragua's Ministry of Culture, as an model to be followed by other poets. The renowned Peruvian poet, **César Vallejo**, stated that the only hope for American poetry was through Whitman and his genuine sincerity, and this is mostly reflected in his work *Human poems*, which contains subconscious Whitmanian contradictions. I also draw attention to the relationship to Whitman of two other Peruvian poets—**José Santos Chocano** and **Juan Parra del Riego**. In fact, Chocano, in his poem *Blasón* (Blazon) proclaimed himself to be *the singer of America, native and wild*. According to his biographers, Chocano was a man of little formal schooling. (He boasted of not knowing French or wanting to learn it to keep himself "free of foreign influences") and notably identified with

---

85 - *Fundación El Perro y la Rana* (the dog and frog foundation), Caracas: 2007, p. XIV.

the Whitmanian parameters *of America and savagery*, revealing an emulation more obvious than mere influence, for he even equated himself with Whitman: *"He has the North, but I have the South"* which he proclaimed with poetic arrogance in a statement that many took as his motto. Although critics pointed out that he did not recognize his essential difference, since his was a Chocano Americanism, and they correctly pointed out his so-called "look in time" in an Americanism of landscapes, of contemplating panoramas and the indigenous and Hispanic past, the monumental and the immobile, whereas Whitman's is one of greatness and universality, and this is lacking in Chocano. By contrast, Whitman looked from the present to the future in an Americanism that was alive and thriving, and this is not a minor difference. Juan Parra del Riego—as Nicolás Magaril points out in his article *"Walt Whitman: a Strange Creature"*—is noted in literary history for having composed the following rant: *That was you Walt Whitman! / The perfect comrade! The Revealer! / Our great source of American strength! Oh dear Walt Whitman! / Oh, Captain, my captain, my captain!* In general, we find that Susan Sontag's assertion about Kafka could be applied to the case of Whitman's influence on Spanish American literature, since there appears to have been a kind of "mass kidnapping" of his work and style. In the above verses we can see the similarity of certain features that appear in various manifestations of Whitman's influence in Spanish-language literature: an out-of-control effusiveness, ultimately a kind of paternalistic apostolate—that bad habit of forever evoking the poet over and over again for what he is, for his life, his mission, what God lovingly calls him, etc., when Whitman himself repeatedly pointed out his reservations in these matters, the American impetus and the reference to the opening verses of the litany he wrote following Lincoln's assassination: *"O Captain! My captain"*, of martial eloquence, a tribute often mentioned in diverse contexts. And we could make mention of many other Hispanic countries and people, from the criticisms by Harvard Spanish philosopher-poet Jorge Santayana, to a defense written by Argentine Luis Franco. Then there is the nationalized Argentine Spaniard, José Gabriel as well as José A. Ramos of Cuba who contradicts Peruvian critic Luis A. Sánchez in his appreciation of the complex democratic genius we know as Walt Whitman and the dialectic of the discourse he engenders.

In addition to Whitman's presence in the Spanish-American literary imagination which we have documented above, he has been reincarnated in numerous and varied **translations of his works in the language of Cervantes** at different times, in different countries, with different theoretical and practical approaches to the praxis of those translations, both literal and academic, including possible linguistic betrayals in controversial and sometimes erroneous Spanish translations of *Leaves of grass*, *Song to Myself* and other poems which have been the subject of entire essays, in the formal and even profound aspect of this great poet of the American democratic epic, admirer of the transcendentalist Ralph Emerson, a Lincoln enthusiast and a precursor of modernism and post-modernism. There are many partial Spanish translations of Whitman's texts such as those by Balbino Dávalos which were unveiled at the Second American International Congress held in Mexico City in 1901; those by Miguel de Unamuno in 1906 (*Canto Adánico* – [Adam's song]) which were included in an article on Walt Whitman's poetry written in 1910 by a Spanish journalist using the pseudonym Ángel Guerra and by other writers such as Cuban poet José de Armas y Cárdenas who is credited with translating select works of Whitman, and the Uruguayan Álvaro Armando Vasseur who had a noteworthy disagreement with Pedro Bonifacio Palacios (Almafuerte) mentioned in an original selection from 1912 (which, according to Enrico Santí was a translation from the Italian), reprinted later in Montevideo in 1939 and later in other editions—translations that were criticized by Fernando Alegría as being too free and erotic but also were defended, by Enrico Mario Santí, among others. In Madrid in 1946 Chilean-born Concha Zardoya published *Selected Works: Critical biographical essay*. (Incidentally, these two translations were referenced by Matt Cohen in his version that I recently corrected for the Whitman Spanish-language page at the University of Iowa). Also that same year in Mexico translations were published in a collection by the Chilean critical poet Arturo Torres-Rioseco entitled *La última vez que florecieron las lilas en el patio* (The last time lilacs bloomed in the courtyard) and an essay by Miguel Mendoza entitled *Walt Whitman, cantor de la democracia* (Walt Whitman, singer of democracy.) Then, in 1949, Chilean poet and translator Gregorio Gasman published *Saludo al mundo* (I salute the world). Between 1950 and 1954 Emilio Abreu Gómez, published a selection, prologue, notes and translations done by the great chronicler of modernism in a work entitled *Enrique Gómez Carrillo: Whitman and other chronicles*. **Leon Felipe**'s translation of *Song of Myself* was most recently published by Losada in 1950 which has been characterized as a "paraphrase" and has vehement detractors as well as defenders. The work opens up with a prologue of nine poems which, according to some critics, reveal all of Whitman's vices and virtues, portraying him as a heroic, revolutionary poet, a denigrator of the absurd laws of man and of the human inequalities of his day and, seemingly, of all time. León Felipe is an undeniable lover of Whitman's poetry whose energetic tone and voice of freedom are reflected in the harangues found in his own verses. There are some who maintain that his is the best translation of *Song of myself*. However, Jorge Luis Borges in his review in the Magazine *Sur* (No. 88, January 1942) expresses his opinion that León Felipe's translation "calumniated" Whitman, affirming that "from his (Whitman's) long psalm-like voice we have now the cocky shouting of *cante jondo*" (The most serious and deeply moving variety of Flamenco, or Spanish Gypsy lament). In 1953, Francisco Alexander of Ecuador published his translation of *Leaves of Grass* (reprinted in Buenos Aires in 2011), whose complete version of Whitman's poetic works, in the words of Rolando Costa Picazo, "reveals a deep knowledge of the American poet and a great respect for the characteristics of his poetry"and "reproduces its rhetorical effects, litanies and repetitions, achieving a veritable feat in the translation of Whitman's lyrical flights"—a critical judgment that I endorse in my own evaluations of the different translations.

Jorge Luis Borges' translation of *Leaves of Grass* (selection) was published in 1969. Borges himself qualifies his approach as a translator by confessing "Meanwhile, I see no other possibility than that of a version like mine which oscillates between personal interpretation and resigned thoroughness." Numerous translations have since appeared and I limit myself to refer only to the following in chronological order: Leonardo Wolfson, *Leaves of Grass* (selection), Buenos Aires, 1976, who for his part compared translations by Vasseur, León Felipe and Borges in his essay "*Three times Whitman*" (1992), as Ana Redondo and Javier Azpeitia had previously done in their "*Versions of Whitman*" (which included, in addition to the above mentioned, translations by Francisco Alexander, José María Valverde, Concha Zardoya, Mauro Armiño as well as his own). See also Pablo Mañe Garzón, *Walt Whitman, Complete Poetry*, 4 vols. (1976-1983). In 1981 Enrique López Castellón translated Whitman's *Song of myself*, *The Quill*, and *Sons of Adam*. In 1984 translations of *Song to Myself* by Roberto Matson were published in Buenos Aires in a bilingual edition and *The Quill* was translated by Rodolfo Rojo in Santiago de Chile. In Madrid, *Song of Myself* was translated by Mauro Armiño, and in Barcelona the two volumes of Walt Whitman's *Leaves of Grass* were translated by Alberto Manzano. Later, in Buenos Aires in 1999 Carlos Montemayor's translation of *Greetings to the world and other poems* appeared. New editions and re-editions of different translations of Whitman's works in the last two decades continue to multiply, cultivating his influence in current Hispanic-American poets—evidence of his genius and immortality.

To conclude this digging up of references, because I believe this subject is for another chapter, I will limit myself to briefly mention some of the most important Spanish-American critical texts that analyze the revolutionary thematic, ethical and aesthetic characteristics of Whitman's poetry in Spanish America, reflecting the complicated presence of his poetic democratic element (many written by other poets), although we have already referred to some of these poems and their translations. This listing includes the above mentioned *Walt Whitman in Hispano-America* by Fernando Alegría published in Mexico in 1954 and numerous later essays that appear, for example, in the corresponding section of *Walt Whitman & the World* edited by Gay Wilson Allen and Ed Folsom (1995); articles and/ or books entitled *"Walt Whitman"* by Armando Donoso (1915), John de Lancey Ferguson (1916), Torres-Rioseco (1922) and Luis Franco (1945), as well as others with more specific slants such as Donoso's essay *"The Free Spirit of Walt Whitman* (1920), essays by Jorge Luis Borges *"The Other Whitman"* (1929), *"Notes on Whitman"* contained in *Other Inquisitions*, 1937-1952; works by Pepita Turnia entitled *Walt Whitman: Day-to-day and Eternal* (1943), *Walt Whitman; the democratic voice of America* by José Gabriel(1944), *Walt Whitman and Latin America* by Elena Aizén de Moshinski(1950), *Walt Whitman: Racist, Imperialist, Anti-Mexican* by Mauricio González de la Garza (1971), and many other books, articles and essays on the subject's life, his referents, his voice and poetic ideals that includes all of us, even in his contradictions, imperfections and immortality.

**My own discovery and experience is embodied in my most recent collection of poems entitled "We are all Whitman."**

In it, I begin by affirming that Whitman himself imparted to me the audacity to proclaim "We are all Whitman,"—and makes me feel proud to be an Hispanic-American. This feeling is born of his insistence and by feeling it I don't encroach on anything or anyone. From this milieu my experiment in Spanish with Whitman resulted in my work **Todos somos Whitman,** [86] based on *Leaves of Grass* and "Song to himself (of myself or to myself)."

Because these texts (containing a minimum of a thousand lines) are born not only of his writings and my own multiple readings of his works and those of many others, but also of the intrinsic multiplicity of the "Song" itself and of the 104 essays written about its 52 sections—a translation task that assigned to me by the University of Iowa and which inspired this new creative reincarnation—possibly ambiguous but certainly opportune—and without any intention of infidelity—quite the contrary. Part of the Whitmanian premise is that there is no periphery: the text is never closed, it is simply rewritten, recreated and we all configure the center and the original, as a loan, a payment and a reward. To paraphrase here the genius of "the Fictions", here literature mimics history and history mimics literature with the elegant recklessness of a Pierre Menard who quixotically boasts about this because of my insistence that I have discovered that "We are all Whitman".

I ask that both he and Borges forgive my irreverence. They justify it even more since Borges poetized that Whitman took "the … infinite / resolve to be all men / and to write a book that includes everyone".

---

86 - *Vaso Roto Ediciones* (broken glass editions), Madrid /Mexico, 2014.

In contrast to this expansive attitude are those who, quite the opposite of Whitman, exalt themselves or believe they are somebodies, but unfortunately they feel the need to bring down others including those that are superior to themselves, or are simply aware of what they are in the estimation of those who really know who they are referring to or who truly know (and we all have to put up with this). Under the guise of being level-headed they claim that someone is nothing or nobody, thus unmasking their intolerance, racism or false sense of superiority. But Whitman, the "friendly and extravagant savage," was much wiser and acclaimed me/us in his verses—me and everyone—that we are one in all and all in one—hence the song and the celebration. How dreadful and vile are the capital sins of envy, intolerance, racism and the false sense of superiority! Wise and good are those who shun these and so wretched are those who succumb to their entrapment which leads them to a sense of low self-esteem. Sadder still are those who make a crowning achievement of their sickly perceptions and beliefs. In more than one sense we are most certainly illusory, and reality is the inevitable punishment. Robert G. Ingersoll and Ezra Pound share this view with their imperfections as I do with mine when I speak ironically of Whitman. Ingersoll points out that he did not subscribe to a creed because he was full of wrinkles, old and had a flowing white beard; but he was very clear in stating that hypocrisy, in spite of having a venerable aspect, relies on appearances and façades, on stupidity and fear. And Pound described himself as "a Walt Whitman who learned how to wear a coat and tie and a dress shirt" even though he was an enemy of both.

Because universal, great and imperfect Whitman is something else, lives differently, breathesthe air, the horizon, the ocean of each and every one the same way, in and of himself. We're all Whitman; and he is everybody and me…

*"I am of old and young, of the foolish as much as the wise,*

*Regardless of others, ever regardful of others,*

*Maternal as well as paternal, a child as well as a man,*

*Stuff'd with the stuff that is coarse and stuff'd with the stuff that is fine,*

*One of the Nation of many nations, the smallest the same and the largest the same;*

*A Southerner soon as a Northerner, a planter nonchalant and hospitable…*[87]

Ironically, while on board a "One World Alliance" flight I wrote the following comment: "The hopeless illusion of an advertisement." But I disseminate

87 - *Song of Myself*, Section 16.

these verses without order, without purpose, without a mission; drops of blood, semen, impulses, outbursts, flowered effects of making love to my imagination seducing me with the exciting promise of life, me and everyone in me, with everyone, without distinction, the poets in each one of us / in me, I seek, I dare, I am liberated, I question, without excess, in heaven and on earth, under the sun, the stars and other sharedatoms. It is the magic and caricature of Whitman in this ambiguous and inclusive dust that has fascinated me once again—a nimble and inclusive democracy. The mystery of reality imposes itself on the individual and, through each one, in the universal present and beyond mistreatment, must be a source of happiness, and I grant myself the right to seek abettors in this wild, seemingly civilized land. Whitman hasconvinced me once again that writing is my significant other, although I do not know if I will be a very good lover. In the end, others will gossip about the final stages of love and death—with details on the cover. The bearded, visionary prophet has freed me from those who are cloistered within all the conventions; I respond to his call to rebellion and endless escape with his lyricism of beginnings—sensual, erotic, courageous and transforming. I graft myself onto him, to his ocean of inclusive enumerations, with the flourishing lilacs of Bloom and Goethe, Blake, Wordsworth, Holdering, Shelley, Keats, as a dreamer, not wishing to escape from his influence and I turn to Allen Ginsberg, Hart Crane, D.H. Lawrence and his spontaneity, T. S. Elliot (his aloofness aside), Wallace Stevens and William Carlos Williams in his narrative, *Ashbery*. He allows me—along with Emerson, Carlyle, Rousseau and other romantics—to transcend.

Thank you, Cosmos, son of Manhattan and Camden: this is my cry in the midst of the crowd, incessantly celebrating and breathingyour own verses: "And what is reason? And what is love? And what is life?" [88]

By living, singing, suffering, attempting in dialogues to embody experiences and words, to enjoy freedom, peace, democracy, to celebrate—today and always—the answers to these questions, you and I, all of us:

We are all Whitman!

And here, too, in conclusion, is my song of the Hispanic-Americans who Whitman inspires, by integrating the universal "me" that Hispanics are as a nation and this was the inspiration for the opening of my book **Todos somos Whitman** justifying its inclusion about the diverse manifestations of the Hispanic United States.

---

88 - *Song of Myself*, Section 42. Section of this charpter in English and the English version of the closing poem has been taken from *Todos somos Whitman / We are Whitman* Brett Aln Sanders tranbslation University of Huston Arte Público Press, 2016

126

# SONG OF / TO / MYSELF

*"What I assume you shall assume"*

**Walt Whitman (1)**

*This scattered Self*
*hispanic, Latin, blond, black, olive-skinned,*
*native and immigrant, was here with everyone,*
*yesterday and today; today and tomorrow; does not stop,*
*virginal atom of nakedness and dust,*
*of Manhattan's universal son*
*the uncaged cosmos*
*and the whirlwindof echoes.*

*Child with the wisdom of questions,*
*offspring of poor and rich, of lettered and unlettered,*
*of rails, planting times, classes and cares,*
*which will sprout, embodied, with nothing forgotten,*
*seed in its newly bloodstained earth,*
*which gathers hands, pupils, voices,*
*the savor of oceans,*
*the smell of sweet jungles,*
*God's pollen, days and nights*
*at center of the Self that dances with many,*
*men, women, young people and old*
*in the light of the infinite's furrows,*
*with open hands, without walls,*
*free roots of mine and everyone's*

*at the foot of the song*
*that now celebrates*
*without creeds or libraries.*

*With all the colors that stir up their race,*
*Roman, Celtic, Hebrew, Moor,*
*Hispanic, Aborigine, with kingdoms of multitudes*
*fresh in the tree of life.*

*Grass, girl or boy child, suppliant germ*
*of love and timepieces in the atmosphere,*
*God of the promise and the future,*
*modern and ancient in the new people,*
*come and gone from among the old people,*
*humanity's heart in the moon, hands' mirror,*
*the breath of syllables.*
*Because it is voice, hum of green and dry leaves*
*that loves equally,*
*in the color of its time, the park that is, am,*
*are, today, here, yesterday and forever,*
*the mystery's imprecise territory.*

*This Self is Puerto Rican, Chicano,*
*from Cuba free dancer of merengues,*
*from Santo Domingo and all the Caribbean,*
*from El Salvador and Nicaragua.*
*It comes from Mexico, Central America,*
*from Costa Rica, Tikal, Guatemala,*
*from their rainforests, lakes of salt and honey,*

128

from Panama, Colombia, Peru and Venezuela,
the corn crops of the Argentine pampas,
Chile's veins of grapes, Bolivia's reed flute,
from the Mayas, Quechuas, Aztecs, Incas,
from the Guaranís, from the Amazon, Ecuador,
from the Uruguay of the Charrúas and its shores,
gauchos, criollos, Europeans, mestizos,
mulattos, the fair-skinned, Turks, Asians, Syrian or Lebanese,
waifs, streetwalkers, huddled masses of Latin America
with their many names.

It is harassed and startled by propellers and shrapnel,
by ashes and the hammer's hard-won pennies.
Boss and day laborer; still the job's slave,
painter of trenches, resourceful creator of roofs, pavement
on the agony of yesterday's blood and the even-now
of the Monday of beginnings and the Sunday of holy days.

It is expressed and is not expressed by welcomes,
the yowls of rejection and the sunless silence
of indifference, every day, gray hands.
It belongs to family and sometimes they invite it, other times exclude it
from family suppers and their menu of dawns;
when the assemblage is gathered, they have become used
to its only cooking, serving, or cleaning up after the meal.

It suffers now, and in the next gust of wind, the discriminating smoke
of random breath, for good or bad of those

*who intoxicated breathe ignorance or haughtiness*

*without clusters of stars, mountains, heavenly clouds,*

*wellsprings of gifts and of meadows.*


*The dream of your creation, fatherland of many fatherlands,*

*at the same time defined and disturbed*

*in the ferment of capricious laws*

*that attacked freedom and happiness in their path*

*and the paths of all who signed your articles.*

*It likes and does not like the words, the eve*

*of silences, words dyed in the antagonism*

*of empires and conquests, welcomes, coffins and slights,*

*gold pieces received and robbed.*


*They will not destroy him, whether he be teacher or student,*

*follower or leader. They tried without luck*

*because history and his soul, to which we belong*

*and it belongs in this cloth of substances and times,*

*do not allow it.*

*I am large, I contain multitudes.*

*They will not manage to deny me or ignore me or declare me undocument-ed:*

*I am written in you, in all,*

*as all are in me,*

*in clay and in the breeze's gentle sky,*

*in the delightful meaning of your body.*


*With the people's wise voice, it complains and does not complain.*

*Like everyone, it triumphs in its defeats and loses, sometimes, in the victories of bridges,*

*because the shank's good fortune carries it inside*

*and outside of agony's navel.*

*It sings with the voice of ravaged fields,*

*the sweat of striae and its gifts,*

*the robust and oppressive body of cities.*

*It aims to be the river's voice and not only of the forbidden,*

*but also strictly unknown voices.*


*It would not wish for entrance to a forest*

*whose roots it must avoid.*


*In everyone's Self,*

*the poem's universal soul,*

*in each innumerable Walt Whitman,*

*cosmos without rubrics,*

*wave among waves, shared worlds*

*inside vibrating yellow,*

*I dance, I smile, I cry:*

*I celebrate myself, and sing myself.*

# CHAPTER V

## PRESENCE AND CREATIVITY:

## THE LITERARY LIFE OF THE HISPANIC UNITED STATES

### FROM 1513 TO THE PRESENT:
### POETRY, PROSE AND THEATER

JUAN FELIPE HERRERA

## Poetry

It is no longer possible to sustain what Miguel Romera-Navarro affirmed in 1917: "The history and exposition of Hispanic literary influence in North America have not yet been written. Not one single study, whether comprehensive or superficial, popular or scholarly, has been devoted to it."[89] Literature written in the Spanish language in the United States—poetry in particular—deserves a prominent chapter in any anthology on the subject of Ibero-American literature that purports to be complete, since works in Spanish are an integral part of American and Hispanic-American literature.

Of the four kinds of Spanish language used in the United States (so-called pure, bilingual, Spanglish and English with salsa) we will focus on documenting the poetry written in "pure" Spanish, without ourselves pretending to be purists and recognizing the dynamics of language with its many adaptations and idiosyncrasies (since we are dealing with a "melting pot" of different Spanish-American roots). In this regard, we will use the classifications created by some literary critics—arbitrary as are all classifications, without further exploring the controversial use of nomenclature to differentiate diverse Hispanic poetry. We will deal with "Hispanic" poets—those of Spanish origin residing in the United States who have chosen to write in Spanish, and "Latinos"—those of Hispanic origin who have chosen to write in English,[90] whose works and creations have not been a part of this compilation in spite of their recognized importance, while sharing many of the discursive and aesthetic characteristics of U.S. Hispanic poetry.

This present work is an inventory in which we hope to document the presence of Hispanic-American poetry even with some formal deficiencies, to contribute to integrating it into a long poetic tradition that enriches so-called

---

89 - *El hispanismo en Norteamérica: exposición y crítica de su aspecto literario* (Hispanicism in North America: exposition and critique of its literary facet), Madrid: Renaissance: 1917, p. 1.
90 - The following works discuss and document these traditions, respectively: William Luis in his book Dance Between Two Cultures: Latin Caribbean Literature Written in the United States, Vanderbilt University Press, Nashville: 1997.

"U.S. Poetry"along with other traditions, because Hispanic contributions have been ignored in the historically antagonistic attitude of the dominant Anglo-Saxon culture, except for the perspectives of certain great thinkers, such as Thomas Jefferson, already documented in Chapter III and the poet of democracy, Walt Whitman in Chapter IV. U.S. Hispanic literature traces its origins to explorers and conquerors who began their incursions into what now constitutes U.S. territory in 1512-1513.

Within the six poetic groupings identified in our research, we began our review of the most representative poetic figures and works during the colonial period, looking at thematic and aesthetic records and their basic importance. We start, in any case, with the premise that there is not just one unique and dominant poetic tradition in the United States. This premise is particularly important because the colonial poetic period is eminently revealed and framed in one (Hispanic) poetic tradition in the context of U.S. poetry along with "official" Anglo-Saxon, native, Afro-American, and other traditions.[91]The Hispanic tradition has been around for more than four and a half centuries in the United States. It connects with the other previously-mentioned traditions in the continual questioning of hegemonic policies, of abuses by those in power in direct, objective language, with a predilection, in the most recent creations, for free verse and, at the same time revealing differences—the most important being the language used metrics and thematic focus.

As we will see and will document more in detail along the way, the literary/ poetic Hispanic/ Latino tradition in the USA is characterized by multicultural enrichment and by old and new voices. It is expressed in different codes (Spanish, English, bilingual, and *Spanglish*) which sometimes appear to mix naturally and give a dimension peculiar to language, to its figures and formal expressions. All angles are considered: Style, images and thematic, reflecting the dynamism of this experience in its various forms: oppression-oppressed-oppressor, struggle, self-preservation, identity, abandonment, race relations, immigration, exile, pilgrimage, melancholy, resentment, wrenching and nostalgia, in a voice that is diverse generationally but geographically concurrent, acculturation—all of the above—in love and in death in this defining context it produced a valuable and unique literary discourse with voices and figures representative of most of the literary movements that have marked poetic creativity throughout the centuries, from the baroque, romantic, symbolist and Parnassian currentsthat pre-

---

91 - The following works document these traditions: Jay Parini (editor), The Columbia Anthology of American Poetry, New York, Columbia University Press: 1995, Duane Niatum, Harper's anthology of 20th century Native American poetry, New York, Harper Collins: 1988 and the anthology of Michael S. Harper and Anthony Walton (eds.), The Vintage Book of African American Poetry, New York, Vintage Books: 2000.

ceded the advent of modernism to vanguard currents, new avant-garde, post-modernism, neo-modernism, modernity, post-modernity and post-globalization.[92]

We begin, then, by limiting ourselves to outlining the scope of these traditions within the colonial period from 1539 to 1810, although the histories and legends place the first expedition of Juan Ponce de León to the Florida peninsula in search of "the fountain of youth" in 1513. In 1528, Pánfilo de Narváez crossed the Gulf Coast where his fleet sank near what is now coastal Texas, from where a group of survivors under the leadership Of Álvaro Núñez Cabeza de Vaca arrived in Mexico after crossing through what is now Texas territory and other areas of the Southwest. There were also expeditions between 1539 and 1543 under the command of Hernando de Soto coming from the west side of Florida to the Appalachian Mountains then to the Mississippi River.

We will take an overview of the six poetic corpus that make up this U.S. Hispanic literary creation /memory, whose beginnings pre-date the founding of the United States[93] and continue vibrantly with far-reaching effects up to the present day, with a future that could surpass expectations, statistics and the possibilities of human exactitude, but not the dim their celebration.

This approach is an imperfect beginning. There is much to do, much to complete, much to cover; hence the vital need for continuous updating by future enthusiasts.

---

92 - I have documented this approach in more detail in my article: *Representantes de los movimientos literarios: en la poesia escrita en español en los Estados Unidos: Modernismo, Pre/Post/Neo y otros ismos* (representatives of literary movements: in Spanish-written poetry in the United States: Modernism, Pre/Post/Neo and other isms). "Alba de América" 30. 57-58 (2011) : 214-27.

93 - I am updating in this presentation my study entitled "Poetry of the United States in Spanish" published in *Hispanos en los Estados Unidos*, edited by Gerardo Piña et al., New York: Columbia University: 2004, pp. 197-213. Then published in www.psicofxp.com/forums/ literature. 62/636564-la-poesia-hispana-en-ee-uu. html In turn, I condense in this and in the following section studies by John H. McDowell, Maria Herrera-Sobek and Rodolfo J. Cortina "Hispanic Oral Tradition: Form and Content", Luis Leal, "Pre-Chicano Literature: Process and Meaning (1539-1959)", Francisco Lomeli: "Contemporary Chicano Literature, 1959-1990: From Oblivion to Affirmation to the Forefront", which are part of the Handbook of Hispanic Cultures in the United States: Literature and Art, edited by Francisco Lomeli, General Editors Nicholas Kanellos and Claudio Esteva-Fabregat, University of Houston: Public Art Press: 1993. I refer to the extensive bibliography to be found throughout this *Handbook* for those who wish to further investigate the periods or themes mentioned here. I refer to poetic texts compiled in *Otra Voz* (another voice). Anthology of Hispanic Literature of the United States edited by Nicholas Kanellos, University of Houston: Public Art Press: 2002, as part of the recovery program of the Hispanic Literary Heritage of the United States.

## Colonial Poetry (1539-1810)[94]

The explorers, friars, travelers and conquerors left a legacy written in different kinds of narrative prose (chronicles, memories, stories, journals, and letters) testimonies of their exploits and discoveries.

The poetic genre began with Bartolomé de Flores in 1571, a native of Málaga and Córdoba, who in Seville published newly-composed work believed to have been written while he was in Florida, according to literary historians, consisting of a poem of 347 verses of *décimas* (tenths) ending with a *Villancico*[95]—poetry with all the arrogant content of Spanish colonialist imperialism of cross and sword, but within its propagandistic rhetoric its verses also reveal admiration, attachment to and the characteristics of Florida—a land at once conquered and promised, the *locus amoenus*, (Latin: "pleasant place"—a literary term which generally refers to an idealized place of safety or comfort) in its depiction of this American landscape, with a confessed curious omission, after using it extensively as a descriptive resource such as in the following verses:

*Curious things I do not tell*

*of animals or groves*

*surrounded by copious fountains*

*and other numberless plants. . .*


Part of the "Invocation":


*Emperor of Glory*

*Powerful, Clement God*

*make my memory acute*

*so that by your grace I may obtain*

*a dazzling victory.*

94 - Based on the essay: *El período colonial en la poesía escrita en español en los Estados Unidos (1539–1810): importancia fundacional* (the colonial period in poetry written in Spanish in the United States (1539-1810): foundational importance) which I presented at the Fourth International *CeLeHis* Literature Congress, Spanish, Latin American and Argentine Literature, Mar del Plata, November 7, 8 and 9, 2011. http://www.mdp.edu.ar/humanidades/letras/celehis /congreso/2011/actas/ ponencias/ambroggio.htm

95 - Popular poetic form of the late 15th to 18th centuries. In the quoting of verses I have used the version of the Universal Virtual Library found at www.biblioteca.org.ar/libros/71351. pdf.

Finishing with praise of Florida's impressive landscapes:

*And to provide a better account*

*I want to tell of the greatness*

*beauty and splendor*

*of this fertile paradise:*

*its people and nature,*

*it is a new world filled*

*with delights and freshness*

*with many and varied landscapes,*

*flowery and pleasant meadows*

*with birds of a thousand kinds.*

Appearing later is a collection of poems entitled *La Florida* by Franciscan friar Alonso Gregorio de Escobedo, written sometime between the years 1587 and 1593 and classified as the first epic poem to be composed in what is now the United States, consisting of approximately 21,000 twelve-syllable lines in royal octaves. It was written, as he himself says, "in uneven language and poorly shaped verse." His first ten poems—hagiographic in nature—deal with the life of San Diego de Alcalá; the following two cantorefer to Juan de Silva's 1595 expedition (Canto 11) and Guale's 1597 revolt (Canto 12). The second part, consisting of 13 poems, begins with the justifications for and the beginning of evangelizing missions, as follows:

*You will go, Christ told His chosen ones*

*to preach to every creature*

*of my divine law the ten precepts,*

*a safe and secure sailing chart.*

Then it speaks of shipwrecks and other vicissitudes and struggles of the Spanish against the English and French, and in a few verses of this section details the depredations of Francis Drake at St. Augustine in Florida, which took place a year before the poet's arrival there. Canto 14 opens up the third part with a description of Escobedo's journey from Havana to the territory of Florida;he also comments on Alonso de Reinoso, a Franciscan friar and religious leader. Starting with Canto 16 descriptions of Florida are interspersed among the verses detailing rites and customs and the local inhabitants' fighting methods, as we see in the following fragments:

*It is swamp-filled Florida,*
*A hundred thousand sea channels penetrate,*
*And you cannot distinguish those nearest*
*From the land in all its expanse.*

*...*

*Because of the abundance of oysters*
*They make of their shells a lime very fine*
*From which they raise walls*

*And repair any remnant of damaged dwellings.*

Descriptions of the native Indians are sometimes pejorative, always revealing the prejudices of the Spanish explorers' religious, moral Christian mentality which distorts or alters their testimonial objectivity. On the one hand, he praises their ability and strength to survive in a hostile environment while facing the "conquerors"; on the other, he asserts their defects (lustful, cruel, and barbaric), as we see in some of his texts:

*The Indian is like a buck in his swiftness,*
*And strong as a hard stone*

*Ingenious,*
*of rare subtlety*

*...*

*They worshipped with gentleness;*
*The beauty of the clear star*
*And the thunder whose noise is dreadful*
*And those known as Cabrillas*
*Worshipped on their knees.*

*...*

*It is a miserable and sinful people.*
*It is a people without truth or government....*

140

*Its womenfolk are malevolent*

*...*

*It is a people without natural speech.*

*It is a people not like rational men.*

The last cantos of the poem contain chronicles of speeches and sermons expressed in verse by the author, with frequent references to both the Old and the New Testament, a chronicle of his campaign of indoctrination and evangelization, as indicated in the verses in Refrain 24 which—in his words—"contain.... as I was describing the most holy incarnation of Our Lord Jesus Christ from the womb of the virgin St. Mary for Christians and infidels. " Raquel Chang-Rodríguez argues that: "from a literary perspective, the poem ... (with its different heroes and events) .... Leads to themes characteristic of the American epic... The variety of episodes, the author's long journey by land and sea, his role as an eyewitness to events and the use of the epic pattern to enhance descriptions make *La Florida* a key text from the northern [Hispanic] frontier and a unique contribution to epic poetry—a style so highly treasured in its day." [96]

It is followed by the creations of Gaspar Pérez de Villagrá—lawyer, soldier, Hispanic-American poet and a legal proxy during one of the expeditions into New Mexico. A native of Puebla de los Ángeles, educated in Salamanca, Spain, who in 1598 began writing a poem in the tradition of Virgil entitled *Historia de la Nueva México* (published in Alcalá de Henares, Spain in 1610). It contains 34 cantos which he expresses in verse form in archaic 16th century Spanish with its twists and remnant phrases,describing the expedition, the natural surroundings and the customs of the New Mexico inhabitants, including stories of courage, love and crises, concluding with the conquest and cruel destruction of the city of Acoma. Critic Manuel M. Martín Rodríguez describes it as "a quite peculiar literary work" because although "it shares many characteristics of the traditional epic . . . it also departs significantly from that genre . . . especially when it tries to interweave official documents into the poem's verses" with hybrid metric structure.[97] The following is an extract from Genaro Padilla's review of the edition of Gaspar Pérez de Villagra's *Historia de la Nueva México 1610*, translated by Gilberto Espinosa with introductory notes by F. W. Hodge. (Los Angeles: The Quivira Society, 1933, Vol. IV) who writes: "What works in this poem is the disclosure of competing claims in the epic structure of

---

96 - From his article *La Florida y el Suroeste: letras de la frontera norte* (Florida and the Southwest: Letters from the northern frontier), in Encyclopedia of Spanish in the United States, Madrid, Santillana: 2008, p. 63.

97 - See his edition of Gaspar de Villagrá. History of New Mexico. Alcalá de Henares: University of Alcalá de Henares, 2010.

intent. It is an epic which celebrates the exploits, intelligence, and courage of the protagonists, but by doing soalso requires honoring the antagonists. Homeric and Greek epics, for example, celebrate conquest and yet dramatize the agony of warfare, making heroes of both the victor and the vanquished thus creating this equal measure in order to immortalize Greece, or—in the case of Villagrá—Spain. Yet, it seems to me that Villagrá in some strange, and I think unintended way, immortalizes not Spain, but Acoma".

An analysis of this poem's stanzas reveals how the poet, from inside the new Mexican landscape, focuses on history with his anecdotes of victories and defeats as well as the feats of the Spaniards; also of the strong men and women who support the survival of a culture which is still very much alive up to the present day; and also on the horse as a symbol of defiance, even when close to defeat, and as a symbol of power and control in the American epic. I quote the following verse from Canto 8, as an example of "Villagrá's lyricism in the style of Garcilaso de la Vega"—so classified by Juan F. Maura in his study "Gaspar Pérez de Villagrá and Sabine R. Ulibarri: past and present of the epic of New Mexico": [98]

*And so, like streams which in passing*

*Refresh their banks and create*

*Graceful groves and adorn them*

*with trembling leaves interweaving*

*A diversity of fragrant flowers,*

*Pleasant meadows,*

*delightful frescoes*

*And pleasing, comforting shade,*

*(Refrain 8, 151).*


These verses echo Garcilaso's first eclogue:


*Flowing waters, pure, crystalline;*

*You see the trees reflected therein.*

*Green meadow, covered in fresh shade;*

*Here among the birds you dissipate your grievances;*

98 - Published in http://www.ucmes/info/especulo/numero20/nmexico.html.

*You pass through the ivy and trees*

*And press through her green bosom.*

Miguel de Quintana continued this poetic tradition after his arrival in New Mexico in 1693 where he remained for the rest of his days. With the influences of ethnic mixing, his writing, which is bold for his time, reveals remnants of religious and social heterodoxy expressing the need to reaffirm himself in metaphysical poetry, as in the following verses:

*Write and be not a coward.*

*Write so that of the immense*

*and supreme good that is God*

*you can experience that movement.*

He had been cross-examined by the Inquisition in 1732, as revealed in the following lines:

*Do not fear interrogation,*

*punishment, pain and effrontery.*

*It is God, Miguel, who heartens you*

*with supreme inspiration. (…)*

In mid-seventeenth century, the Tale of Alonso de León (1649) was written. He was the captain of the expedition to the Bay of the Holy Spirit in the territory of Texas. The work was concluded by an anonymous author in 1690 and contains the elegy of a soldier "standing beside a corpse", with a notable influence on later poems, such as those of the romantic Mexican poet Manuel Acuña (1849-1873) bearing the same title, in the following typical verses:

*Dismal, sad site*

*where gloom alone is with you;*

*because sad fortune brought your inhabitants brutal death.*

*I only contemplate you here*

*as a casualty and sad instance*

*of the capriciousness of life; (…)*

*And you, cold corpse,*

*which once showed so much mettle*

*I see you as gentle*

*and of unhappiness a living paradigm.*

Also in this narrative context, the poems of Fray Manuel de Arroyo and those of an anonymous author (possibly Pedro Bautista Pino) of the chivalric play "*Los Comanches*" with its characters and hero *Cuerno Verde* (Green horn) deserve special mention.

Simultaneously with this written legacy, a fruitful oral tradition was generated and maintained among U.S. Hispanics. The significant literary body of different genres in the oral tradition can be seen in sayings, rhymes, riddles, *corridos*(i.e. ballads), *décimas*, (a type of poetic composition whose metric requirement is that it contain ten octosyllabic verses where the first must rhyme with the fourth and fifth; the second with the third; the sixth with the seventh and the eighth with the ninth), songs, allegories (for example "*La Llorona*" – [the crying woman],). The *corridos* and ballads referring to Gregorio Cortes are classics—symbols of the Hispanic/ Latin resistance against oppression by the dominant Anglo culture:

*Said Gregorio Cortez*

*with his soul truly on fire*

*"I'm not sorry I killed him.*

*Defense is allowed."*


Or another one: *Valentín de la Sierra* (V of the mountain range):


*I'm going to sing a* corrido

*about a friend from my land,*

*he was called Valentín*

*and was shot and hung in the mountains.*

And the following is an example of a popular rhyming riddle (rhymes in the original):

*Avo passes by my house,*

*cado\* of my heart.*

144

*If you don't guess this one*

*you're just a dumb donkey.*

*(i.e. avocado – rhyme missing).

In concluding our commentaries on this period, we must point out the importance we attach to the rescuing of U.S. Hispanic culture, literary creations and history whose relevance cannot be ignored nor can its premeditated exclusion from "official history" remain unchecked. This is changing now because Hispanic contributions are being acknowledged more and more with the appearance of numerous, well-documented critical editions of foundational texts, even by non-Hispanic Anlgo scholars who include those works in the canons of U.S. Literature, beyond the aversion that certain subject matter in the compositions of this epoch might produce in the mind of the present-day reader. José Rabasa addresses this issue in his work "The aesthetics of colonial violence"[99]Also, Harold Bloom argues that the art of poetry is of interest in and of itself regardless of "political correctness."[100]Raquel Chung-Rodríguez has posed the following question: "Why, in the study of early contact between Spain and America, have these voices been relegated or ignored? Why are they excluded in recounting the cultural history of the United States? In reflecting on recent trends in the field of interdisciplinary studies in colonial and transatlantic themes, it becomes clear that it is urgent for this legacy to be recovered and incorporated into critical deliberations showing its complexity, ramifications and validity. Given the importance of the "northern border" as it stands now, which paradoxically annuls—and at the same time sets— boundaries, we must include the voices of those who wrote to record the narration of events 'worthy of the pen that writes them' (Pérez de Villagrá, *Canto* 1, 4). because 'historical truth . . . is not what happened; it's what we judge to have happened. (Borges, 1970: 59)"[101]

In the second place, despite the desire to distance oneself from the events of conquest under the Cross and the Sword preserved in these texts, it is a reality of the past which prefigures constitutive elements of Hispanic culture and identity such as the Catholic religion with its values or lack thereof, institutions, influence, vernacular content and historical and cultural reference, sources of conflicts with the values and defects of the dominant culture and its Protestant ethic and historic religious antagonism, which even today is the footing for articles such as those by Samuel Huntington when

---

99 - Rabasa, José (1993). "Aesthetics of Colonial Violence: The Massacre of Acoma in Gaspar de Villagrá's 'History of New Mexico". College Literature 20 (3): 96-114.
100 - Harold Bloom, "The Anxiety of Influence: A Theory of Poetry". New York: Oxford University Press, 1973; 2d edition, 1997.
101 - Op. Cit., p.72.

he speaks with bias and intolerance of "the Hispanic threat to the American dream." The above-referenced poems by Fray Gregorio de Escobedo and, especially, those of Gaspar Pérez de Villagrá, correspond to the baroque period of Hispanic literature—a period in which society admired the figure of the soldier/poet during those centuries of imperial expansion with contributions from poetic figures such as Garcilaso de la Vega, Miguel de Cervantes and Alonso de Ercilla, among others.

Finally, it is important to emphasize the sequence already seen during this period from discourses of conquest, the efforts to evangelize, writings about customs, populations and topography, to those of rebellion reflected by, among others, Miguel de Quintana, against religious authority and later a critic of the dominant culture, with satiric expressions characteristic of the romantic movement. These articulations will become sharper in the nineteenth century and will exemplify Hispanic poetic creativity in the United States up to the present time, using symbolic language to challenge restrictions on religion, gender, sexual orientation, etc. in the post-modern era. It will also be a starting point for valuable antithetical discourses and worldviews including protest, nostalgia and struggle against hegemonic discourse, shaping memories of a different social order in the United Stateswith an unbiased national consciousness. It is a foundational element of reality and expression, in the given context, in which Hispanic poets in the United States express themselves today, recording the present, envisioning the future.


## Mexican-American poetry

In the evolution of Mexican-U.S. poetry, a series of stages or epochs with well-defined characteristics and four presences in their literary heritage are evident in each one: indigenousness, Creole cultures, inter-ethnic procreation and Anglo-Americanism.[102]

The years from 1810 to 1848 correspond to the **period of independence and literary autonomy** which although it persists in the poetry of the colonial period in romances and *corridos*, also witnesses the appearance of other forms of popular poetry such as the *indita*, the *trovo* (poetic duel), the *cuándo* (when), *décimas* (tenths) and those used in dramatizations called *Pastorelas*. One of the oldest anonymous *corridos* belonging to this period is entitled *Condenado a Muerte* (Condemned to die) which refers to a real event, dated in the poem. An excerpt is quoted below:

102 - Luis Leal, "The Four Presences in the Literary Heritage of the Chicano Populace", in the *Anthology of Latin Literature, Cruzando Puentes* (crossing bridges) II, *Ventana Abierta* (open window), Vol. VII, No. 25, Fall 2008, pp. 8-18.

*Wednesday, July 20th*

*Year eight hundred and thirty two*

*They carry me to the grave*

*To answer before God*

Another *corrido* of the time is dedicated to Juan Nepomuceno Cortina, a popular hero in the defense of abused workers:

*That general Cortinas*

*Is free and very supreme,*

*They have enhanced his tributes*

*Because he saved a Mexican man.*

Father Florencio Ibáñez, in his *Pastorela*, writes in verse…

*Silvio, on this serene night*

*With its beautiful radiance*

*Manifesting loveliness*

*On Christmas Eve (…)*

*In the meadows, on summits and hills*

*All the birds warble*

*Singing in soft echoes*

*Silver-tongued are the mocking birds.*

In the Mexican-American literature known as **"territorial" created from 1848 to 1912**, of note are the poems of Manuel Clemente Rojo de los Ángeles, José E. Gutiérrez and from the publishers of *El Clamor Público: Literario e Independiente* (Public outcry: literary and independent), the poets José Elías González and Francisco P. Ramírez. The latter in one of his verses, states:

*Over there in the Supreme Court,*

*Where integrity reigns*

*I see that there is not equality.*

The before mentioned poem by New Mexico poet José María Alarid expresses a theme that will be repeated constantly in this tussle among three cultures alluded to in verses cited in Chapter II: *Beautiful Spanish Language / They want to ban you?/I think there is no reason /Why you should cease to exist.* And the poem also previously cited, published in California under the pseudonym initial V, sarcastically referring to the difficulties of different languages coexisting:

*/Here in Californial met*

*A really beautiful country woman*

*/. . . /*

*Englished certain phrases*

*That smelled foreign from far away.*

*She was often heard*

*To call a basket* basqueta,

*Talked of blocks as* squares,

*Called a fence a* fensa

*Called coffee* café

*Called markets* markettes

*The corner store a* grosería(vulgarity).

As Victor Fuentes points out in his book *California Hispano-Mexicana*[103] there are numerous poems published in the newspaper *El Clamor Público* (now included in the 465-page Reynaldo Ruiz anthology *La poesía Angelina* (Los Angeles Poetry – 1850-1900),[104] most of which are anonymous but are nonetheless impressive because of the level of their similarity to those published in Spanish and Hispanic-American newspapers of the day, with a "variety of short poems in the genre of *letrillas*, romances, sonnets and epigrams" (VF 140-141), "a variety of topics: satirical poems in the vein of Quevedo, such as in *A un chato* (To a pug-nosed guy) (p. 185), "*Una viuda*"(A widow) (251), and amorous poems, such as *El ángel de amor* (The angel of love - 147), others about pastoral love, (154), or fables, such as "*La gota de agua*" (Drop of water – an Arabic fable), exotic legends such as *Ritja o Balada* [Ballad] (157-162), and poetry of romantic ethos such as "*El pirata*" (The pirate) by Ignacio Teneroio Suárez 239-240) reminiscent

103 - New York: North American Academy of the Spanish Language, Plural *Espejo* (mirror) Collection, 2014.
104 - Lewiston: The Edwin Mellen Press, 2000.

of Espronceda's *La canción del pirata* (the pirate's song) or social poetry, such as *"El jugador"* (The player) (215-216) or *Lo de hoy* (what's happening today) (284) and the very surprising "¿Será verdad – mujeres?"(Could it be true, women?) (221-224) *avant garde* poetry and in the vein is the poem *Hombres necios que acusáis* (foolish men whom you accuse) by Sor Juana Inés de la Cruz:

*The Camilos and Soteros*

*Live only to eat,*

*And you must know*

*That the sum total of all men*

*Including the dead ones*

*Aren't worth even one woman (224)*[105]

In addition to *El Clamor Público* (Public outcry) from Los Angeles, numerous poets are published in newspapers of the day, in New Mexico, California, Texas and Nevada, such as Juan B. Hijar and J. M. Vigil in San Francisco's *El Nuevo Mundo* (The new world -1864), Luis A. Torres and José Rómulo Rivera in the New Mexico's*Boletín Popular* (1856 and 1892 respectively), Luis Tafoya in *El Nuevo Mexicano* (The New Mexican - 1898) and the *Revista de Taos* (Taos Review - 1911); several anthologies by both regional poets (such as *Los pobladores Nuevo mexicanos y su poesía* (New Mexican settlers and their poetry) by Anselmo F. Arellano) or themes such as the *Colección de Cantos Espirituales* (Collection of spiritual songs) by Father Railliere or *Flores Teológicas* (Theological flowers) by Father Cabello. Worthy of mention is the poetry of José Escobar and, especially, that of Santiago de la Hoz de Laredo for his use of *Silva*, (Renaissance Spanish versification—a strophe, consisting of eleven- and seven-syllable lines), in his *Sinfonía del Combate* (Combat symphony):

*People! Time to wake up! Your children grow up*

*with an inheritance of hatred they do not deserve…*

We see in these early pre-modernist stages of Mexican-U.S. poetry (1810-1912), written in classical metric style in the form of romances, *corridos*, and other popular poetic forms such as the *indita*, the *trovo* (thunder), the *cuando* (when), *décimas* (tenths) characterized by respect for traditional customs and the struggle for the vindication of social ideals typical of romanticism and post-colonialism.

---

105 - Victor Fuentes, Op. Cit., p. 141.

In the **period between 1912 and 1959**, among the poets writing in Spanish, Felipe Maximiliano Chacón, with his *El cantor neo-mexicano: Poesía y Prosa* (New-Mexican singer: poetry and prose (Albuquerque, 1924) and Vicente Bernal's, *Las primicias* (First fruit - 1916) and otherpoets with pseudonyms like PG (Pero Grullo) who, for example, in 1914 published these verses:

*Oh, Solicitorwayfarers!*

*Oh, formidable Licurgus!*

*You who are clever and crafty,*

*Listen carefully*

*To these morning verses*

*….*

*/You will receive great honor*

*That will shine even as the sun*

*If you make sure that Spanish*

*Is taught all around us*

*With zeal and devotion.*

From that time, in the late 20's and early 30's, *corridos* "about immigration" became popular. The following are two samples of such documentary poems by anonymous writers:

*The dishwasher*

*…*

*I did any kind of bicoca*(work)

*So I headed off to Sacramento*

*Without even one zoca,*

*I had to get onto the cement.*

*…*


And *The deportee:*


*I will sing for you gentlemen,*

150

*I will sing for you gentlemen*

*about all I have suffered.*

*Since leaving my homeland,*

*since leaving my homeland*

*to come to this country.*

...

Enrique Flores Magón (1877-1954) in his "Revolutionary Hymn" exhorts...

*Proletarians: To the cry of war,*

*And for ideals, fight on with courage*

*And expropriate,*

*brave ones,*

*the earth*

*held captive in the hands of our exploiter*

In addition to the revolutionary militancy of the Flores Magón brothers, Nicandro Flores, Juan Bonilla, Servando Cárdenas, are linked to these recurrent themes, and dominant during this period, there is the issue of identity as reflected, among others, by Américo Paredesin his poem *Alma Pocha – tres faces del pocho* (*Pocho* soul – 3 phases of the *Pocho*)* and Rodolfo Corky González with his "*Yo soy Joaquín*" (I am Joaquin); addressing the topic of cultural and socio-economic enslavement we find a work by A. Ortiz Vargas entitled *Las torres de Manhattan* (Towers of Manhattan), Boston, Chapman and Grimes, 1939):

* (Pocho: Mexican living in the U.S.)

...

*They corrupted their language*

*With bizarre mixing*

*Of the foreign tongue*

*Which they never learn.*

*And in the permissive shadow*

*Of the strange flag*

*Pathetic in defeat*

*They sank forever.*

**The 1950's mark the beginning of contemporary Chicano Literature** characterized by the need for that culture to find its own space, its own militancy and its own expression within that community and way of being in the face of rejection on several fronts—a phenomenon that became consolidated in the 1960's. We cite two fragments of poems from that period, one in English by Abelardo B. Delgado ("Chicano: 25 Pieces of a Chicano Mind", 1969): . . . .

*America, remember that Chicanito*

*flunking math and English*

*he is the Picasso*

*of your western states*

*but he will die*

*with a thousand masterpieces*

*hanging only from his mind.*

And the other bilingual pioneer, Alurista (*Floricanto en Aztlan*, 1971):

*My puffy eyes*

*Flooded with tears*

*Of brass*

*Melting on the cheek bones*

*Of my concern*

*Indigenous features*

*The scars of history of my face*

*And the veins of my body*

*That aches*

*Vomits blood*

*And I cry freedom*

*I do not ask for freedom*

*I am freedom*

152

This duality of codes and semantics—resulting from biculturalism—will be a constant in these poetic expressions with a greater or lesser presence of one or the other of the two languages depending on what is intended to accentuate in a particular poem.

Also among these poet pioneers we find Jesús Flaco(thin man) Maldonado with his *Oda al molcajete* (Ode to the mortar and pestle) and "*Oda al frijol*" (Ode to the bean). And, in this Chicano renaissance, I would also mention Ricardo Aguilar, Juan Bruce Novoa, and José Antonio Burciaga.

Then come **the eighties and post-modernity** during which a group of Chicanas (i.e. females) such as Lorna Dee Cervantes with *La Emplumada* (Female feathered one)

*The little houses near the gray cannery ... are gone now ... old gardens come back more robust than they were, / trees have been left standing in the yards. / apricot trees, cherry trees, walnut trees ... old ladies come here with paper bags to gather greens. / Spinach, purslanes, peppermint / Maybe it's here / in the strange fields of this city / where I'll find it, that part of me /. . .*

Or in *Barco de Refugiados* (Refugee boat):

*Like the corn starch / I slip, passing through the eyes of my grandmother, / Bible at her side. She removes her glasses. / The pudding thickens. / Mama raised me without a language. / I am orphaned by my Spanish name. / The words are strange, / Stuttering is on my tongue. / My eyes look in the mirror, at my reflection: / The bronze skin, the black hair. / I feel I am a detainee / aboard a refugee boat. / A boat that never docks.*

The figure of the "gringo" in the poems of Bernice Zamora, beginning with her poem *Sunday's Faith*. Or Gloria Anzaldua who versifies in her poem *Borderlands / La frontera. The New Mestiza* (Mixed-blood girl), 1987,*drowned, sculpturing the dark / floating with our very own shadow / the silence buries us.* Cheri Moraga who in her poem has Malinche confront Cortez whom she blames for the 500 years of suffering:

*Hah!—and for that I gave you*

*my blood and my people!*

*Yes, I see you, vulgar gringo,*

*you love me so much*

*that you married me off to your subordinate, Don Juan,*

*just like that*

*as if I were*

*a kilo of meat—well, even if you were my father*

*to sell me off however you please*

*you wretched man…*

*(from "La Malinche to Cortez and Vice Versa,*

*that is," Love does not forgive, not even for love," Woman, Woman.)*

And with typical bilingualism, a poem by Gloria Perez *Mi hombre* (my man):

*like the sumptuous*

*pyramids of tenochtitlán*

*mi hombre*

*you stand in my mind*

*y en mi corazón*

*erect*

*. . . . . . . . .*

*como la adelita*

*siempre al lado*

*del guerrillero*

*i'll live with you*

*i'll hunger with you*

*i'll bleed with you*

*and i'll die with you*

and the Mexican immigrant Lucha Corpi, perhaps in one of the greatest poetic works, writing in proper Spanish *Palabras de Mediodía* (Words at-noon). *From the branch hangs an orange / Still not promising an orange blossom* (from the poem *Romance Negro*). She also refers to Malinche's role in "*Marina Madre*" (Sailor mother):

*Already you did not like her and he turned her down*

*and when he was a kid, mama, he shouted at her!*

*when he grew up, he called her a "fuck-up".*

154

Then we have Sandra Cisneros, Ana Castillo, Pat Mora and the poem *Legal Alien,* ironic in the contradictory meaning of its title: *Bi-lingual, Bi-cultural, able to slip from "How's life?" To "They're driving me crazy",/ sliding back and forth / between the fringes of both worlds / by smiling / by masking the discomfort / of being pre-judged / Bi-laterally.*

We add the San Antonio poets Ángela de Hoyos, Evangelina Vigil-Piñón and Carmen Tafolla. And from other places: Yolanda Luera, Alma Villanueva, and Demetria Martínez. Judy Lucero and her poetic memoirs that were penned while in prison. There are others like Diana Marie Delgado, Sheryl Luna, Alivia Nada, Emy Pérez, María Meléndez, Carolina Monsivais, Brenda Cárdenas, Lisa Chávez, Xanath Caraza and Margarita Cota-Cárdenas: *I am a chicana macana / or gringa marrana, the ink paints / or the inked painting.*

Male voices include those of Roberto A. Galván, Reymundo Gamboa, Juan Gómez Quiñones, with their *Canto al Trabajador* (Song to the worker) and *A León Felipe,* the visual poetry of Louie "the Foot" González, Rafael Jesús González, Juan Felipe Herrera, Nephtali de León, Jesús Maldonado, José Montoya, Ernesto Padilla, Raymundo Pérez, Rubén José Rangel, Raúl R. Salinas, Rolando Hinojosa-Smith, Gary Soto, angry Ricardo Sánchez, Luis Talamentez, Tino Villanueva(*...there is another voice that wants to speak; / there is a profile of bronze skin...*),Heriberto Terán, Sabine R. Ulibarri, Jimmy Santiago Bacca, Américo Paredes, Víctor Martínez, Francisco X. Alarcón, Alberto Huerta, Humberto Garza, Rigoberto González, Eduardo Corral, Tim Hernández, Blas Manuel de Luna, the *"Alurist"* Alberto Baltazar Heredia Urista, Anthony Robinson, Luis J. Rodriguez, Alejandro Murgui and many others.

Worth a special mention is the edition by Tino Villanueva entitled *Antología Histórica y Literaria* (Chicanos: a historic and literary anthology)[106] and a set of critical essays by Rafael Pérez-Torres: *Movements in Chicano Poetry. Against Myths, against Margins* (Cambridge Studies in American Literature and Culture)[107], who, in addition to making a detailed study of the works of some of the above mentioned poets, makes a critical incursion into the Chicano poetic memory and its discursive axes from post-colonization to post-modernity.

In short, in the most recent periods of the Mexican-U.S. poetic body, we find paradigmatic examples of the post-modern era, such as thoseof a group of female Chicano poets including Lorna Dee Cervantes (*Emplumada* – Female feathered one), Bernice Zamora with the figure of *el gringo-*

---

106 - Tino Villanueva, editor. *Chicanos: Antología Histórica y Literaria* (Chicanos: Historical and Literary Anthology). Mexico, *Fondo de Cultura Económica*: 1980.
107 - Cambridge, Cambridge University Press: 1995.

and Gloria Anzaldúa in her verses *Borderlands / La frontera. The New Mestiza* (Mixed blooded woman), 1999: "*Drowned, we spat at the dark / fighting our own shadow / we are buried in silence*" (76). Cheri Moraga in her verses regarding Malinche's confrontation with Cortez, and his guilt in bringing about 500 years of suffering, and the Mexican immigrant Lucha Corpi when she too refers to Malinche's role in *Marina Madre*. Pat Mora with her poem *Legal Alien* with the irony of the double meaning in the title: *Bilingual, Bi-cultural, / able to slip from "How's life?" To "They're driving me crazy,"* ... (39), Lila Downs' *Border / La línea*. As we pointed out earlier, in many cases, these Chicana writers, in an act of rebellion, use the border, among other subjects, as a socio-cultural metaphor rather than a geographic boundary, with peculiar and varied bilingual and even tri-cultural language to refer to a mixed and divided identity, to pose an ethno-religious and internal questioning of values and "otherness" in a personal, sexual and stereotypical context, with accessible feminine models (Gloria Anazaldúa, "*compañera, cuando amábamos*" (female friend, when we used to love), generally with iconographic reference to Mexican roots, as we have shown by citing some of her verses.

In this specific attempt to redefine identity or subjectivity in this post-globalization period, we again use the example of Margarita Cota-Cárdenas' second poem *Noches despertando inConciencias* (Nights awakening unConsciousness), entitled *Crisis de identidad* (Identity crisis) or *Ya no chingues* (No more fuck-ups) and hericonographic verse:*Soy chicana macana/ o gringa marrana, /la tinta pinta/o la pintura tinta*(I am chicana macana / or gringa marrana, / the ink paints/ or the ink paint). In this context, we must allude to and contrast with, as an example of the dialectic of literary movements, essays on the "post-trans-border" from the now classical book by Néstor García Canclini, entitled *Culturas híbridas. Estrategias para entrar y salir de la Modernidad* (Hybrid cultures. Strategies to penetrate and exit from modernity) and criticism of the enthusiastic application of postmodernist theories regarding "the border", as well as hybridity as part of hegemonic discourse designed to explain other notions and environments with a conservative rather than an innovative cultural strategy. Note the antithesis.

## Puerto Rican poetry in the Continental United States[108]

Despite Puerto Rico's political inclusion in this overview as a non-state member of the U.S., commemorating Hispanic poetry, we have so far

108 - Adapted from the chapter "Puerto Rican poetry" which the author wrote for the *Enciclopedia del Español en los Estados Unidos* (Encyclopedia of Spanish in the United States. New York: *Instituto Cervantes* and *Editorial Santillana*, 2008, pp.672-77.

not included poetry from the Island itself. In the 19th Century there was a breaking away from Romanticism and *costumbrismo* (i.e. referring to customs) in the works of José Gautier Benítez with his trilogy of poems that are so revealing in their very titles alone *A Puerto Rico (ausencia)* (to PR [Absence]), *A Puerto Rico (regreso)* (to PR [return]; *A Puerto Rico (canto)* (to PR [song]) and many others, taking it to anti-romanticism and pre-modernism—a period from which we mention only Lola Rodríguez de Tió (1848-1924) who, in one of her many exiles, lived in New York and was a precursor to José Martí with her poems *Versos Sencillos* (Simple verses). Among her best known works are *Mis Cantares* (My songs) -1876), *Claros y nieblas* (Clear and foggy) (1885), *A mi Patria en la muerte de Corchado* (To my country in the death of Corchado -1885) and *Nochebuena* (Christmas Eve - 1887). From her brief decasyllabicpoem entitled *Autógrafo* (Autograph) we have: *I never feel foreign; / Everywhere home and shelter / The blue sphere opens wide for me; / My temples always a bosom friend / They attain on one side or the other / Because the Fatherland is inside me,* as well as her famous verses from *A Cuba*(to Cuba), which proclaim a feature of the brotherhood of the Caribbean nations in their struggle for independence:*Cuba and Puerto[Rico] are two wings / of the same bird, / they receive flowers or bullets / in the very same heart.*

In addition to her name, we must add those of the essayist Eugenio María de Hostos (1839-1935), the hero, diplomat and vast poet Ramón Emeterio Betances (1827-1898), Afro-Puerto Rican Sotero Figueroa (1851-1923) and Francisco Gonzalo "Pachín" Marín (1897-1963), author of *Los Romances*.

We must also include here Puerto Rican nationalist poet Juan Antonio Corretjer (1908-1985), who spent time in prison in the United States, later living as a free man in New York where he produced most of his nationalistic poetic works, concentrated in *Agueybaná* (1932) and *Ulysses* (1933) in which he undermines the thesis of literary and political insularity with his postulate of *"verses to the sea from a man of the land"*, *Love to Puerto Rico* (1937), *Canticle of War* (1937). In 1950 he composed *El Cantar Épico de Puerto* (The epic song of Puerto [Rico]), and *Alabanza en la Torre de Ciales* (Praise in the tower of Ciales); published in 1953, to which we add the poetry of social protest by Alfredo Ortiz Vargas, author of *Las torres de Manhattan* (Towers of Manhattan - 1939).

Another of the best-known poet activists is Clemente Soto Vélez (1905-1993) who wrote mostly in New York in the 1950's. His *Obra poética* (Poetic work) was published in San Juan in 1989 by the Institute of Puerto Rican Culture): *"Hands with hands that have / five-pointed stars / five-pointed stars / with starless stars"* His books: *Escalio, Abrazo interno* (The climb,

Internal embrace), Árboles (Trees), *Caballo de palo* (Wooden horse) and *La tierra prometida* (Promised land). Also Julia de Burgos (1914-1953) with her *Poema en 20 surcos, Canción de la verdad sencilla y El mar y tú* (Poem in 20 furrows, Song of simple truth and The sea and you) containing noble verses about the essence of Puerto Rico: *Morir conmigo misma, abandonada y sola/En la más densa roca de una isla desierta.* (Dying with myself, abandoned and alone / In the densest rock of a desert island). To these we add more names: Tomás Gares (1892-), active in New York from the 1920's to the 1940's *"They say the sonorous Spanish language / Lies mortally wounded in the land.../ As long as I can remember my mother country / The language of Castile shall be spoken ...".* ("Arts and Letters" - 1934), Clara Lair (1895-1974), José I. de Diegogo Padró (1896-1974), of the avant-garde movement known as *"diepalismo"*, Erasmo Vando (1896-1988), who lived in the south before moving to New York, composed the poem *United States* and a collection of verse: *Amores: poemas* (Loves: poems -1996), Jesús Colón (1901-1974), with his sonnet *The Flapper. "Like a young hip girl, New-York style / the "flapper"scratches the air shaping everything. / Her suit, a futuristic look at the latest fashion, / with her divine silk hinting a thousand things.* Also Emilio R. Delgado (1901-1967), founder of *Noismo* (no-ism) in 1925, Felipe N. Arana (1902-1962), José Dávila Semprit (1902-1958), author of *Brazos Bronce* (Bronze arms -1933), Juan Aviles, president of CEPI, the influential "Circle of Ibero-American Writers and Poets", Ángel M. Arroyo (1908), Graciani Miranda Archilla (1908) founder of the *Altayalista* movement, Ramón Ruiz de Hoyos (1908), Pedro Carrasquillo (1909-1964), one of the outstanding exponents of *jibarismo* in poetry, CEPI's César Gilberto Torres (1912), with his poem *Al Presidente Roosevelt* (To President Roosevelt), which resonates with a similar one by Rubén Darío; Poliana Carranza (1917), José Emilio González (1918-1990), with his Hegelian avant-gardism, Carmen Puigodllers (1919), with her poem *Dominio de Alas* (Dominance of wings -1955), Diana Ramírez de Arellano (1919) with her poems *"Salmo penitencial de desterrados"* (Exiles' penitential psalm) and *A Puerto Rico* (to PR).

Coming later on the scene is Roberto "Boquio" Alberti (1930-1985) with his *Canciones de un febrero* (Songs of February) (1965), Jaime Carrero (1931) with his poem *New York Jet* (1964), precursor of the *Niuyorricano* (Puerto Rican New Yorker) movement, Ernesto Álvarez Valle (1937) author of *Sobre el Puente de Brooklyn* (On Brooklyn bridge), the Spaniard, but essentially Puerto Rican, Alfredo Matilla Rivas (1937), Olga Nolla (1938-2001), Rosario Ferre (1938- ?), who lived in several places in the continental United States, mostly in metropolitan Washington D. C. while working on her doctorate at the University of Maryland marking her self-identity as a female literary critic and author of poetic works. At the time she wrote her well-known poems *Fábulas de la garza desangrada* (Fables of the heron that bled to death).[109] I add the name Juan Manuel Rivera (1943) who wrote *Poemas de la nieve negra* (Black snow poems -1986) and other representative works in the *Proto-Niuyorricano,Niuyorricano* and *Post-Niuyorricano* periods; also the poet and anthologist Iván Silen (1944-), from the poetic subculture and noted for his nihilistic anarchism with an altered poetic ego (discussing otherness) and *A la deriva* (Drifting)[110]with Victor Fragoso (1944), Brenda Alejandro (1947), Lourdes Vázquez[111] (1949) and Orlando José Hernández (1952), who are all included in the anthology *Los Paraguas Amarillos* (Yellow umbrellas)[112]as are both Ferre and Soto. Not to be left out isAlfredo Villanueva Collado (1944) with his many poems, among them, *En el imperio de la papa frita* (In the empire of French fry).[113] José Luis Colón Santiago (1945-2001), with his poems *La primera vez que yo vi el paraíso* (The first time I saw paradise - 1989) and *Aquí, mi sur del Bronx* (Here, my south Bronx - 1990). Also included in the anthology *Herejes y Mitificadores: muestra de la poesía Puertorriqueña en los Estados Unidos* (Heretics and mythmakers: a sampling of Puerto Rican poetry in the U. S) [114] compiled by Efraín Barradas and Rafael Rodríguez, (not previously mentioned), although some of them write primarily in English and could be typecast as Newyorican poets: namely, Roberto Marquez (1942), Luis Reyes Rivera (1945), José Ángel Figueroa (1946) with his *Noo York*, David Hernández (1946), Julio Marzán (1946) with *Puerta de*

---

109 - Mexico, J. Mortiz, 1982.

110 - Some of his poems: *Después del suicidio* (after suicide), Santo Domingo: 1970. *El pájaro loco* (crazy bird), Puerto Rico, *Ediciones Puerto*: 1972.The Poems of Fili-Melé, New York, *El Libro Viaje* (the travel book): 1976. *La poesía como libertá* (poetry as freedom), Puerto Rico, Institute of Puerto Rican Culture: 1992.Casandra & Yocasta, Puerto Rico, Institute of Puerto Rican Culture: 2001.

111 - Widely anthologized and published in magazines. Her book of poems *Las hembras* (the females), *Chile, Papeles del Andalicán*: 1987 (Chile, papers of the *Andalicán*) Puerto Rican critics called it one of the ten best books of the year. In 1988 The Omar Rayo Museum of Colombia published *La rosa mecánica* (mechanical rose) in its series on Latin American female poets. From 1995 to 1997 it published *Plakettes, el amor urgente* (urgent love), "The Broken Heart" and *Erótica de bolsillo* (pocket eroticism). In 1999 they published her storybook *Historias de Pulgarcito* (Histories de Pulgarcito – little thumb) (Cultural Editions), also *Bestiary*: Selected Poems 1986-1997 (2004), *La estatuilla* (the statuette - 2004), *Salmos del cuerpo ardiente* (psalms of the burning body) (Mexico: *Chihuahua Arde* (Chihuahua's burning - 2004); (May the transvestites of my island who tap their heels exquisitely - 2004); *Obituario* (obituary) (2004); *Desnudo con Huesos* (naked with bones - 2003), Park Slope (2003).

112 - Hanover, NH and Binghamton, *Ediciones del Norte* (Northern Editions) and Bilingual Press: 1983.

113 - Collado has eleven published works of poetry, among which, in addition to the above, we can mention *La guerrilla fantasma* (the ghost guerrilla fighter - 1989), *La voz de la mujer que llevo dentro* (the woman's voice inside me - 1990), *Pato salvaje* (wild duck - 1991), *Entre la inocencia y la manzana* (between innocence and the apple - 1996), *La voz de su dueño* (the owner's voice - 1999), and *Pan errante* (errant bread - 2005).

114 - Río Piedras, Puerto Rico, *Huracán* (hurricane) Editions: 1980.

*Tierra*(door of earth - 1998), Luz Maria Umpierre[115] , Carmen Valle (1948), writing poetry of contrasts in Spanish: *Un poco de lo no dicho* (A bit of what is not mentioned - 1980), *Glenn Miller y varias vidas después* (Glenn Miller and several lives later - 1983), *De todo da la noche al que la tienta* (The night gives all to him who tempts it - 1987), *Preguntas* (Questions - 1989), *Desde Marruecos te escribo* (I write to you from Morocco - bilingual edition, 1993) and *Entre la vigilia y el sueño de las fieras* (Between the vigil and dreaming of wild beasts - bilingual edition, 1996), *Esta casa flotante y abierta* (This open floating house - 2004), Jesús (Papoleto) Meléndez (1951) , Néstor Barreto (1952) and Orlando José Hernández (1952).

The social and political poetry of the *Newyorican* Movement was founded by Jesús Colón (1901) and has been anthologized in two fundamental works: *Newyorican Poetry -An Anthology of Puerto Rican Works and Feelings*, Miguel Algarín and Miguel Piñero editors. (New York: Morrow, 1975) and *Aloud. Voices from the Newyorican Poets café*, Miguel Algarín and Bob Halman, editors. (New York: H. Holt, 1994), which was dedicated to the writer of this book in 1995, with authors such as Miguel Algarín (1941), Pedro Pietri (1944- 2006), José Ángel Figueroa (1946), Miguel Piñero 1988), Sandra María Esteves (1948), Martita Morales, Lucky Cienfuegos and others, characterized by anti-intellectualism and anti-aestheticism. The poems were mostly written in the vernacular English of the Puerto Rican *"barrios"*—which are a concept rather than definite physical places, in New York, and that is why we don't pause there too long, despite a plethora of words in Spanish and occasionally published in original bilingual versions. A recent example is provided by the prominent Puerto Rican poet Jesús Papoleto Meléndez (1950), born in the East Harlem *Barrio*, with his bilingual anthology entitled *Hey Yo! Yo Soy!* (Hey me! it's me!)and *40 Years of Nuyorican Street Poetry* (2012).

We do not prejudge here the question of whether or not Puerto Rican poetry not composed in Spanish is still Puerto Rican. This was heatedly discussed in the wake of this movement which sought to preserve that peculiar Puerto Rican New York language which, in Victor Hernández Cruz (1949) gave way to a re-encounter with Spanish and the roots of Puerto Rican Spanish identity, as Francisco Cabanillas points out in his article *"España desde la poesia Nuyorican"*[x] (Spain as revealed in *Nuyorican* poetry)."[116]

This movement allowed other Puerto Rican poets in the U.S. to develop their own distinct styles within the movement, both in one subject matter

---

115 - Beginning with his book of poems *En el país de las maravillas* (in wonderland - 1979) he has continued to publish articles on literary criticism, narratives and poetry.

116 - In *Espéculo* (Speculum). Journal of literary studies. *Universdad Complutense de Madrid*, No. 33.

and literary forms in what Frances Aparicio[117] catalogs as post-*Newyoricanpoetry*: Here we find poets like Tato Laviera (1951), the aforementioned Víctor Hernández Cruz, Luz María Umpierre, and Martin Espada (1957). It is poetry of amalgamations and code changes. Some of these poets, such as Laviera and Víctor Hernández Cruz, at times "expand"their use of Spanish, and the poems by Víctor Hernández Cruz in *Maraca* (2001), *Federico García Lorca*, *De tres raíces* (Of three roots), *Bobadilla, España* and *Semillas* (Seeds), have a marked meta-poetic progression from *Niuyorqueño* Afro-centrism to an appreciation and praise of what is Hispanic—Caribbean Spanish.

Simultaneously with these movements, we look to the creations of Puerto Rican continental poets such as Joaquín Torres Feliciano (1945) with *Cachivache* (junk - 1976), Vilma Byron Brunet (1946) with *Semblanza y Colma Pópulo* (Semblance and *Colma Pópulo*), Olga Casanova Sánchez (1947) with *Raíz al aire* (Exposed root), Elizan Escobar (1948), Manuel Ramos Otero (1948-1990) with *El libro de la muerte* (Book of death - 1985) and *Invitación al polvo* (Invitation to dust) (1991), Carlos A. Rodríguez Matos (1949)[118], David Cortes Cabán (1952) with *Poemas y otros silencios* (Poems and other silences) (1981), *Al final de las palabras* (At the end of words) (1985), *Una hora antes* (One hour before - 1990), *Libro de los regresos* (Book of the returnings) (1999) and *Ritual de pájaros* (Bird ritual): *Antología personal* (Personal anthology)*1981-2002* (2004) Giannina Braschi (1953), with *El imperio de los sueños* (Empire of dreams) in multiple editions[119], Luz Ivonne Ochart (1954)[120], Jan Martínez (1954), with his poems *Minuto de silencio* (Minute of silence) (1977), *Archivo de cuentas* (Accounting archive) (1987) and *Jardín, obra escogida* (Garden, selected works - 1977), Marithelma Costa (1955), who published three works of poetry under the title *De Al1vión* (1987), *De tierra y de agua* (Of earth and water - 1988) and *Diario oiraí* (1997), Arnaldo Sepúlveda (1956) with *El Libro de Sí* (The book of yes). They include, among many others already mentioned, the work entitled *Papyrus of Babel: An Anthology of Puerto Rican Poetry in New York* (published by the University of Puerto Rico, 1991), one of the most complete to date, edited by the outstanding poet and critic Pedro López Adorno (1954)[121], and author of numerous well-known poems

117 - In the discussion of Proto-Newyorikan, and Post-Newyorikan poetry, I base myself on and complement Frances R. Aparicio's study "From Ethnicity to Multiculturalism: An Historical Overview of Puerto Rican Literature in the United States", included in "The Handbook of Hispanic Cultures in the United States: Literature and Art", edited by Francisco Lomeli, General Editors Nicholas Kanellos and Claudio Esteva-Fabregat, University of Houston, Public Art Press: 1993.

118 - With his poetry on transsexuality.

119 - Barcelona, Anthopos, *El Hombre*(man) publishers: 1988; University of Puerto Rico, publisher, Rio Piedras: 2000; Amazon Crossing, Seattle, 2011, 3rd edition.

120 - Poems *Ritos de muerte* (rites of death - 1975) and *Obra poética* (poetic work).

121 - Author of *Rapto continuo* (continuous rapture - 1999), *Viaje del cautivo* (captive's journey -

to which I have added the names of some not previously mentioned such as Marta Magaly Quiñones (1945)[122], Judith Ortiz Coffer (1952) who writes mostly in English[123] Myrna Nieves (1949) with *Viaje a la lluvia poemas* (Trip to the rain - poems - 2002), Egla Blouin, Maria Juliana Villafañe with *Dimensiones en el amor* (Dimensions in love) (1992) and *Entre Dimensiones* (Between dimensions) (2002), Paul González with two small works of poetry *Poems for May, June or April* and *Confundido por el Mar Caribe y el Rio Culebrina*, (Poems for May, June or April and Confused by the Caribbean Sea and the Culebrina River); Naomi Ayala (1964) who writes poems in Spanish and has published works with Bilingual Review Press, although her first poems *This Side of Early* (2007) and *Wild Animals on the Moon* (1997), were written in English, Rebecca Villareal and others with anthologized poetry and award-winning works.

The different trends of post-*Nuyoricanism* have had different scenarios and unequal productions regard their aesthetic quality. One of them has been captured by Juan Flores and Jorge Matos in his 1999 edition of the *Revista de Estudios Puertorriqueños* (Magazine of Puerto Rican studies) with their selection of "*diasporripocano*" poets (i.e. poets of the Puerto Rican diaspora). Other new poetic generations, now referred to as "*Neorriqueños*", publish in anthologies, Hispanic or multicultural magazines such as *Ratallax, The Americas Review* and others, with "new" stylistic and thematic proposals, by doing away with geographies and other distinctions since they express a more complex reality in fluid territory and, therefore, address issues broader than those of mere identity which—in the words of Juan Flores and Mayrna Santos Febres—"are no longer definitively seen as a monolithic block, coherent and tied to a language or a specific geographic space, ethnicity or race. They see it, instead, as porous territory, full of contradictions and juxtaposed experiences that also define that terrible and beautiful reality that is:'being Puerto Rican.'"[124]

The anthology *La ciudad prestada: poesía post-moderna en Nueva York* (The borrowed city: post-modern poetry in New York - Dominican Republic: 2002), compiled and edited by Pedro López Adorno, includes the Puer-

---

1998), *Concierto para desobedientes* (concert for the disobedient) Rio Piedras - 1996), *Los Oficios* (the professions - 1991), *País llamado cuerpo* (a country called body - 1991), *Las glorias de su ruina* (the glories of its ruin - 1988), *Hacia el poema invisible* (toward the invisible poem - 1981).

122 - With numerous poems published, among them: *Entre mi Voz y el Tiempo* (between my voice and time - 1969), *Era que el mundo era* (it was that the world was - 1974), *Zumbayllu* (1976), *Cantándole a la noche misma* (singing to the night itself - 1978), *En la pequeña antilla* (in the little Antille - 1982) *Nombrar* (nominate - 1985), *Razón de lucha* (reason for struggle - 1989), *Sueños de papel* (paper dreams - 1996), *Patio de Fondo* (back yard - 2003), *Mi Mundo* (my world - 2003).

123 - Like *A Love Story Beginning in Spanish*: Poems, "Silent Dancing", "Terms of Survival", "Reaching for the Mainland" and "The Latin Deli": Prose and Poetry.

124 - Hostos Review: *Micrófono abierto: Nuevas literaturas puertorriqueñas* (open mike: New Puerto Rican Literature, Issue 2: 2005, Introduction, p. XII.

to Rican poets Juan Manuel Rivera, Giannina Braschi as well as Pedro López Adorno himself, whom I have referenced earlier.

We conclude this review with the very novel Puerto Rican poetry of the so-called generations of the 80's and 90's, highlighted in an edition of the *Hostos Review* under the title *Open Microphone: New Puerto Rican Literature*, edited by Juan Flores and Mayra Santos-Febres (Issue No. 2: 2005 ) which includes poets other than those previously cited with regard to other groups or movements, such as New York's *"Mariposa"* (Butterfly) Fernández with her "Ode to the Diasporican (*pa mi gente* [for my people])", Moisés Agosto-Rosario (1965) with poetry entitled *Porqué la construcción de los profetas* (Why the prophets'edifice -1988), *Poemas de lógica inmune* (poems of immune logic - 1993), Puerto Rican-Costa Rican Kattia Chico (1969), Caridad de la Luz, alias *"La Bruja"* (Witch); poet, actress and singer Maria Luisa Arroyo, author of *Raíces de Silencio* (Roots of silence -2005), Chiara Merino Pérez Carvajal (1973), "the rapper" Gallego (1974), Uroyoán Noel (1976) with his work *Las flores del mall* (mall flowers - 2000) and *La lógica kool* (Kool logic - 2006), Willie Perdomo, a voice from East Harlem *barrio* who says ¡*Yo soy Boricua!* ¡*Yo soy africano! I ain't lyin'*(I am a Boricua! I am African! I ain't lyin'). *Pero mi pelo is kinky y curly y mi skin no es negro pero it can pass.* (but my hair is *kinky* and *curly* and my skin is not black but it can pass...) and his poem *Nigger-Reecan Blues* (1996); he writes his blog in Spanish but his poetry is mostly in English, Guillermo Rebollo-Gil (1979), who published the poems *Veinte* (Twenty - in 2000), *Sonero* (2003) and *Teoría de Conspiración* (Conspiration theory - 2005); he has gotten important critical reviews as have poets David Caleb Acevedo (1980), Nicole Cecilia Delgado (1980) and Raquel Z. Rivera.[125] The poetry of the 80's 90's generations and later is, as we stated before, hybrid in nature with new subject matter, new styles, new experiences and hip-hop-performances, with multiple forms of artistic expression, but authentically Puerto Rican, Diasporic or Newyorican in its inspiration and poetic creation.

---

125 - The poets mentioned below write almost exclusively in English, although they insert phrases or verses in Spanish in their works: Edwin Torres (1958), Tony Medina, now at Howard University, the Puerto Rican-Ecuadorian Emanuel Xavier (1971) with his poems *Pier Queen* (1997) and *Americano* (2002) Nydia Rojas in Wisconsin, Ed Morales, Frank Varela, "Shaggy" Flores, Anthony Morales, Sandra García Rivera, the new *niuyorricano* "Flaco" (Skinny) Navaja, Héctor Luis Rivera and Ray Ramírez, founders of Welfare Poets, Puerto Rican-Ecuadorian resident of Philadelphia, and the Afro-Puerto Rican Aya de León, Magda Martínez, Hugo J. Ríos Cordero, John Rodríguez and Bonafide Rojas, author of Pelo bueno (good hair). Very few of the poets of this anthology have had their works published but their literary creations have appeared in magazines, in papers or virtual anthologies. Some of the authors in Juan Flores' and Mayra Santos-Febres' anthologies have not been mentioned herein either because they reside outside the continental United States, write in other literary genres or do so only in English.

This approximation and brief review of Puerto Rican poetic reminiscence written in Spanish[126]in the continental U.S. covers a variety of verse that mingles linguistic expressions and indigenous influences, from the Boricua (Arawak) and Jíbaro, Spanish (with characteristics of identity and metrics such as African and U.S. contributions *décimas* and *corridos*) from New York and elsewhere—poetry and poets that have expressed themselves in the trends of modernist, post-modernist, and later movements typical of North America with their changes of codes and idiomatic mixtures, with idiosyncratic themes of national identity and Creolism, patriotic, nationalism and social struggle based on the complicated realities of the *barrios* and of a nation in conflict with its own political makeup, of romance, nostalgia, the countryside and nature, of cultural and personal identity in a continuous flow from here to there, of physically or spiritually leaving from and returning to the Island, as the roots of identity and the source of the imagery of the two branches of a single population in a continuous dialectic of prefiguration, configuration and re-figuration.

## Cuban-American Poetry[127]

The complex and rich body of Cuban-American poetry also traces its origins to the nineteenth century with the contributions of greats like the neoclassical José María Heredia (1803-1839): *Oda al Niágara* (Ode to Niagara), *Himno del Desterrado* (Hymn of the exile), Miguel Teurbe Toulon (1820-1857): *Himno de guerra cubano* (Cuban war hymn), *Mi propósito* (My purpose) *El pobre desterrado* (The poor exile) Leopoldo Turla (1818-1877): *Perseverancia* (Perseverance), *Degradación* (Degradation), Pedro Ángel Castellón (1820-1856): *A Cuba* (to Cuba),*A los mártires de Trinidad y Camagüey* (To the martyrs of Trinidad and Camagüey)", Pedro Santacila (1826-1910): *A España, El arpa del proscripto* (To Spain, the harp of the excluded), José Agustín Quintero (1829-1885)*El banquete del destierro* (The banquet of exile),*Poesía bajo la tiranía* (Poetry under tyranny), "Juan Clemente Zenea (1832-1871), the best poet of the elegiac tradition during the romantic period with his compositions *El filibustero* (The filibusterer), *El 16 de Agosto de 1851*(Aug. 16, 1851) and *En la muerte de Narciso López*

126 - We have omitted references to anthologies in English like The Puerto Rican Poets (1972) by Alfredo Mantilla and Yván Sillén, Borinquen: An Anthology of Puerto Rican Literature (1973) by María Teresa Babín and Stan Steiner, Inventing a Word: An Anthology of Twentieth Century Puerto Rican Poetry (1980) by Julio Marzán, Boricuas: Influential Puerto Rican Writings (1995), an anthology edited by Roberto Santiago, Puerto Rican Writers at Home in the USA, by Faythe Turner.
127 - In my presentation of these poetic works I have summarized and updated the study by Rodolfo J. Cortina, entitled "History and Development of Cuban American Literature: A Survey, "in the Handbook of Hispanic Cultures in the United States: Literature and Art", edited by Francisco Lomeli, General Editors Nicholas Kanellos and Claudio Esteva-Fabregat, University of Houston, Public Art Press: 1993.

(Upon the death of N. L), and his later poems *Cantos de la Tarde*(afternoon songs) and the posthumous *Diario de un mártir* (Martyr's diary). I must add to this list of romantics, Nicholas Cárdenas y Rodríguez, Isaac Carrillo O'Farril (who died in New York in 1901), Rafael María Mendive and José Jacinto Milanés.

In the post-Romantic period, we have those belonging to the Idealistic trend such as the Sellen brothers (1838-1907), in *Poetry*; Antonio Sellen (1839-1889) *Cuatro poemas* (4 poems) and both *Estudios poéticos* (Poetic studies) which they made available in Spanish with their translations of works of European poets and writers whose influence was noted in later Impressionistic generations.

José Martí (1853-1895), the best-known Cuban poet and militant for Cuban independence, closes this century as a spokesperson of Modernism which has its maximum expression in Nicaragua's Ruben Darío his famous *Ismaelillo*, as well as *Versos Sencillos* (Simple verses), composed in New York, are already part of poetry's universal heritage.

*"I am a sincere man*

*from the place where the palm trees grow*

*and before I die I wish*

*to transmit the verses of my soul"*

Then we have the modernist Bonifacio Byrne (1861-1936), an exile in Tampa, author of the famous poem *Mi bandera* (My flag).

A copious Cuban-U.S. poetic tradition continues into the 20thcentury with several generational manifestations not only in relation to time frames but to aesthetic characteristics labeled as the Vanguard, the Generation of Origins, the Pre-revolutionary Generation of 1953, the 70's Generation, the *Puente* (Bridge) Group the Conservatives, the *Mariels*, the *Atrevidos* (Daring ones) and other more recent movements.

Among the Cuban-American representatives of the avant-garde, Eugenio Florit stands out with his poems *Hábito de esperanza* (Habit of hope): *Poemas, De tiempo y Agonía* (Of time and agony), *Castillo interior y otros versos* (inner castle and other verses). Recapturing the first expressions of feminist Cuban-U.S. poetry, I refer the reader to Emilia Bernal (1884-1964), with her publication of *Alma errante; América* (Errant soul; America), in 1990 the respective facsimile editions of two her poems were recovered (the first originally came to light in Havana in 1916 and the second in Chile in 1938). I also draw attention to Clara Niggeman, *En la puerta dorada* (At the golden door), *Como un ardiente río* (Like a fiery river), widely anthologized and belonging to this time although difficult to place in any early century movement.

Two poets residing in the United States (in addition to Gastón Baquero who also lived in Madrid) are considered to be the most important representatives of the Origins Generation. They are Lorenzo García Vega who has resided in Miami since the Cuban Revolution and has published *Ritmos acribillados* (Bullet-torn riddles), *Rostros del reverso* (faces of the other side) and *Los años de Orígenes* (Years of origins) and Justo Rodríguez Santos, a New Yorkresidentwith his works *El diapasón del ventisquero*(the pitchfork and the snowdrift), *Los naipes conjurados* (The conjured playing cards) and *Las óperas del sueño* (the dream operas). The 1953 Generation *Grupo Renuevo*, (Renewal group) led by Ángel N. Pou opposing the baroque language of the *Orígenes* (Origins) Generation, is widely represented in the United States with some outstanding poets: Carlos Cancio Casanova's *Sale del verso el corazón ileso* (The heart emerges from the verse undamaged). Ana Rosa Núñez is the force behind this group with creative and critical production in *Las siete lunas de enero* (7 moons of January), *Requiem para una isla* (Requiem for an Island), *Escamas del Caribe: haikus de Cuba* (Fish scales of the Caribbean: Cuban haikus). Ángel Cuadra Landrove—a Cuban political prisoner freed because of international pressure along with other poets from this group: Jorge Valls and Armando Valladares—published several poems in the United States, including *Fantasía para el viernes* (Friday fantasy), *Esa tristeza que nos inunda* (This sadness that engulfs us) and has received numerous awards and acknowledgment.

Heberto Padilla (I still remember my last telephone conversation with him) is one of the most important poets of this group. He has resided in and published in the United States since his arrival in 1980. His numerous works, poem collections and critical studies are well known and too numerous to list in this brief review, but I can't resist including lines from *Fuera del juego* (out of bounds)

*To the poet, fire him!*

*That guy has no business being here.*

*He's not in the game.*

*He has no fervor at all.*

Mauricio Fernández and Orlando Rossardi have published poetry in Miami, and prior to that in Washington D. C. and have given numerous recitals, such as those presented at the Congress I helped organize at Georgetown University in which Rita Geada, Matias Montes Huidobro and his wife Yara González—as professors, critics and prolific writers with prestigious

166

awards and recognition for their creative work—all took part. Also, Juana Rosa Pita who now resides in Miami. I close this brief mentionof this poetic generation that had so many important exponents by adding the names of Gladys Zaldívar, Carmen Valladares, Benigno Nieto, Teresa María Rojas, Antonio A. Acosta, Rosa Cabrera, Carmen R. Borges, Ernesto Carmenate and José Corrales.

The 70's Generation includes several poets such as Rodolfo Cortina who has classified it into three subgroups: In the first, *El Puente* (Bridge) and the *Conservadores* (Conservatives), outstanding among them José Kozer, Isel Rivero, Reinaldo García Ramos, Enrique Marquez, Omar Torres, Magaly Alabau, Uva Clavijo, Manuel Santayana, the well-received Octavio Armand, Amando Fernández, (one of the most important and award-winning poets of the group) and, finally, Vicente Echerri with his poems *Luz en la Piedra, Casi de Memorias, Fragmentos de un discurso amoroso* (Light on the stone, almost memories, fragments of a loving speech).

Secondly, the Mariel Group, which includes Jesús Barquet, Rina Lastres Beritán, author of the posthumous anthology, *A cal y canto: Poesía y prosa* (Masonry lime and melody: poetry and prose, 2005-2011), Roberto Valero (who worked with me in Washington D. C. in the early 90's in founding the "*Horizonte 21*" group and the local Chapter of the Ibero-American Poetry Academy), Carlota Caulfield, Belkis Cuza Malé, who still publishes—in addition to her own work—the prestigious *Liden Lane Magazine*as well as pages on the Internet. From Roberto Valero, in a tribute to a life that ended too soon, here are a few lines from his unpublished work ...*pero nadie sabe su nombre* (But nobody knows his/her name) the manuscript of which he gave to me:

"...*and its blood is the five oceans*...

*that's why there is warfare beneath the gentle waves*...

*every single fish lives on the edge of misery*

*every aquatic living thing is terrified of all the others*

*the monsters devouring the small fish, themselves being devoured by other monstrous ones*"

Thirdly, we have the *Grupo de los Atrevidos* (group of audacious ones) according to the classification by Carolina Hospital in her anthology of very diverse poets. In addition to her, the most outstanding of this group are Ricardo Pau Llosa, Mercedes Limón, Pablo Medina, Iraida Iturralde, Lourdes Gil, Jorge Guitart, Bertha Sánchez Bello, Elías Miguel Muñoz and Gustavo Pérez-Firmat. Unfortunately the poets within this group whom this writer knows personally (Hospital, Pérez-Firmat and Pau-Llosa) have cho-

167

sen increasingly to write in English only, so they do not fit into the criteria of this review. However, Elías Miguel Muñoz *En estas tierras* (in these lands), Iralda Iturralde *Hubo la viola* and *Tropel de espejo* ('There was the viola' and 'The mirror throng') and Lourdes Gil's *Manuscrito de la niña ausente, Vencido el fuego de la especie y Blanca aldaba preludia* ('Manuscript of the absent girl', 'The fire of the species is overcome' and 'White latch prelude'), have opted to publish their works in Spanish as mentioned earlier.

Complementing this poetic body are the creations of some later poets whose efforts are more "cosmopolitan"in nature as is the case with Maricel Mayor, author of several poems and editor of the Journal *Baquiana*; and other young voices are coming forth with recently-published poems or inclusions in important poetic anthologies such as those of Rafael Catala, Jorge Oliva, Rafael Bordao, Maya Islas, Alina Galliano, Rafael Román Martel, Pablo Medina, Alexis Romay, Ernesto R. del Valle, Madelín Longoria, Yanitzia Canetti and others including Yosie Crespo of Miami—a member of the so-called Generation Zero. In summarizing this section I call to mind the occasion when I shared Spanish-language poetry readings in Washington D. C. many years ago with the now recognized Cuban-American poet Richard Blanco, who was the poet chosen for the second inauguration of President Obama in 2012. As a footnote, this writer represented the United States with recitations in Spanish at the most recent 11th annual International Poetry Festival in Granada, Nicaragua, in February, 2015. As an example of the cultural diplomacy of the Hispanic United States, Richard and I proudly used the motto *Estamos Unidos* (We are united)—which rhymes with *Estados Unidos* (United States).

Excellent work on this body of poetry, detailing publications of poetry and poetic anthologies year after year, has been produced by Orlando Rodríguez Sardiñas (Rossardi) and Jesús J. Barquet in their studies on Cuban poetry which were published in the *Enciclopedia del Español de los Estados Unidos*.[128]


## The poetry of other exiles[129]

We have grouped the exile poets geographically in order to organize the

128 - Yearbook of the Cervantes Institute 2008, López Morales (coordinator), Madrid: Santillana publisher: 2009: pp. 678-718.
129 - Numerous studies have been published about each one of the exiles to which we shall refer in this section, although they refer to literary output in general, not specifically to the poetic genre. An extensive bibliography can be found in the article by Chilean professor Juan Armando Epple "Hispanic Exile in the United States" in the *Handbook of Hispanic Cultures in the United States: Literature and Art*, edited by Francisco Lomeli, General Editors Nicholas Kanellos and Claudio Esteva-Fabregat, University of Houston, Public Art Press: 1993.

information about them without dwelling too much in categorizing currents, chronologies or movements to which the members of these exile groups belong and with very few biographical references.

We also define the term "exile"very broadly, the criteria being that the individual reside in the U.S. and compose poetry in this country, that is, other than that written in his/her country of origin from which he/she is exiled, whether for political, socio-economic, professional or personal reasons. Aware of the possible controversy surrounding the meaning of this broad definition, we stand by it in light of the following lines from poet Octavio Paz: ". . . I traveled the world. My house was my words. the air my grave," and from César Vallejo" Get away! Remain! Return! Leave! The entire social apparatus is in these words!"The poets referred to here are victims and expressions of the experiential reality of having left the lands of their birth, uprooted themselves, living in a new culture with a different language, far from their "homeland" and now find themselves in a different place, a new country and a different culture and language having to more or less adapt themselves through "acculturation"—rather like "stepchildren"—as will be seen in the selected verses of some of the representative poets of this diaspora.

The experience of this exile process, the complexity of any diaspora, the conditions leading to exile, the departure, the hopes, the difficulties of going back, the more or less traumatic consequences of exile—all will vary according to the circumstances of each individual. The whys and wherefores of an exile can be due to political persecution, to being expelled or threatened, but all have certain similarities as well as considerable differences. Exile can also happen for economic or professional reasons, including self-exile.

The poets listed here include representatives of a whole range of different kinds of exile or diaspora, including the voluntary leaving from one's country, imposed exile, emigration / immigration, in any case, but all exiles as we will observe, suffer the effects of so-called "exile devaluation,"including a keen sense of departure, loss, feelings of defeat, guilt, false expectations, transience, identity crisis, dualism, friction and the challenges of adaptation. Living in this state of affairs, they create poetry as a way of helping themselves to not disappear, to deplore and proclaim change, to cling to their roots, their people, their ancestors in a kind of corporality, remembering their homelands as a referent to create a certain sense of solidarity, speaking to a lost audience in a cry of abandonment inside a culture that is not really an audience or a public for their poems. In their verse they also speak of remoteness, estrangement in a new environment, uprooting, loneliness, desertion, de-acculturalization and acculturation in a process of searching and reconstruction of the identity of their poetic self, with the dream of returning and a rescuing of referents and continuous nostalgic probing. A study of the positive aspects of exile in the literary creations of some of the representative figures of the Hispanic-American exile is also possible, and yet the cruelly poignant question posed by Cuban exile Herberto Padilla persists: *"How can you continue to live with two languages, two houses, two nostalgias, two temptations, two melancholies?"* This is a question that other exiled poets such as Gustavo Firmat ask, not only as an epigraph to his own poem *"Provocations"* but also to discuss its occurrence among exiled literary scholars like Rafael Rojas in his article entitled *"Diaspora and literature. Symptoms of post-national citizenship."*

Dissociations are found in poetic footprints, including inter-culturalism, hybridization, and unsuspected façades in poetic subject matter in the process of surviving exile with its attendant syndromes that accompany the process of trying to integrate into a new country in a dialectical progression of an imperfect synthesis of life and death. We will look at samples of poetics that return and take refuge in childhood, the task of building things/relationships/city/land/landscape/history/ socio-political order / ideal order / family with words. These poet exiles in the United States also write with echoes of Spain, South America, Central America, the Caribbean, to fail to remember, yet evoking memories. Both pain and tragedy are masked in parody, in irony, in images of un-realism—even the absurd—as an echo of the experience of apparent meaninglessness, the congenital incongruence of uprooting in a continuous tone of denunciation and social and political commitment as seen in poems that travel,that reach out to a distant country and to the country of residence which, in turn, reigns over that distant country and the world. Hence these poetics have an international look and rhetoric, a multiplicity and are a metaphor of interaction and an eagerness to behold. In fact, a large portion of 20th Century Hispano-American literature has been written by exiles. Pablo Antonio Cuadra defined this as literature that receives "its most valuable contributions from the dual native and foreign vision of exile" validating the assertion of philosopher Leszek Kolakowski that "Creation is the child of insecurity, of a kind of exile, of experiencing that which has been lost" (Solís 161).

## From the Spanish Exile Community

The poetry of Spanish exiles in the U.S.is extensive[130] and includes representatives of the numerous and varied schools, generations and move-

---

130 - The author has written more in detail about this exile in his essay, *Poesía del exilio español: figuras, registros y contribuciones* (poetry of the Spanish exile: figures, records and contributions), in a paper presented at the Poetry Congress at the University of Virginia in November, 2008.

ments, from modernism, avant-garde, post-avant-garde, the 50's generation, current, post-modern and post-globalization.

In addition to widely-known figures such as Max Aub, Francisco Ayala and Américo Castro, we begin this section by highlighting some milestones of a representative of modernism, the Nobel Prize winner Juan Ramón Jiménez, referring to essays and poems written in Maryland, Miami, and Puerto Rico. In the opinion of his disciple, Graciela Palau de Nemes in her work *Espacio y Tiempo* (Space and time), Juan Ramón's two long prose poems written in Florida, shed light on the background of his exile, that is to say, his true exile.[131]Although with different poetic resources, the city of New York that initially impacts the poet as seen in his poem *Moguer,* and in the process of his poetic creativity and memory time frame, we see trans-textual references to this new city with reference to its annoying, inhuman dimensions and commercialism, compelling Juan Ramón's in his poetic "I" to configure the language in terms of questioning, inner dissonance and personal rebirth. Martha López-Luaces[132] speaks of an "aesthetic rupture" in this regard. We allude to the heartbreaking verses of his poem *"Con vexidades"* (With vexities): *The sky turns its back, / turns its back to the sea, and between this double nakedness / the day slips by behind my back,* and then there is the refigured return to his homeland in *Moguer*which he refers to as "his truth": *My pit, fatal Moguer, / with its bushlands, its gate and pine forest, / with stone and peace; / solid ground there / living and the dying place of the real / lover, from which it returns to its reality.*[133]

"From these Americas—Juan Ramón Jiménez wrote to Enrique Diez Canedo—"I began to see myself and others in the days of Spain: from the outside and far away, in the same time and space. A profound change took place in me, something similar to what I underwent when I first arrived in 1916."[134]

The same phenomenon can be seen in the other figures of the genera-

---

131 - Graciela Palau de Nemes, *El fondo del exilio de Juan Ramón Jiménez* (background of the exile of Juan Ramón Jimenez), in *El exilio de las Españas de 1939 en las Américas: ¿adónde fue la canción?*(the exile of the 1939 'Spains' in the Americas: what happened to the song?) by José Maria Naharro Calderón, Anthropos Publisher, Madrid: 1991, pp. 241-250.

132 - Martha Luaces, *Nueva York como motivo de ruptura estética en la poesia española* (New York as a motive for the aesthetic rupture in Spanish poetry): Juan Ramón Jimenez, Garcia Lorca and Jose Hierro, New York, June 2007. See also Dionisio Cañas, *El poeta y la ciudad, Nueva York y los escritores hispanos* (the poet and the city, New York and Hispanic writers). *Cátedra Madrid* publisher: 1994.

133 - Juan Ramón Jiménez, *En el otro costado* (on the other side), edition prepared by Aurora de Albornoz with prologue. Madrid: *Ediciones Júcar*, 1974, p. 29.

134 - Juan Ramón Jimenez, *A Enrique Diez-Canedo, Cartas literarias* (to Enrique Diez-Canedo, literary letters), p. 65, written in Washington, DC, August 6, 1943.

tion of 1927 who wrote poetry in the U.S.: Pedro Salinas, Jorge Guillén and Luis Cernuda, whose verses from his poem *Un español habla de su tierra* (A Spaniard speaks of his homeland)—from the book of poems *Las nubes*(clouds) reveal the epicenter of tragedy:

*They, the winners*

*persistently cruel,*

*stripped away everything from me.*

*Leaving me an exile.*

Here we have manifestations of that tendency in the exiles of the Spanish Civil War to shape memory to elicit place and non-place.

In the same context and to complete this historical panorama one cannot omit Federico Garcia Lorca's brief sojourns in the U.S. with his exemplary surrealistic poem *Poeta en Nueva York,* as well as Alberti's *Banca de Sangre, Versos suelos de cada día* (Blood bank, daily earthy verses), which make up a significant body of his indelible poetic creation. Others journeyed through that same city (New York) as well as several other places in the U.S.: Dámaso Alonso, León Felipe, Concha Espina, Claudio Rodríguez and José Moreno Villa. In 1927 the latter wrote the poem *Jacinta la pelirroja* (Jacinta the redhead) and in prose *Pruebas de Nueva York* (Trials of New York). Later, two great poets, Rosa Chacel and Gloria Fuertes, lived there for a few years; Rosa Chacel from 1959 to 1961 while on a Guggenheim scholarship; and Gloria Fuertes from 1961 to 1963, who said that those were the best years of her life, on a Fulbright scholarship as a professor of Spanish Literature at Bucknell University.

Subsequently, among the new avant-garde, the figure of Ángel González Oviedo (1925-2008), who grew up in the midst of the Spanish Civil War, stands out as a representative of the so-called 50's Generation. He was a "social" poet who, paradoxically, was a critic of this genre and insisted on the meaninglessness of words: s*angre: no sangres más* (Blood: bleed no more) from his poem *Otra vez* (Again). In the context of post-war defeatism, he expressed himself in a tone of denunciation wrapped in a kind of lyrical essentialism without idle trappings but with realism and rigorousness, with an effective use of irony to distance himself firmly in order to say exactly what he meant and used the almost obsessive themes of the oppressiveness of city life, the passage of time, and questions of love and civility, as reflected in the poems entitled "Áspero mundo" (Harsh world)(1956), *Sin esperanza, con convencimiento* (Without hope, with conviction - 1961), contained in the different editions of *Palabra sobre Palabra*(Word upon word) and, among others, a poem titled *El derrotado* (The defeated one):

172

*You embark on an outward journey, towards*

*a time, a well-named future.*

*Because you have no country,*

*because no land*

*is or will ever be yours,*

*because there is no country*

*where your empty heart can put down roots.*

Worth mentioning is the contribution of José Hierro of the 50's generation, with several sojourns in the United States where he wrote his poems in *Cuaderno de Nueva York* (New York notebook - 1998), one of his most important and successful compositions for which he won the national poetry prize.

Contributions to characteristic uprooted poetry have also been made by Manuel Mantero, Gonzalo Sobejano, Juan Marichal, José F. Montesimos, José María Fonollosa, and later Manuel Durán and Odón Betanzos Palacios. In this post-modernity and post-globalization period, we must also add the names of Ana Merino, María Paz Moreno, Alicia Giralt, Fernando Operé (director of the Center for Hispanic-American poetic studies), Ignacio Barrero, Santiago García Castañón, María del Águila Boge Pineda, Tina Escaja, Alberto Acereda, Ignacio López-Calvo, Ramón Díaz-Soliz, Benito del Pliego, José Molina, Alberto Avendaño many of whom have been included in the *Piel Palabra* (Skin word) anthology (A sampling of Spanish poetry in New York, Francisco Álvarez-Koki, editor, 2003) which includes, in addition to the above-mentioned, a few others, such as Hilario Barrero, Dionisio Cañas, Antonio Garrido Moraga, Francisco Álvarez-Koki, Alfonso Armada, Josefina Infante and Marta López-Luaces. To these we add the works of other important contributors such as Alfredo Gómez-Gil. More are listed in a recently-published anthology entitled *Escritores Españoles en los Estados Unidos* (Spanish writers in the United States) edited by Gerardo Piña-Rosales who has compiled texts written by Ana María Fagundo, Santiago García Castañón, in addition to the above-named poet.

**From the South American Exile Community**

Equally important is the building of and neutralization of memory in Spanish poetry composed by South American exiles in the United States who in their need to write again have created a hybrid discourse with disas-

173

sociated poetic markers, multiple references to the past, to their roots, to symbols, to the causes of suffering caused by defects and contradictions in the human condition which has been a theme in Dostoyevsky's writings.

Beginning with countries of the "Southern Hemispherie": first, Argentina, our short list will include only a few poets: Silvia Molloy, Juana de Arancibia with *Alba de América* (Dawn of America), then Mariano Gowland, José Anibal Yaryura Tobias, María Negroni, Zulema Moret, Mercedes Roffe, Gladys Il-larregui, Emma Sepúlveda (who lived in Chile prior to emigrating to the U. S), Alicia Portnoy, Alicia Borinski, Alicia Ghiragossian, Nela Río, Margarita Feliciano (the last two now Canadian residents), Lila Zemboraín, Cristina Iglesias Kinczly, Margarita Drago, Elena Smidt, David Lagmanovich, Diana Bellesi and this writer—Luis Alberto Ambroggio, having had the good fortune of being honored in a volume entitled *El cuerpo y la letra* (Body and text) - *Poética de Luis Alberto Ambroggio*, edited by Mayra Zeleny and published by the North American Academy of the Spanish Language in 2008.[135]

Juana Arancibia, founder of the *Instituto Literario Cultural Hispano* (ILCH - Hispanic Literary Institute), wrote a canonical poem titled "Chañi" in which she expresses the following:

*Millennial stone*

*of my childhood*

*you are here with me*

*because he who knows everything*

*placed in my path*

*another tiny Chañi*

*in an out-of-the-way place.*


*And in spite of the surroundings,*

*the maelstrom*

*and the trickeries of absence,*

*you watch over me as before*

*through a landscape*

---

135 - A more complete essay on this poetic body can be seen in Luis Alberto Ambroggio, *Poesía del exilio argentino en los EE.UU.: registros y figuras* (poetry of Argentine exiles in the USA: records and figures", in the *Isla Negra* Magazine 3/128, pp. 19-28: http://www.ildialogo.org/poesia/islane-gra128especialeupoen.pdf.

*of alienated*

*time*

Just as Juana Arancibia nostalgically and allegorically evokes a topographical reference, others do this differently, such as Mariano Gowland by way of a guitar, or a musical style (Ambroggio and Nela Rio – a tango :), *yerba mate* or a *siesta* (nap) (Lila Zemborain),a particular city (for Silvia Tandeciarz, Buenos Aires). Ambroggio's poetry has been analyzed by critics specifically from the point of view of identity memory and in the context of discourse on power; for example, Adriana Corda's article entitled *Identidad y memoria en la lírica de Luis Alberto Ambroggio* (Identity and memory in the lyrics of LAA) as well as others[136] ranging from *Poemas Desterrados* (Exile poems), *Oda Ensimismada* (Self-absorbed ode), *El Testigo se desnuda* (The witness undresses), *Laberintos de Humo* (Smoky labyrinths), *La desnudez del asombro* (Astonishment's nakedness), *La arqueología del viento* (The wind's archeology) to *Todos somos Whitman* (We are all Whitman) and the volume published in 2014 by the North American Academy of the Spanish Language, *En el Jardín de los Vientos* (In the garden of the winds), *Obra poética* (poetic work) - 1974-2014—a critical edition by Carlos Paldao and Rosa Tezanos-Pinto. From the work *Habitantes del Poeta* (The poet's inhabitants)—a source of verses that connects with prevailing poetic themes in written in Spanish in the USA: Language as the homeland for identity memory:

*Two opposing languages live inside me;*

*I feel like a slave in my own flesh.*

*I disinherit the sweet words,*

*I obey, yet rebel, against orders*

---

136 - In the First International Literature Congress, Buenos Aires, October, 2006. Also from Adriana Corda, *El Discurso de la Identidad en los habitantes del poeta* (identity discourse in the poet's inhabitants) by Luis Alberto Ambroggio, 10th National Linguistics Congress, Catholic University of Salta (Argentina) July, 2005 ; *El discurso del poder, la memoria y el exilio en los textos poéticos de Luis Alberto Ambroggio* (the discourse on power, memory and exile in the poetic texts of LAA)", Universität Zu Köln, School of Philosophy, 2006; "The poetic writing of Luis Alberto Ambroggio as resistance to the discourse of power", 13th National Literature Congress, Argentina, School of Philosophy and Letters, National University of Tucumán, August 2005; *Disociación del signo poético en Laberintos de Humo de Luis Alberto Ambroggio* (dissociation of the poetic sign in Labyrinths of Smoke by LAA), *XXVI Simposio Internacional de Literatura Presente y Futuro de la Literatura Hispanoamericana Universidad de Los Lagos* (16th international symposium on present and future of Hispanic-American literature, *Los Lagos*University), Puerto Montt, Chile August 8-13, 2005. In addition to works entitled *El Cuerpo y la Letra, La poética de Luis Alberto Ambroggio* (the body and the letter. The poetics of LAA - Mayra Zeleny Publisher), New York: North American Academy of the Spanish Language, 2010. And *El exilio y la palabra. La trashumancia de un escritor agerntino-estadounidense* (exile and the word. The migrations of an Argentine-U.S. writer) Rosa Tezanos-Pinto Publisher), Buenos Aires: Editorial Vinciguerra, 2012.

*Let them disdain me with their deadly syllables*

*I reek of a loud discordant scream*

*Like burnt toast.*

There are references to dictatorships, dirty wars and torture, expressions of historical and political memory, as in the collection of poems *La Celda* (The cell), *El peso de los cuerpos* (The weight of the bodies) which begins with Vicente Huidobro's epigraph: "*To the bottom most tombs / To the very bottom of the seas / Beneath the murmur of the winds*" and concludes:

*The sentencing of a body*

*overcomes the apathy of the gods*

*/. . . /*

*Body-spirits rise up,*

*defying death*

*like a raging fire*

*To their bodies we bestow wings!*

We also highlight Zulema Moret who emphasizes attachment to the figures of memory, language, culture, family, to figures of love and loved ones as a shared characteristic in her *Mujeres mirando al sur - Antología de poetas sudamericanas en US* (Women looking south – an anthology of South American feminine poets in the U.S.).[137] Included in this anthology. Alicia Portnoy refers to the traumas of imprisonment and torture in her poem *Venganza de la manzana* (Revenge of the apple):

*They threw me*

*like a stone,*

*a weed,*

*a bad one;*

*removing,*

*the subversive*

*rotten apple…*

*But now*

*the remaining*

137 - Madrid, Ediciones Torremozas, S. L: 2004.

*apples*

*rot,*

*that is to say,*

*they have been rotting*

*since before*

*I even appeared*

In that poem we have verses displaying denunciation:

*They dug me up from the ground*

*from down below*

*—that's what they call exile—*

*that is,*

*suddenly,*

*I had to have dirt*

*and I was too far away*

*/. . . /*

*and then,*

*when I tried to breathe*

*there were too many bars. . .*

… and in *Canción de la exiliada* (Song of the female exile):

*They cut my voice:*

*I have two voices*

*. /. . /*

*They isolated me from my loved ones*

*and for them today*

*my song returns twice*

*as an echo.*

In *Los molinos de la memoria* (The memory mills) she writes: *on which among the dead shall we place what blame? / when the plot of silence is unraveled before us they will extract me from, my coffin.*[138]

From Bolivia: Eduardo Mitre is considered the catalyst of a late-blooming Bolivian avant-gardism. His significant poetic production in terms of prefiguration, configuration and re-figuration of memory is grouped under several titles such as *Morada* (Dwelling - 1975), *Desde tu Cuerpo* (From your body - 1984), *El Peregrino y la Ausencia: antología* (The pilgrim and the absence: an anthology (1988), *La Luz del Regreso* (The light of the return - 1990), *Camino de cualquier parte* (Road from anywhere - 1998) and *El paraguas de Manhattan* (The Manhattan's umbrella - 2004). We add Yolanda Bedregal who studied at Barnard College Columbia Univeristy; also Marty Sánchez Lowery Edith Graciela Sanabria and Ricardo Ballon.

From Colombia we have Luis Zalamea, Ramiro Lagos, Albalucia Ángel, Agueda Pizarro, Alonso Mejía, Armando Romero, one of the founders of *Nadaismo* (Latin American nihilism), Jaime Manrique, Consuelo Hernández, Miguel Falquez Certain, Gabriel Jaime Caro, Fabio Velázquez, Manuel Cortés Castañeda, Medardo Arias Satizabel, Juan Carlos Galeano, Don Gellver de Curra Lugo, Antonieta Villamil (organizer of the LA Poetry Festival), Carlos Aguasaco (anthologist of ten Latin American poets in the U.S., director of *Artepoética Press* and co-editor of anthologies from the Latin American Poetry Festival, New York City, 2013, with his poems *Conversando con el Ángel, Nocturnos del Caminante, Antología de poetas hermafroditas* (Conversing with the angel, Nocturnes of the hiker, Anthology of hermaphrodite poets); Elisa Dávila, Oscar Osorio, Rafael Saavedra Hernández, Andrea Cote Botero, Nicolás Linares Sánchez, Diego Rivelino, Lucia de Garcia, Arturo Salcedo, José Jesús Osorio[139] and the winner of the recently awarded "Carmen Conde" poetry prize, Clara Eugenia Ronderos, with her poetry *Estaciones en exilio* (Seasons in exile). Her poem *Tierra Firme* (Firm ground), based on the epigraph of the *Libro del Buen Humor* (Book of good humor) *"One's feet can be bound; one's will, not so"*, expresses the range of emotions:

---

138 - For more information see the article by Luis Alberto Ambroggio, *Poesia del exilio argentino en los EE. UU: registros y figuras* (poetry of the Argentine exile in the USA: records and figures) at www.ildialogo. org/poesia/islanegra128especialeupoen. pdf.

139 - See *15 Poetas colombianos en Estados Unidos. Poesía Migrante* (15 Colombian poets in the U.S. Migrant Poetry. Bogota: *El Tiempo*: 1998.

*I step on the ground of my dreams*

*and let my foot sink*

*deeply into the sticky stuff.*

*I want to say everything.*

*And let all the drool,*

*light darkness come out.*

*But from below, gravity pulls me*

*and terrifies the warm dampness*

*of recent death,*

*of life barely emerging,*

*of convulsing belly,*

*of death's rattle.*

*And now I don't want to, I don't want to, no.*

*I grab the rope tightly*

*where every morning I dry out my misery*

*and in disgust I pull,*

*and shake and dry and wash*

*and run toward the dense wake of fear.*

From Chile, Gabriela Mistral, who lived for extended periods in several places in the United States and died in New York. Details of her life are to be found in the volume *Gabriela Mistral y los Estados Unidos* (G. M. and the United States - 2011) by the North American Academy of the Spanish Language. The presence of this distinguished representative of the 1938 Generation is described by Fernando Alegría, a recognized critic and poet who documented the Nerudian contribution and the outstanding poets of the Chilean post-vanguard such as Humberto Díaz Casanueva, Gonzalo Rojas, Enrique Lihn, Oscar Hahn and Pedro Lastra in *Baladas de la memoria* (Ballads of memory - 2010), whose poetry has been categorized under *neomanierismo* as formulated by Dubois,[140] because it reveals in its poetics the struggle of the self against repressive instincts, as a way of restating the past. From Pedro Lastra, for example, we have these verses from his poem *Ya hablaremos de nuestra Juventud* (we will now speak of our younger years):

140 - Dubois, Gilbert. *El manierismo* (mannerism). Barcelona: Peninsula: 1980.

*We will now speak of our younger years*

*almost having forgotten,*

*confusing the nights and its descriptions,*

*what was taken away from us, the presence*

*of a murky battle with our dreams.*

And numerous other renowned poets such as Enrique Giordano, Raúl Barrientos, David Valjalo, later Marjorie Agosín, Juan Armando Epple, Javier Campos, Lilianet Brintrup, Alvaro Leiva, Cecilia Vicuña, Jesús Sepúlveda, Miriam Balboa, Mary Rosa Moraga Barrow, Oscar Sarmiento, Luis Correa-Díaz, Alicia Galaz Vivar, Andres Fisher, Marcelo Pellegrini, Francisco Leal.

From Ecuador: Jaime Montesinos, Yvon Gordon Vailakis, and José Ballesteros.

From Paraguay: Gustavo Gatti, Lourdes Espínola.

From Peru: Antonio Cisneros, Eduardo Chirinos, (who calls himself an 80's person, an exponent of culturalism in his poetics), Cecilia Bustamante, Miguel Ángel Zapata, Isaac Goldenberg (founder and director of the Latin American Writers Institute of New York), Raúl Bueno, José Cerna Bazán, Jaime Urco, Pedro Granados, Marita Troiano, Mario Montalbetti, José Antonio Mazzotti, Julio Ortega, Rafael Dávila-Franco, Sandro Chiri, Rocío Silva-Santisteban, Roberto Forns-Broggi, Reñato Gómez, Jorge Frisancho, Mariela Dreyfus, Oswaldo Chanove, Roger Santiváñez, Alfredo Ejalde, Lorenzo Helguero, Ericka Ghersi, José Luis Falconi, Victoria Guerrero, Odi Gonzales, Rocío Uchoffen, Luis Chávez, Enrique Bernales, Chrystian Zegarra, Carlos Villacorta, Enrique Bruce and Ulises González, among others.

From Uruguay: Roberto Echavarren, exponent of Androgynism whose poetic style has been described as *Gonzogongorism*, Eduardo Espina (director of the *Hispanic Poetry Review*), inventive Uruguayans who in their poems perform wild and bold feats with language; add the name Cristina Rodríguez Cabral.

From Venezuela there are many who have resided in the USA for different lengths of time: Antonio Arráiz of the "Generation of 18", Rufino Blanco Fombona, Ana Teresa Torres, Lydia Zacklin (essayist and translator), Arturo Gutiérrez Plaza, María Auxiliadora Álvarez, Josefina López and Carmen Rojas Larrazábal.

# From the Caribbean and Central American Exile Community

In the poetry of the Caribbean-Central American exile we find:

From Costa Rica: Aquileo J. Echeverría whom Dario called Costa Rica's national poet and who served as an Attaché to the Costa Rican Embassy in Washington, D. C. , Julián Marchena, who was a long-time resident of the United States in the 1930s and also Laureano Albán, who obtained his doctorate in New York and held diplomatic positions in Washington, D. C. ; Alexander Obando, the Mark and Alan Smith-Soto brothers of Costa Rica (the latter being the author of the poems *Libro del lago* and *Fragmentos de alcancía* (Book of the lake - piggy back fragments) and editor of the International Poetry Review.

From El Salvador: Gustavo Solano (1886), modernist and now more like a spokesman of social realism as seen in his drama in verse, published in California *La sangre: crímenes de Manuel Estrada Cabrera* (blood: the crimes of Manuel Estrada Cabrera). We note Claudia Lars whose father is a U.S. citizen. Then Lilian Serpas, who has resided in in the U.S. has created conceptual poetry in postmodernist sonnet format. In our time, Mayamérica Cortés, Jorge Argueta and more recently Oscar Morales Aguilar, Julio Valencia, Karla Coreas, Mauricio Campos, director of *La Revista Cultural Hispanoamericana* (Hispanic-American cultural magazine), Juana Ramos, author of the collection of poems *Multiplicada en mi* (Multiplied in me), which represents the city as a cannibalistic monster that devours the subject of the verse as indicated here: *Aquí, desde este lugar/ que me tragó entera,/ que me eructa, me vomita* (here, from this place / who swallowed me whole, / who belches me up, vomits me); Also Arío Salazar, Quique Áviles, Carlos Parada, Wladimir Monge, whose inspiration is based on the previously mentioned "*guerrillerismo*" and the characteristics of that genre's literary and cultural evolution.

From Guatemala: Luis Cardoza y Aragón in an interval in between his multiple exiles; Efraín López Rodriguez.

From Honduras: Rafael Heliodoro del Valle, who during several years of diplomatic activity in the U.S. (1915-1921), wrote a collection of poems entitled *El perfume de la tierra natal* (Perfume of the homeland - 1917), which made him one of the most outstanding voices of youthful Central American poetry. Also, Aida Ondina Sabonge Gutiérrez who divided her time between her homeland and the U. S; and the publisher-poet Amanda Castro.

From Nicaragua, among many, names such as that of Santiago Argüello (1871-1940), a romantic-modernist poet who wrote *El alma dolorida de la patria* (The pained soul of the fatherland) Salomón de la Selva who according to Emilio Pacheco[141]is the founder of *La otra vanguardia*(the other van-

---

141 - From his essay *Nota sobre la otra vanguardia* (notes on another vanguard), *Casa de las Améri-*

guard,); also in critical moments of their formation and literary creation, we include Salomón de la Selva, Ernesto Cardenal and Claribel Alegría. Then as typical of the prefigurative, configurative and refigurative times of memory the poets Gioconda Belli and Daisy Zamora, both long-term California residents whose literary discourse, after disappointments, failures, new peace agreements, abandoned *guerrillerismo* and concentrated on redefining aesthetic paradigms in cultural models and projects, new priorities and new identities, with an ever-present magnetism of an ideal revolution. Also: Rubi Arana, Horacio Peña, Yolanda Blanco, Conny Palacios, Nicasio Urbina, Milagros Terán, Silvio Ambroggi, Francisco Larios and Roberto Cuadra.

From Panama: José S. Cuervo, Afro-Panamanian Yvette Modestín, poet-professor Eduardo Ritter Aislán who lived there and modernist José Guillermo Batalla, who resided in U.S.

From the Hispanic Caribbean: In addition to the aforementioned Puerto Rican and Cuban-U.S. poets, we add, from the Dominican Republic, Pedro Henríquez Ureña who had several periods of residency in the U. S.; Sherezada "Chiqui" Vicioso, Fabio Fiallo, Andrés Francisco Requena, Rei Berroa, Yoseli Castillo Fuertes, Miriam Ventura, Carlos Rodríguez, Teonilda Madera, Josefina Báez, René Soriano, Leonardo Nin plus representatives of the 80's Generation, the post-modernity of the so-called Post-war Group, among whom are Marienela Medrano, Yrene Santos and the youngest of this generation, Alexis Gómez Rosas. Then there are the "meta-poets" Joel Almonó and Jorge Piña who stand out. Also Juan Tineo who annually organizes the cultural event known as the Hispanic-Latin Book Fair in New York which has honored authors such as Junot Díaz, Carmen Boullosa, among others. Also in this context and as a reference we cite only the *Antología de poesía hispano-caribeña escrita en los Estados Unidos* (Anthology of Hispanic-Caribbean poetry written in the U.S.),- by William Luis.[142]

It is important to note that although some of the authors mentioned above have had limited periods of residency in the United States, many of the exiles included in these necessarily incomplete listings have been noted not only for important poetic creations, but also for being involved in activities, institutions, publications, or relevant editorial initiatives in promoting Hispanic poetry in their places of residency and centers of influence.

**Current poetic movements and trends**

It is impossible to cover all current activities and movements related to U.S. Hispanic poetry.

---

*cas* 118 (January-February, 1980).

142 - Bulletin published by the Federico García Lorca Foundation, 18 (December, 1995), 17-93.

However, we will start this short list by highlighting the presence of bilingual magazines and bilingual (Spanish-English) publications such as *Tameme* edited by the award-winning author C. M. Mayo of Washington D. C. , in which she cites the works of Elizabeth Miller Gamble of Texas; *Terra Incognita*, *The Bilingual Review Press* of the University of Arizona; *Literal* Founded by Rose Mary Salum; contributions such as the *Alba de América* (Dawn of America) a journal of the University of California edited by the Argentine-American Juana de Arancibia; conventions organized by The Hispanic Cultural Literary Institute of California; *Baquiana* headed by Maricel Mayor; the *Gaceta Iberoamericana de Cultura* (Ibero-American gazette) published in Washington, D. C. by Dr. Miranda Rico of Bolivia; George Mason University's *Hispanic Culture Review*; the *International Poetry Review* of the University of North Carolina at Greensboro; *Ventana Abierta* (open window) at the University of California's Institute of Chicano Studies and, finally, the leading publisher, *Arte Público Press*, associated with the University of Houston and their outstanding and exhaustive pioneering research on Hispanic literature in the U.S. embodied in an important collections of papers and texts (some mentioned herein), as well as prestigious bilingual editions of poetry works created in the U.S.—activities carried out under the leadership of Professor Nicholas Kanellos and colleagues.

We also note the active role of poetic groups, such as *Para eso la Palabra* (That's why words) the Ibero-American Academy of Poetry which I helped organize twenty years ago in Washington, D. C. embracing all literary genres and promoting discourse and poetic memory in Spanish in the United States. And we edited a recent anthology published by the American Language Academy entitled *Al pie de la Casa Blanca Poetas Hispanos de Washington DC* (At the foot of the White House Hispanic poets in Washington DC - 2010). Also in Washington, the *Teatro de la Luna* (theater of the moon) has organized over twenty "Poetry Marathons" in Spanish, an event which has been echoed by other organizations. For example, in Los Angeles, *La Poesía Festival* under the direction of Colombian poet Antonieta Villamil; *Poesía para la gente* (Poetry for the people); the cultural organization known as *La Luciérnaga* (Firefly), in which Salvadoran poet Mauricio Campos participates as director of the *Revista Cultural Hispanoamericana* (Hispanic-American cultural review); San Francisco, with the holding of Children's Poetry Festivals organized by "San Francisco Poetry Workshops" under Salvadorian poets Jorge Argueta and René Colato; in Chicago, the *Pura Palabra* (Word alone) recitals; Boston with the initiative Hispanic Writers Week which has been honored with the presence of outstanding poets Marjorie Agosín, Claribel Alegría, Luis Alberto Ambroggio, Martín Espada, Naomi Ayala, Rosario Ferre, Demetria Martínez, Daisy Zamora and Juan Felipe, and has produced anthologies such as *A Toda Luz* (all lit up), in 2011, and 2013; the *Hispanic Writers Week Anthology*; New York: New Poetry Festivals - Poets in New York, *Latino Poets* NY, and a prolific series of poetic readings such as those held in the *Centro Cultural Rey Juan Carlos* (King Juan Carlos cultural center) by Lila Zemboraín as well as those organized by Roger Cabán, *Hijo legítimo del Barrio* (legitimate son of the Barrio)"; *Poetas con Café* (Poets with coffee) for eighteen years, which in 2014 was sponsored by the *Museo del Barrio* (*Barrio* museum) with literary and poetic encounters such as those organized by CUPHI in Los Angeles in 2014; those of the O-MIAMI poets and writers, under the International Association of Hispanic Poets and Writers (AIPEH), led in Miami by Pilar Vélez as well as the International Poetry Festivals *Grito de Mujer* (Woman's cry); the O-Miami festival with its promotion of the "Spanish book month" and other activities such as an Hispanic poetry competition sponsored by Miami's Spanish Cultural Center and Miami Dade College (MDC) in collaboration with the National Poetry Series Poetry Peace Prize, which honors the best works in Spanish by U.S. residents; the magazine *Suburbano* featuring U.S. Hispanic writers edited in Miami by Cuban-American Daina Chaviano, which features poetic texts; the *Tintero* (Inkwell) reading cycle held at the *Talento Bilingüe* (Bilingual talent) cultural center in Houston, headed by Mexican-American poet Guadalupe Méndez. Speaking of cities and the presence of Hispanic poetry therein, it's worth to mention is the book by the Peruvian poet Sandro Chiri, *Para Español, Marque 2: Escritores Hispanoparlantes en Filadelfia* (For Spanish, mark 2: Spanish-speaking writers in Philadelphia) (Latino Press 2010).

Here are some examples of poetry activities like those I had the honor of "curating" for the Smithsonian Institution in Washington D. C.: Celebrating Roots, Creating Community: a Night of Music and Bilingual Poetry" and "Celebrating the Bicentennial: Argentine Poets in the United States" and the annual celebration (now nearly 20) of Spanish poetry written in the United States, held at the Library of Congress during Hispanic month. Also those organized by Zulema Moret at Grand Valley State University entitled "Building Community Through Poetry." The Cervantes Institutes in New York, Boston, Chicago and Albuquerque have supported and promoted poetry recitals and discussions of Hispanic poetry in the United States.

Other poetry groups have expressed themselves in joint anthologies such as *Los Paraguas Amarillos* (Yellow umbrellas)"Latin Poets in New York", edited by Iván Sillén (Bilingual Press - 1983), *Cool Salsa and Red Hot Salsa*—successful bilingual editions by Lori Carlson- (1994);the previously cited anthology *Piel Palabra* (Skin, word) and the recently released *Al fin del siglo: 20 poetas* (end of century: 20 poets) edited by Francisco Álvarez-Koki and Pedro R. Monge Rafuls (Ollantay Press, 1999). Also *La Ciudad Prestada, Poesía Latinoamericana posmoderna en Nueva York* (The borrowed city, postmodern Latin American poetry in New York, edited by Pedro López Adorno - 2002); *Cruzando Puentes* (Crossing bridges)—an anthology of Latin Literature (Center for Chicano Studies, University of California Santa Barbara; *Ventana Abierta* (Open window - 2001) edited by Luis Leal and Victor Fuentes[143] and *Encuentro* (encounter): Ten Latin American Poets in the USA (New York 2003);[144] the anthology *Poetas sin fronteras* (Poets without borders - Verbum, Madrid: 2000) edited by Colombian poet Ramiro Lagos which includes a sampling of poetry written in Spanish by poets residing in the United States; in addition to Lagos and others already mentioned, Antonio Barbagallo of Italy, Louis Bourne of the USA and Andres Berger-Kiss of Hungary. We refrain from a more detailed reference to the well-received *Paper Dance* anthology because it contains poems written in English by Latin authors such as the recently published anthology entitled *Looking Out, Looking In* (Public Arte Press, 2013) compiled by William Luis. In Chicago, *Desarraigos, cuatro poetas latinoamericanos en Chicago* (uprooted - four Latin American poets in Chicago)—an anthology that includes works by Jorge Hernández, Febronio Zataraín, Juana Iris Goergen, León Leiva Gallardo; *Voces sueltas* (loose voices) *Editions* (2008) and the activity of *Contratiempo* (Setback) publishers and a magazine which, for example, in 2014 collaborated with the Cervantes Institute of Chicago and DePaul University in the organization of the 7th International Festival of Poetry in Spanish held in April: *Centenarios* (Centennials), and other poetry competitions. Finally, there is the recently published anthology *Malditos Latinos, Malditos sudacas* (Damned Latins, damned South Americans), *Ibero-American Poetry made in USA*[145] which includes poets born in the U.S. or in Spanish-American countries who write in Spanish, as well as those mentioned in some of the previous groupings such as Gabriela Jaúregui, Roberto Tejada, Rodrigo Toscano and *Nostalgias de Arena* (Nostalgias of sand - 2011), an anthology of writers from Dominican communities in the USA.

I conclude this review of the Spanish-U.S. poetic genre, celebrating the recent appointment of Juan Felipe Herrera as Poet Laureate of the United States—the first Californian Hispanic of Mexican origin, to occupy such a distinguished and iconic position, recognized nation-wide and internationally.

## Prose

In addition to the rich poetic production that we have reviewed, many works

---

143 - Poets included in anthologies not previously mentioned: Jorge Antonio Buciaga, Gabriela Gutiérrez, Omar de León, Ángel Luis Méndez Ramos, Ángel González, Gabriela Tagliavini, Renato Rosaldo, Jorge Simán, Aracelis Collazo Mapa, Alfonso Rodríguez, Rusmesa and Estela Morena.
144 - David J. Labiosa, a poet not mentioned above. included in the anthology.
145 - Mexico, *Ediciones El billar de Lucrecia* (Lucrecia's billiards), National Fund for Culture and the Arts: 2009, Publisher: Rocío Cerón, Selection and prologue by Mónica de la Torre and Cristián Gómez.

in the narrative genre have also been published in Spanish in the United States, beginning in the Colonial period and in the following centuries up to the present.

In the Colonial period, we saw the publishing of a literary text called *La Relación* (The telling) by Álvar Núñez Cabeza de Vaca, written during his passage through U.S. territory between 1528 and 1537, published in Zamora, Spain in 1542 and *El descubrimiento de las siete ciudades de Cíbola* (Discovery of the seven cities of Cibola) by Fray Marcos de Niza, probably written in 1539 during his mission to New Mexico. On page 150 of this text we can find the following fragment: "… in this first province there are seven quite large cities . . . whose inhabitants are very well dressed. And later [the man] provided me with many other particulars about these seven cities as well as about other provinces each of which claims to be even much larger than those seven cities; also I learned from him how he knew these things. We made many requests for answers and found them to be well-founded. "

Following this present short section devoted to prose texts written in those days, I will also cite two examples of figures, themes and specific motifs from the literature of the period. Pedro Menéndez de Áviles is also on this list of the epistolary genre exemplified by a letter he wrote to his nephew, dated 1574 (quoted in *San Agustín de la Florida*, p. 205), in which—as Víctor Fuentes points out—he expresses one of the central themes of the literature of immigration: namely, attachment—in this case love for the new land. A more extensive text about this migrant experience in the territories of the Americas is what has come to be regarded as the first book written within these territories: that of Álvaro Núñez Cabeza de Vaca, entitled *Los naufragios* (Shipwrecks), published in 1542, about events that took place between 1527 and 1536. These nine years are highlighted in this literary text and later on in others with thematic and aesthetic characteristics that are typical of the immigration literature of this period and of the United States—themes to which we have alluded previously and will touch upon in the conclusion of our analysis of poetic creations such as that of Cabeza de Vaca, incorporated into American literature in what we could now call its Spanish-American dimension—the entire extent and bordering territories of what would be the two Floridas, as well as the territories and places of the Southwest (New Mexico, Colorado, Texas and Arizona), with significant chapter titles such as: "How we entered into the land," "How we got to Appalachia," "The lay of the land," "How we left the town of Aute," "What happened to us in Villa de Malhado,""How we followed the path of the corn" and others that typically refer to the fauna and flora of indigenous communities, as well as their customs, characteristics, daily life, appreciations—though sometimes biased—"How the Indians brought us food,""How we moved about and how we were received," "How they gave us the hearts of deer," "How we saw remnants of Christians. "

Literary creations such as these continued in the following centuries. At this point we will take a brief tour of these genres created during the Nineteenth, Twentieth and Twenty-first centuries to briefly point out areas for further expansion, following a generalized summary based on an article appearing in the newspaper *El País* (The country) on Jan. 25, 2014, by Eduardo Lago entitled, "Hispanic literature becomes a cultural force In the United States,"[146] and by other writers, including Jesús J. Barquet, in his article, "Reflections on Hispanic Literature in the United States."[147]We begin by referring to the historical novel *Jicotencal* by Spanish immigrant Félix Mejía, published in Philadelphia in 1826, in addition to another of his works, *Vida de Fernando VII y Los retratos políticos de la revolución de España* (Life of Fernando VII and Political portraits of the Spanish Revolution) as well as translations of works by Félix Varela, a Cuban priest, who was a figure with significant impact during the Nineteenth Century as he helped promote Hispanic and Catholic culture in the U.S. He resided in both Philadelphia and New York and translated *A Manual of parliamentary practice* written by Thomas Jefferson, and was the founder of the newspaper *El Habanero* (The Havana citizen), the first Spanish-language newspaper at the beginning of the 20th century and also founded *El Mensajero Semanal* (the weekly messenger). In 1851 a book written by Antonio Maria Osio entitled *La Memoria de la California Mexicana* (Remembering Mexican California) was published; it contains suggestive references to Spanish literary tradition from *Don Quixote* to *Lazarillo de Tormes* as well as many others. The novel *The Squatter and the Don* (1885), written in English by Amparo Ruiz de Burton, describes the situation of the defeated inhabitants after the signing of the Guadalupe-Hidalgo Treaty.

In the Twentieth Century, exile prose literature and that of Hispanic-American immigrants in the United States, including fiction, biographies and essays expanded exponentially. Like those of the poetic genre, prose has its own special characteristics, defined and identified in the concert of world literature including the trauma of uprooting, remembering, nostalgia, having the freedom to protest and clinging to memories. Special studies have been made of literary characters, authors, histories, culture and other subjects. For example, the works of Colombian author José Eustasio Rivera and his novel *La vorágine* (Whirlwind). He died in New York in 1928 while writing the manuscript of *La mancha negra* (The black stain),

146 - http://cultura.elpais.com/cultura/2014/01/23/actualidad/1390479980_742205.html.
147 - The Window. Casa de las Américas, http://www.google.com/
url?sa=t&rct=j&q=&esrc=s&frm= 1&source=web&cd=1&ved=0CB4QFjAA&url=http%3A%
2F%2Flaventana.casa.cult.cu%2Fmodules.php% 3Fname%3DNews%26file%3Darticle%26si
d%3D6340&ei=3PQSVbTyHsHSgwTsmISoBQ&usg = AFQjCNGAVAsE4retJ1_8u BtZo-rQ-
4mO5w&sig2=OOSeE2VP2lCmH1Ay-SJoYQ & bvm=bv.89184060, d. Exy.

his second novel. Also in 1928 a novel by Daniel Vanegas: *Las aventuras de Don Chipote o, cuando los pericos mamen* (The adventures of Don Chipote or, when the parakeets suckle) was published. Eduardo Marceles in his essay *The Literature of Exile: Latin American writers in New York*[148]stated, "José Yglesias is the patriarch of Latin American authors in New York." Yglesias, the son of a Galician immigrant to Havana, was born in Tampa, Florida in 1919 and settled in New York in 1937. Although he wrote in English, he deserves mention here because of his interesting subject matter and the quality of his writing which exemplifies the idiosyncrasies of Hispanic writers in the United States. His first autobiographical novel, *Home Again*, recounts his childhood in Ybor City, the Cuban district of Tampa, known for its tobacco industry. His most recent novel *Tristan and the Hispanics* (1990) is a humorous account of a young man in search of his nearly forgotten Hispanic roots. According to Yglesias, assimilation to U.S. culture does not mean abandoning one's own heritage but, in fact, makes it even richer. His thesis is that Hispanics in the United States do not lose Bolivar or Martí; instead they add Jefferson and Lincoln.

To the review of authors previously discussed, there is a narrative by Spanish-American Felipe Alfau entitled *Locos* (The crazy ones - 1936)—a refined and avant-garde collection of stories, followed in 1948 by *Chromos*—a novel about the adventures of a Spaniard in the United States. Then, *Mexican Village* (1945) by Josephina Niggli, of European ancestry born in Mexico, offers a vision—more idealized than lived—of Mexican culture through ten heart warmingly intertwined stories. Jesús Colón (1901-1974) a Puerto Rican author of humble origins and a contemporary of Alfau, was an African American communist sympathizer who composed brilliant journalistic works in both English and Spanish, including his most characteristic work, *Un puertorriqueño en Nueva York y otras estampas* (A Puerto Rican in New York and other traces - 1961). It is a work sprinkled with immense humanity and a sense of humor that initiates a *Newyorican* literary scene which, together with the emergence of Chicano identity, marks the beginning of a movement of political resistance and an affirmation of Hispanic cultural values. In 1962 John Steinbeck received the Nobel Prize for Literature as the author of a bewitching and heartbreaking novel, *The Grapes of Wrath*(1939) the Spanish title of which is *Las uvas de la ira*, dealing with the ordeals of California Mexican migrants. During the sixties, works of decisive importance by Hispanic writers appeared on both the East and West coasts. Puerto Rican judge Edwin Torres offered his description of Latino delinquency in his novel *Carlito's Way* (1963), which was made into a movie at least twice. That same year, Chicano author John Rechy published *City of Night*, which paints a grim picture of the world of male prostitution in New York, Los Angeles, San Francisco and New Orle-

---

148 - http://www.qcc.cuny.edu/foreignlanguages/rvci/marcelesliteratura.html.

ans. In the autobiographical novel *Down These Mean Streets* (1967), Piri Thomas writes about life in Spanish Harlem—a suburb of Upper Manhattan. Although it did not appear until 1984, the best chronicle of the history of New York's Puerto Rican colony is Berne Vega's *Memorias* (Memoirs)—a document of significant sociological and literary value.[149]

To these must be added three works considered to be the pinnacle of Mexican-American literature: *Y no se lo tragó la tierra* (And it was not swallowed up by the earth - 1971), by Tomás Rivera; *Bless Me, Última* (Last - 1972), by Rudolfo Anaya, and *Estampas del valle* (Imprints of the valley - 1973) by Rolando Hinojosa-Smith. The first and third of these three novels were originally written in Spanish. The *Autobiografía de un búfalo marrón* (Autobiography of a brown buffalo - 1972) by Chicano activist Óscar Z. Acosta, although different in character from the above, received positive reviews by critics. The above-mentioned trilogy is classic Chicano literature written by Anaya, Rivera, and Hinojosa-Smith who acknowledge a forerunner in a work entitled *Pocho* written by José Antonio Villarreal(1959), as well as follow-up works by Sabine Ulibarri, author of a collection of stories published under the title "*Mí*".

Although some of these works were written in English (or in Puerto Rican English-Spanish *barrio* mix) I include them, as well as the works of *Newyorrican* Nicholasa Mohr, who wrote *Nilda* (1973), *The Bronx Remembered* (1975), *In New York* (1977), *Abuela fumaba puros y otros cuentos de Tierra Amarilla* (Grandma smoked cigars and other tales of *Tierra Amarilla* [Yellow land] - 1977), '*Rituals of Survival*' (1985), to which critics have attributed significant testimonial and literary value. I would like to emphasize the special merit of the literature produced by New York Puerto Rican writers as they represent the pioneer Hispanic-American community in the United States, which we have previously touched upon in the analysis of continental Puerto Rican poetic writings. Historically, the genre of Hispanic prose writing is headed by Eugenio María de Hostos, Ramón Emeterio Betances and more recently the testimonial narratives by authors including Nicholasa Mohr, Pedro Juan Soto with '*Spiks*' and Edward Rivera with '*Family Installments*'—a literary genre that is increasingly well-known in its diverse expressions as can be seen in the following works: '*Yerba Buena*'(Good herb) by Sandra María Esteves, and the novels by Esmeralda Santiago:- *Casi una mujer* (Almost a woman), *Cuando era puertorriqueña* (When I was Puerto Rican), *Las Mamis* (The moms), *Conquistadora* (Female conqueror), *El sueño de América* (the American dream), *Las Christmas*: *escritores Latinos recuerdan las tradiciones navideñas*(Latin writers remember Christmas traditions), Tato Laviera's experimental theater and the combative novels of Edgardo Vega, to cite just a few examples.

---

149 - https://es.wikipedia.org/wiki/Literatura_de_Unidos_en_espa%C3%B1ol.

From the eighties: In 1983 the outstanding writer, and this author's beloved friend, Óscar Hijuelos—a Cuban resident of the Bronx—debuted with his excellent novel *Our House in the Last World*, which together with *Los reyes del mambo tocan canciones de amor* (The mambo kings play love songs), received the Pulitzer Prize in 1990. In this context, some critics point to Sandra Cisneros, a Chicana living in Chicago who wrote *La casa en Mango Street* (The house on Mango St. - 1984)—which is not a novel but rather a collection of short stories whose influence continues to be felt today (translated into Spanish by Elena Poniatowska).

Another important New York writer of the 1980's and early 1990's is Cuban-born Reinaldo Arenas, (1943) who was a participant in the 1980 Mariel exodus, who after his death in 1990, in addition to his poetry, left a legacy of a dozen novels, plus his biography entitled *Antes que anochezca* (Before nightfall) based on which, Eduardo Marceles pointed out, 'Julian Schnabel directed the film *Before Night Falls*, starring Javier Bardem in the role of the novelist and he received an Oscar nomination for best actor for his great interpretation of that character.[150] In 1997, his book of stories entitled *Las historias prohibidas de Marta Veneranda* (The forbidden stories of Marta Veneranda) won the *Casa de las Américas* Extraordinary Hispanic U.S. Literary Prize.

In the 1990's, in addition to Hijuelos' Pulitzer prize, other finalists in the *Chromos* National Book Awardscompetition (almost half a century after its publication) included Spanish author Felipe Alfau with his work *Locos* (Crazy ones)—a comedy of gestures—and Elena Castedo, also from Spain with *Paradise*, which she herself translated into Spanish, (*Paraíso*) encouraging other writers to do the same. In 1992, which commemorated the fifth centenary of the discovery of the American Continent, Abraham Rodríguez, Jr. published *The Boy Without a Flag: Tales of the South Bronx*. Cristina García published *Soñar en cubano* (Dreaming in Cuban), focusing on the concept of identity as did Julia Álvarez and Sandra Cisneros. In 1993 Chicano Dagoberto Gilb, author of *Gritos* (Cries - 2003), *Hecho en Tejas* (Made in Texas - 2006), foreshadowed his talent as revealed in his collection of stories *The Magic of Blood* (1993)—a work highly praised by critics—and in 1994 AbrahamRodríguez published the novel *Spidertown*, with a cris-crossing of languages about the troubling drug world of upstate New York. In 1997 *Marinero raso* (Sailor with the rank of private) ratified Francisco Goldman as an author of international standing. A year later, Rolando Hinojosa-Smith, a university professor and the son of a *campesino* who fought in the Mexican Revolution and himself a veteran of the Korean

---

150 - See his essay *La literatura del exilio: Escritores latinoamericanos en Nueva York", Revista Virtual de Cultura Iberoamericana,* 2003 (the literature of exile: Latin American writers in New York", a virtual journal of Ibero-American culture, 2003), http://www.qcc.cuny.edu/ForeignLanguages/RVCI/ensayomarsales1.html.

War, was nominated for the Cervantes prize for his work *Ask a Policeman*, culminating the long series entitled *Klail City,* a quarter century later with *Estampas del valle* (Valley imprints). Hinojosa, according to information provided by Eduardo Lago, amalgamates diverse influences. He says that his novels are like choirs, full of characters who become an authentic collective voice in *Klail City.* The beautiful classical Spanish of his first five books is impressive, but the sixth installment, *Rites and Witnesses*, Hinojosa-Smith wrote in English.[151]

In the final decades of the 20th and in the early 21st Century, another Cuban writer, Fernando Velázquez Medina, made his debut with his novel *Última rumba en Havana* (Last rumba in Havana - 2002). There are other novelists and poets of note, such as the Colombian-American, Jaime Manrique, author of the novel *Latin Moon in Manhattan* (1992) and my esteemed Peruvian colleague and friend, Isaac Goldemberg, who wrote *La vida a plazos de Don Jacobo Lerner* (DJL's life in stages - 1978), *El nombre del padre* (Name of the father - 2002) and other novels, the most recent being *Acuérdate del escorpión,* (Remember the scorpion - 2010), as well as Dominican Julia Álvarez whose works she wrote in both English and Spanish: *Había una vez una quinceañera* (There once was a quinceañera [15-year-old girl]), *En el tiempo de las mariposas* (in the time of the butterflies), *Yo* (I), *Negocios* (Businesses), in addition to her well-known novel *How the García Girls Lost Their Accents* as well as her book of essays, *Algo que declarar* (Something to declare); Ecuadorian Ernesto Quiñónez, creator of the novel *El vendedor de sueños* (The dream seller - 2001), Bolivian writer and Cornell University professor Edmundo Paz Soldán, a writer who effectively promotes Hispanic literature in the United States with his novel *La materia del deseo* (The substance of desire) which explores themes shared by all immigrants and exiles trying to put down roots in the U.S. without any desire to sever the ties that connect them to their native lands; and Honduran Roberto Quesada with his novel *Nunca entres por Miami* (Never enter by way of Miami). Peruvian Daniel Alarcón,—a U.S. resident since childhood—produced a collection of stories entitled *Guerra en la penumbra* (War in the half-light). Dominican-American Junot Díaz, was the second Hispanic to be granted the prestigious Pulitzer Prize for his novel *La breve y maravillosa vida de Oscar Wao* (The short, wonderful life of O.W.), and other works published under the title *Así es como las pierdes* (That's how you lose them). At the Frankfurt Book Fair in 1997, publishers around the world were pushing for the rights to his book of short stories entitled *Drown*. Mexican novelist and poet Juvenal Acosta, who at the time of this writing resided in Berkeley, California, wrote the novel *Terciopelo Violento* (Violent velvet). Ray Loriga, a Spanish author and screenwriter published

151 - See his previously quoted article: "Hispanic literature becomes a cultural force in the US", in *El País*, 25-I-2014: http://cultura.elpais.com/cultura/2014/01/23/actualidad / 1390479980_742205. htm.

his first novel, *Lo peor de todo* (The worst thing of all) in 1992, in a style of writing reminiscent of the Beatnik generation of Keouac and Bukorsby, and who since then has written about urban themes, plus he has a passion for music as noted in his work *El hombre que inventó Manhattan,* (The man who invented Manhattan), *Lo peor de todo* (The worst thing of all) and *Héroes* (Heroes). Chilean-American Alberto Fuguet, one of the founders in the 1990's of the McOndo group, is the author of several works, among them, his best known, *Por favor, rebobinar* (Please rewind) published in 1998. Then there is the Peruvian Eduardo González Viaña with, among others, *El amor de Carmela me va a matar* (Carmela's love is gonna kill me - 2010) and *Vallejo en los infiernos* (Vallejo in hell- 2010). Cuban-American Antonio Orlando Rodríguez, winner of the prestigious Alfaguara Prize for novels written in 2008 including his work *Chiquita*, short stories, children's stories and essays. Peruvian by birth, the prolific Chilean Isabel Allende writer raised in and a resident of the U.S. has some outstanding novels beginning with *La casa de los espíritus* (House of spirits), *Eva Luna, Cuentos de Eva Luna* (Tales of Eva Luna), *El plan infinito* (The infinite plan), *Paula, Afordita, Hija de la fortuna* (Daughter of fortune), *Retrato en sepia* (Portrait in sepia - 2002), *Mi país inventado* (My invented country), *Amor* (Love), *Zorro* (Fox), *El juego de Ripper* (Ripper's game), *La Ciudad de las Bestias* (City of beasts – 2002), *El Reino del Dragón de Oro* (Kingdom of the golden dragon - 2003) and *El Bosque de los Pigmeos* (Pygmies' forest - 2004), a trilogy reissued in the recent publication of *Memorias del Águila y del Jaguar* (Memories of the eagle and the jaguar).

A listing of other well-known Hispanics who have published biographies or essays with major publishing success in the United States includes journalist and Mexican reporter Jorge Ramos who has passionately investigated the experience of Hispanic immigration in the United States, with his several essays, including *La otra cara de América* (The other face of America). Cuban Cristina Saralegui wrote *Pa'arriba y pa'delante Mis secretos para triunfar en tu carrera, tu relación y tu vida* (Upward and onward - my secrets for success in your career, your relationships and your life - 2014); actress Cameron Díaz contributed in English with *The Body Book: The Law of Hunger, the Science of Strength, and Other Ways to Love Your Amazing Body*- 2014). Eddie "Piolín" Sotelo poses the question: ¿A qué venimos? (Why are we here?), which he himself answers, ¡A triunfar! (To overcome!), *Cómo encontré mi voz entre la esperanza, la fuerza y la determinación.* (How I found my voice through hope, strength and determination - 2015), to mention just a few significant literary contributions, whose very titles explicitly address many of the concerns of immigrants.

There are many more excellent writers in the U.S. Spanish literary world today, such as Cuban Daína Chaviano, a Miami resident, with more than a dozen books dwelling on the theme of female fantasies and works of science fiction, among them: *Historias de hadas para adultos* (Stories about fairies for adults - 2007), *La isla de los amores infinitos* (The island of infinite loves, *Los mundos que amo* (The worlds I love), *Fábulas de una abuela extraterrestre* (Fables of an extra-terrestrial grandmother), *Gata encerrada* (Walled in cat), *Casa de juegos* (House of games), *El hombre* (The man), *la hembra y el hambre* (The lady and the craving), *Confesiones eróticas y otros hechizos* (Erotic confessions and other delights); Jorge Majfud, from Uruguay, a professor at Jacksonville University is the author of novels, stories and essays such as *Hacia qué patrias del silencio / memorias de un desaparecido* (Toward what countries of silence / memoirs of a disappeared one, *Crítica de la pasión pura* (Criticism of pure passion), *La reina de América* (The queen of America), *El tiempo que me tocó vivir* (The times I lived in), *La narración de lo invisible / Significados ideológicos de América Latina* (The narrative of the invisible / ideological meanings of Latin America), *Perdona nuestros pecados* (Forgive our sins), *La ciudad de la Luna* (City of the moon), *Crisis, Cyborgs, El eterno retorno de Quetzalcoátl* (Cyborgs, the eternal return of Quetzalcoátl), *Cuentos* (Tales), *Cine político latinoamericano* (Latin American political cinema), *Hermenéutica* (Hermeneutics), *El pasado siempre vuelve* (The past always returns); Teresa Dovalpage, a Cuban resident in Taos, New Mexico, (*A Girl like Che Guevara, El Difunto Fidel* (dead Fidel), *Habanera* (female Havana resident), *Muerte de un murciano en La Habana*(a Murcian dies in Havana), *Posesas de La Habana* (Possessed women of Havana), ¡Por culpa de Candela! (Because of Candela!), *El retorno de la expatriada* (The return of the female expatriate), *La Regenta en La Habana* (The female regent in Havana), *Llevarás luto por Franco* (You will mourn for Franco), *Orfeo en el Caribe* (Orpheus in the Caribbean);Peruvian Pedro Medina León, editor and author of the books *Streets de Miami, Mariana no te veré en Miami* (Mariana I won't see you in Miami), *Lado B* (side B) and publisher of the anthology *Viaje* (travel) *and One Way*; Peruvian writer Ani Palacios McBride (publisher of *Contacto Latino*in Columbus, Ohio and author of *Nos vemos en Purgatorio* (see you in Purgatory), *Plumbago Torres y el sueño americano* (P. T. and the American dream), and *99 amaneceres* (99 sunrises).

The list of Hispanic essays and essay writers is quite long, so I arbitrarily chose to limit the numbers of authors apart from those already mentioned: José Martí and his scholar Roberto Agromonte, Humberto Piñera Llera, José Olivio Jiménez, Enrique Anderson-Imbert , Germán Arciniegas, Amado Alonso, Fernando Alegría, Emir Rodríguez Monegal, Ángel Rama, Jorge Rufinelli, Ariel Dorfman, Julio Ortega who, among others, had temporary residence in the United States,including Octavio Paz, Pedro Henriquez Ureña; also Federico de Onís, Américo Castro, Francisco Ayala, Gonzalo Sobejano and José Ferrater Mora. Their essay topics and analyses of more or less academic character cover fields, figures, creations and events, including historical, literary, philosophical and socio-political ones, relating to all the Hispanic American countries as well as universal culture, mainly Western, in all their eras and traditions.

In this context, I cannot fail to highlight the contributions of some publishers, including the production staff and writers at *Arte Público Press*, who, in addition to some of the above-cited works, have published prizewinning editions in Spanish or in both languages (English-Spanish), such as *Bailando en silencio: escenas de una niñez puertorriqueña*: (Dancing in silence: scenes from a Puerto Rican childhood) by Judith Ortiz Cofer, *La lucha por la justicia* (Thefight for justice) by César Chávez, *Mariposas en la calle Carmen* (Butterflies on Carmen Street)by Mónica Brown, *Tiro en la Catedral* (A gunshot in the cathedral) by Mario Ben Castro, *Mi querido Rafa* (My dear Rafa) by Rolando Hinojosa, *El corredor de Dante* (Dante's corridor) by Eduardo González Viana, *Colored Men* and *Hombres Aquí* (Men here): *Hernández v. Texas and the Emergence of Mexican American Lawyering,* edited by Michael A. Olivas, *Fronterizas: una novela en seis cuentos* (Border ladies: a six-story novel) by Roberta Fernández, *En otra voz: Antología de literatura hispana de los Estados Unidos* (In another voice: an anthology of Hispanic literature of the United States) edited by Nicholas Kanellos, *La flor de oro: un mito taíno de Puerto Rico* (The golden flower: aPuerto Rican *Taino* myth), *Mi sueño de América* (My dream of America) by Yuliana Gallegos, *Salsipuedes* (Get out if you can) by Ramón Betancourt, *Sangre en el desierto: Las muertas de Juárez* (Blood in the desert: the dead women of Juárez) by Alicia Gaspar de Alba. They have also published numerous editions of children's literature, many of which have received awards, among them: *Estrellita se despide de su isla* (Little star says goodbye to her island) by Samuel Caraballo, *Clara y la Curandera* (Clara and the female healer), *Lupita's Papalote* (Lupita's kite) by Lupe Ruiz-Flores, *El chocolate de abuelita* (Grandma's chocolate) by Pat Mora, *Los tamales de Ana,* the English version of which is called *Growing up with tamales*by Gwendolyn Zepeda, *Soy René* (I am René), *El niño* (The boy) by Rene Colato Lainez, *Pateo el balón* (I kick the ball) by Gwendolyn Zepeda, *Juan y el Chupacabras* (Juan and the goatsucker) by Xavier Garza, *La fiesta para papá Luis* (The party for dad Luis) by Diana González Bertrand, *No hay tiempo para monstruos* (There's no time for monsters) by Spelile Rivas, *René tiene dos apellidos* (René has two surnames) by René Colato Lainez, *Girasoles* (Sunflowers) by Gwendolyn Zepeda, *La guerra de las raspas* (The battle of the snow cones) by Lupe Ruiz, *El cochinito fugitivo* (The runaway piggy) by James Luna, *El regalo del leñador* (The woodcutter's gift) by Lupe Ruiz, *De cabeza y al revés* (Upside down and backwards) by Diane Gonzales Bertrand and Karina Hernández.

Another publisher with an important role in publishing Spanish books in the United States, is Vintage Spanish, a division of Random House, founded in 1994, which presents itself as "a hallmark dedicated exclusively to the publishing of selected fiction and nonfiction In Spanish," written by Hispanics of the United States and elsewhere, including the complete poems of Jorge Luis Borges, Federico Garcia Lorca, and major works by other authors such as Gabriel García Márquez, Roberto Bolaño, Isabel Gómez-Bassols, Jorge Amado, Cristina García and other works previously mentioned by Isabel Allende and Junot Díaz, as well as others of current interest such as a work entitled *Mi mundo adorado* (My beloved world) by the first Hispanic member of the U.S. Supreme Court, Sonia Sotomayor.

Also the prestigious publishing house Santillana USA (Now Prisa Publishers) with headquarters in Miami which has released numerous titles, many of them contracted locally, like *Conquistadora*, (Female conqueror) by Esmeralda Santiago—one of the most outstanding innovations in this area is *Sam no es mi tío* (Sam is not my uncle)—an anthology of essays and chronicles of Spanish authors who have lived in the United States including Daniel Alarcón and the aforementioned Edmundo Paz Soldán. Prisa also published *La Enciclopedia del español en los Estados Unidos* (Encyclopedia of Spanish in the United States). All this is taking place because, as Andrea Aguilar pointed out in her article appearing in the newspaper *El País* dated February 14, 2012, *"Estados Unidos lee en español"* (The United States reads in Spanish).

## Drama and theater

In this overview of Hispanic dramatic genre and theater in the United States, detailed studies have been made documenting the presence and activity of Hispanic-Americans in this artistic endeavor, such as those by Beatriz J. Rizk,[152]Nicolás Kanellos,[153] and Matías Montes Huidobro (as documented by University of Texas Press,Austin).I will mention certain other authors by citing plays, events and theaters, without including critical or detailed analyses of texts, montages, activities, and organizations.

---

152 - Beatriz J. Rizk *El teatro de las comunidades latinas en Estados Unidos y su relación con un contexto social determinado (Centro de Investigaciones del Nuevo Teatro)* (Latin community theater in the United States and its relation to a particular social context" [New Theater Research Center], pp. 179-193, which can be seen in its digital version at http:// dspace.uah.es/dspace/bitstream/handle/10017/4460/El%20Teatro%20de%20las%20Comunidades%20Latinas%20en%20States%20Units%20y%20su%20Relation%20Social%20Determined. pdf?Sequence=1.
153 - *A History of Hispanic Theater in the United States: Origins to 1940.*

## Theater in the colonial era and in the later Mexican-American scene

In the Introduction, we already alluded to the origins of Hispanic theater in the earliest dramatic works presented in U.S. territory, according to Jorge Huerta. One of the first was of a religious nature written in 1598 in El Paso, Texas,[154] and there was a second one dated around 1599 in the area of what is now Santa Fe, New Mexico entitled *Moros y Cristianos* (Moors and Christians), written by Marcos Farfán de los Cobos—a captain in one of Oñate's expeditions—in collaboration with Gaspar de Villagrá. Kanellos points out: "This popular form, like others of a religious origin such as the *Pastorelas* that are put on during the Christmas season came into the New World and was strongly implanted in the oral tradition of the people born under the practices of the new Hispanic culture" and, as documented by Parra J. Samora and P. Vandel Simón,[155] even today they are still stared during Christmas celebrations and on other occasions in the U.S. South-west including places in New Mexico such as Alcalde, Jémez Pueblo, Taos Pueblo, and Bernalillo. Author Douglas Kent Hall has written extensively about the *Matachines*[156] tradition and Eva Jane Matson has written about *Los Pastores de Valle Mesilla*,[157] (The pastors Little *Mesa* Valley)—two rep-resentative examples of these traditions which are the forerunners of the so-called itinerant theater of the American Southwest, such as that of the dance company known as *Los Nuevos Maromeros*, (The new Maromer-os). Currently they also show short skits based on matters of present-day relevance, such as the plight of Central American refugees, interspersed with dances, native songs and imagery. These activities have proliferated since the early Twentieth Century in the form of variety shows performed in large tents. The best-known have been described by T. Ybarra-Fraus-to, such as the *Carpa García* (García tent) of San Antonio, which put on shows from 1914 to the late 1940s, the *Carpa Escalona* (Escalona tent), and the famous Tanda Company's Noloesca "*Chata*" (Flat, pug-nosed) whose popularity led to its being introduced and presented on New York stages. T. Ybarra-Frausto mentions the 1920s and 1930s as the Golden Age of Southwestern Spanish-language Theater.[158]

---

154 - Jorge Huerta, Chicano Theater: *Thenies and Fornis*, Ypsilandi, Michigan, Bilingual Press / Editorial Bilingüe, 1982, 192.

155 - *A History of the Mexican American People*, Notre Dame, Univ. of Notre Dame Press, 1977, 2003.

156 - Douglas Kent Hall, "The *Matachines*: Dancers Keep Listening to World Tradition Alive," New Mexico Magazine, December, 1986, 43.

157 - Eva Jane Matson, *Los Pastores del Valle de Mesilla* (the Mesilla valley shepherds): "Packing Them in for 25 Years," New Mexico Magazine, December, 1985.

158 - Thomas Ybarra-Frausto, "I can Still Hear the Applause. *La Farándula Chicana: Carpas y Tandas de Variedad* (Chicana showcase: tents and variety shows) ", *Hispanic Theater in the U. S.,* Ed. Nicols Kanellos, Houston, Public Art Press, 1984.

This large tent entertainment tradition continues in Texas with the San Antonio Actors Company directed by Jorge Piña, founded in 1986, with headquarters at the Guadalupe Arts Center, where they put on the play *Las Tandas de San Cuilmas- Los Carperos* (The San Cuilmas tent people series - 1989), commissioned to playwright José Manuel Galván.

The authors agree, however, that Chicano theater began in 1965 when Luis Valdez founded the *Teatro Campesino* in Delano, in response to the San Joaquín Valley workers' strike in California, inspired and driven by social commitment, the César Chavezmovement and the urge to establish a Chicano-rooted cultural identity by staging protests in the midst of worrisome societal and political situations of the day, with works like *Vietnam Campesino* and *Soldado Raso* (The Private). As Beatriz J. Rizk put it, "...the group's structuring, based on the collective participation of its members, the influence of Latin American popular theater, the so-called *Nuevo Teatro* (New theater), already developing well, is clear. Valdez recognizes the influence of the comedy genre on his own activities with the San Francisco Mime Troupe with whom he worked for a number of years, as well as his other theatrical experiences that marked his entrance onto the scene, such as his involvement in Spain with F. García Lorca and the *Barraca* group. . .

Beginning the 1980's, Valdez experimented with a new drama form known as *corridos** (see definition below), with notable success. In 1987, he adapted four such works (*El Corrido de Rosita Álvarez*, *Delgadina*, *Soldadera* and *El corrido del lavaplatos* – [Female soldier and the Corrido of the dishwasher]) under the title *Corridos: Tales of Passion and Revolution*, produced for the public television network, subsequently obtaining several Emmy nominations for television excellence. *(*Corridos* are theatrical productions based on popular ballads known by this same name, which have accompanied and documented the people of Mexico—including Chicanos—based on Spanish romantic traditions.")[159]

Limited space will allow us to refer only to a small sampling of Chicano theater groups that stage Chicano or Hispanic works such those held in Minnesota, Indiana, (*El Teatro Desengaño del Pueblo*– [The peoples' disillusionment theater]), Illinois, Nebraska and many other States by Hispanic playwrights like Jorge Huerta in Santa Barbara, San Francisco with Rodrigo Duarte Clark author of *Brujerías* (Witchcraft), *Hijos* (Children) and

---

159 - Beatriz J. Rizk, *El teatro de las comunidades latinas en Estados Unidos y su relación con un contexto social determinado* (the theater of Latino communities in the United States and their relationship to a particular social context - New Theater Research Center), pp. 183-184 http://dspace. uah.es/dspace/bitstream/handle/10017/4460/El%20Teatro%20de%20las%20Comunidades%20 Latinas%20en%20Estados%20Unidos%20y%20su%20Relaci%C3%B3n%20Contexto%20So-cial%20Determinado.pdf?sequence=1.

*Once a Family*. In California there is also the so-called National Theater of Aztlán under the direction of Carlos Morton, author of the *Corrido de Pancho Diablo*, played at the *Teatro libre* (Free theater). *El Tolteca, Troka*, the Zapata Theaters, Juan Felipe Herrera's *Teatro ambulante de salud* (Travelling health theater), *El Teatro de la Gente* (Peoples' theater) directed by Andrián Vargas, whose staging of *El Corrido de Juan Endrogado* (The *corrido* of druggie Juan – 1973), had lasting repercussions. The *Los Topes* (Tops, stops) and Urban Theaters were all founded in the 1970's in different California cities. Later, there was the "Culture Clash"group (1984) in San Francisco and Latins Anonymous (1989) in Los Angeles, representing theatrical trends, as in the case of *Chusma* (Riffraff) and the group known as the *Chicano Secret Service*. In Denver, *Su Teatro* (Your theater - 1971) directed by Tony García which premiered its own center in 1989 with the musical work *Intro to Chicano History 101* (1986). The *Libertad* (Liberty) Theater of Arizona (1975) whose presentation of *La vida del cobre* (Life of copper) championed the copper miners' struggle in Texas and Arizona in 1983 including those in Chile. Also in Tucson, the Chicano Theater (1981), now called *Teatro del Sol* (Theater of the sun - 1987) with works dramatizing the discords between Hispanic and Anglo cultures as well as others, based on Chicano mythology and modern Spanish-American picaresque comedy as seen in works such *Anhelos por Oaxaca* (Yearnings for Oaxaca - 1984) and *Amor de hija* (A daughter's love) 1986). In addition to the aforementioned Guadalupe Theater which has been directed by Jorge Piña since 1986 in San Antonio, Texas, there is the *Teatro de los Pueblos* (People's theater) of El Paso, Texas , *El Teatro de los Niños* (Children's theater), directed by Viviana Aparicio Chamberlain, with its well-known production *La Bella y la Migra* (The beauty and ICE). In New Mexico, the National Company of Albuquerque (1977), for example, with its play *Tito* (1987) by Rómolo Arellano that deals with the physical and cultural threat of alcohol to the greater community. There are other groups, writers, important playwrights in this group not mentioned herein, for example, Estella Portillo Trambley who wrote *Sor Juana*, Silvinia Wood, Arturo Martínez and the plays *Cuentos de Barrio*(neighborhood tales - 1980), *Lavida dulce de los compadres Mascazate* (The sweet life of the Mascazate godfathers - 1983).

In conclusion, as Manuel M. Martín Rodríguez points out in his article, *El teatro chicano a través de los siglos: panorama critico* (Chicano theater over the centuries: a critical panorama),[160] the revitalization of Chicano theater today has many manifestations, one of which is a feminist revisionism symbolized by the prolific playwright Cherrie Moraga. Also, jointly authored works produced by, among others, E. A. Mares, Denise Chávez, Josefina López, Rudolfo

---

160 - http://www.raco.cat/index.php/arrabal/article/viewFile/229320/327859.

A. Anaya, Rick Nájera, Judith and Severo Pérez, Edit Villarreal, Guillermo Reyes and Milcha Sánchez-Scott plus the well-known and controversial figure of protagonist Guillermo Gómez-Piña with his original comic performances and obsessions with multicultural, multilingual and border issues.

I finish with the words of Manuel M. Martín Rodríguez in his previously-mentioned article: "Contemporary Chicano theater . . . is the result of a long history of ritualistic, religious and folk representations, as well as regular contribution by native and international playwrights who have kept the flame of Hispanic drama alive in the Southwest and in the great urban centers of the United States. During its long history, Chicano theater has been able to balance and appropriate elements from different cultures as well as different ways of presenting scenography, resulting in a product that at this point is bilingual, multicultural, transnational, border-friendly and also decidedly original. Also it has been able to accommodate the different audiences that support it, from communities that take ownership of the folk and religious presentations to the growing middle class that promotes the development of works of different authors through the most popular or politicized elements, favoring a lower-class aesthetic in their presentations. This historical malleability is undoubtedly the greatest guarantee of a good future for Chicano theater."[161]


## Puerto Rican theater[162]

The first steps: From the Island to the Continent, back and forth. At the end of the 19th Century, and with considerable presence, theatrical groups in Puerto Rico, because of the Island's very history, produced political and critical *sainetes* (comic operas) critical of the Spanish government in the Island's struggle for self-determination and independence. As of July 25, 1898, the invasion of Puerto Rico by U.S. troops and the new reality of the Island's political dependence as a U.S. Commonwealth territory signalized the end of one era of Puerto Rican theater and the beginning of another with its own special opportunities and complications.

With the U.S. government already imposing itself on the Island, this led to a displaying of Puerto Rican culture and artistic expressions by theatrical companies presenting works in English with very little acceptance by the local population, which directed its attention to local and Spanish companies offering dramaturgy in Spanish more in tune with the prevailing situa-

---

161 - http://www.raco.cat/index.php/arrabal/article/viewFile/229320/327859.
162 - Adapted from the article "Puerto Rican Theater" which I wrote for *La Enciclopedia del Español en los Estados Unidos* (the Encyclopedia of Spanish in the United States). New York: Cervantes Institute and Santillana Publishers, 2008, pp. 738-742.

tion. Critic Frank Dauster, among others, affirms that Puerto Rican theater did not have a strong tradition during the late 19th and early 20thcentury and that only from around the year 1938 did Puerto Ricans seriously engage themselves in promoting professional theater on a larger scale with issues related to the new bicultural identity of the Island, its problems and its colonial experience which formed the subject matter of many theatrical expressions.

Hence, well into the 20thcentury, these issues inspired such works as *Tres banderas* (Three flags), by Eugenio Astol (1912); *Don Pepe*, by Jesús M. Amadeo (1913); *El Grito de Lares* (Lares' cry), by Luis Lloréns Torres (1914), and *Por mi tierra y por mi dama* (For my land and my lady), by Matías González García (1929)—themes that reappear years later in *La Resentida* (The resentful lady) by Enrique Laguerre (1944).

In addition, even in the first decades of the 20th Century, despite the Island's depressed economic situation and its difficult social and political reality, movements in Europe with its social revolutions and class struggles were all reflected in Puerto Rican theatrical works with two quite distinct slants; that is, there was 'high society theater'—a nostalgic expression of bygone Spain and the works of well-known Spanish playwrights, in which genre the comedies of José Pérez Lozada predominated; and then there was the 'Workers theater', which sought to inspire workers to defend themselves from being exploited. The most outstanding authors and actors in this trend were Ramón Romero Rosa with *La emancipación del obrero* (The worker's emancipation - 1903), Enrique Plaza and José Limón de Arce's *Redención* (Redemption - 1906), Magdaleno González and Luisa Capetillo, who spent time in New York and Tampa between 1912 and 1913, presenting works such as *En el campo: Amor libre* (In the countryside: free love) and *Matrimonio sin amor* (Marriage without love), *Consecuencias del adulterio* (Adultery's consequences - 1906), and the activities of Franca de Armiño who became especially important in promoting Puerto Rican theater in the continental United States.

In addition to that period's ruinous economic depression, the 1920s and 1930s were characterized by a climate of marked political instability as a result of U.S. government campaigns on the Island to repress growing nationalism that was intent on reaffirming Puerto Rican identity in the face of the sway of U.S. culture, inspired by patriotic campaigns for independence and autonomy. In this context, on the one hand audiences frequented the theater for enjoyment, and, on the other, to show support for the presenting of controversial issues in theatrical performances. The playwrights and actors who best articulated these insistent sentiments in their works were: Nemesio Canales, with *El héroe Galopante* (The galloping hero); Luis Lloréns Torres, with his above-mentioned highly successful work *El Grito de Lares*, Juan Nadal Santa Coloma—a Puerto Rican actor and playwright who was a great promoter of the most recognized Puerto Rican national theater in the first thirty years of the 20th Century, whose efforts were influential also New York, where at the *Variedades* Theater, in 1932, he mounted a Puerto Rican *zarzuela* titled *Días de Reyes* (Kings' days) and other works in 1933 and 1934. The production of *El Grito de Lares* in New York's *Teatro Hispano* had a great impact on and importance for Puerto Rican theater in the United States.

The drama competition at the Puerto Rican *Ateneo* in 1938 was one of the most important activities of the 20th century in terms of its influence on the thematic characteristics and productions of subsequent Puerto Rican theatrical works. With the call for playwrights to submit plays of real significance for Puerto Rican identity, works of national pride touching on matters of current relevance, the response was significant, and some outstanding winners emerged such as Manuel Méndez Ballester, with his work *El clamor de los surcos* (The clamor of the furrows- 1938), Fernando Sierra Berdecía, with his play *Esta Noche juega el jóker* (Tonight the joker plays), and Gonzalo Arocho del Toro, with *El desmonte* (The dismantling)—three works that marked a new era in Puerto Rican theater, with fundamental and still valid themes for Puerto Rican society, such as the usurpation of land, the emigration of locals to New York and the countryside versus the city.

Manuel Méndez Ballester would later write the most important Puerto Rican tragedy to date entitled *Tiempo Muerto* (Dead time - 1940)—one of the key works attempting to express the essence of "Puertoricanism." He founded a group which joined up with important theater companies such as *Tinglado Puertorriqueño* (PR platform). In 1940 the notable playwright Emilio S. Belaval y Marrero Núñez wrote *Areyto*. For him—in the words of Belaval himself—the slogan was to 'create a Puerto Rican theater in which everything is ours'. With enthusiasm and determination to form a national theater, several actors, playwrights and designers left the Island in search of new horizons, knowledge and experiences—a spiritual and psychological action of leaving and returning—so characteristic of contemporary Puerto Rican identity.

Manhattan is another island with novel scenarios. René Marqués and Afro-Puerto Rican Francisco Arrivi moved to the United States. Actor José Luis 'Chavito' Marrero moved to Spain. Acting director Leopoldo Santiago Lavandero came back from the United States. In the mid-1940's he created, the *Teatro Rodante Universitario* (University theater on wheels). Under his tutelage young people received training and later became outstanding theatrical directors, for example, Victoria Espinosa, Nilda González and, later, Myrna Casas, who is arguably the most outstanding Hispanic playwright of the 20th century. Her work and achievements will be detailed below. Her drama training took place in the United States at Vassar College, Boston College and New York University and she lived for an extended period of time in New York City.

In these different settings, the activities of the most outstanding playwrights of contemporary Puerto Rican theater took place. The above-mentioned Francisco Arrivi and René Marqués were immersed in *El Teatro de la Resistencia* (Resistance Theater)—so called for its involvement in the common themes of cultural, social and political resistance of the people of Puerto Rico in the face of continental U.S. influence and the struggle to define and defend a Puerto Rican identity.

Following the establishment of the Institute for Puerto Rican Culture, a Theater Division was formed, headed by Francisco Arrivi. It established the Puerto Rican Theater Festival and an International Theater Festival both of which have had a significant impact and influence in the cultivation and promotion of Puerto Rican dramaturgy both locally and internationally. Among Arrivi's works are *Vejigantes,*("Old giants"—an invented word) *Sirena* (Siren), *Bolero y Plena* (renamed *Cóctel de Don Nadie* (Bolero and full –Mr. Nobody's cocktail), the latter being included in the third volume of *Spanish-American Contemporary selected Theater* written by Orlando Rodriguez Sardiñas and Carlos Miguel Suárez Radillo (1971). One of the best-known and most important pieces by René Marqués, which inaugurated Puerto Rican theater in New York, was *La Carreta* (Wagon), which premiered at Ateneo Hall. The play was enthusiastically received and had a great impact on the development of Puerto Rican theater in the United States and it was also performed at the San Sebastián Church in that same city in 1953 under director Roberto Rodríguez. Of this, Beatriz J. Rizk wrote, "The play was so well received by the public that one of the young actresses, Miriam Colón, together with director Roberto Rodríguez, decided to organize a theatrical company which—despite its short existence of only four years—was able to create its own headquarters under the name *Nuevo Círculo Dramático* (New dramatic circle)."[163] Playwright Manuel Méndez Ballester also lived in New York for a time, producing works of social criticism such as *Arriba las Mujeres* (Hurray for the ladies), *Bienvenido Don Goyito* (Welcome DG) and *Los cocorocos* (The coconuts).

Myrna Casas was among the Puerto Rican playwrights who experimented with the 'theater of the absurd', with her works *Absurdos en soledad* (The

---

163 - Op. Cit. p. 186, quoting Pablo Figueroa, *Teatro* (theater): Hispanic Theater in New York City / 1920-1976. Publishers by Off-Off Broadway Alliance Inc. and *Museo del Barrio* (neighborhood museum), New York, 1977.

solitude of the absurd ones- 1963) and *Tres* (Three - 1974), and Luis Rafael Sánchez, who combines universalist influences with insular experience in works such as *La pasión según Antígona* (Passion according to Antigone -1968), or *Casi el Alma* (The soul, almost) and *Sol 13, interior* (Sun 13, inside). But Myrna Casas also experimented with other forms of expression and dramatic styles throughout her long, multi-faceted and successful career as a playwright, beginning in 1960. She continues into the 21$^{st}$century, as does Luis Rafael Sánchez. These two playwrights exemplify one of the many cases in which Puerto Rican theater on the Island and in the continental United States is as one and the same spirit. Myrna Casas created an innovative series of pieces in which she criticizes current Puerto Rican society, as in her successful play *Este país no existe* (This country does not exist -1993)which she staged during the Fourth Hispanic American Theater Festival in Miami in 1989, receiving high praise from New York critics, as did her work *El Gran Circo Eucraniano* (The great Ukrainian circus). Other works of hers include *Cristal roto en el tiempo* (Glass broken in time -1960), *Eugenia Victoria Herrera* (1964), *La Trampa* (The trap- 1963-1964), *El impromptu de San Juan* (The San Juan impromptu -1966), *Voces* (Voices - 2000), and some still unpublished plays: *No todas tienen* (Not all of them have - 1975, revised in 1994), *Al Garete* (Messed up - 1994), *Flash* (1997) and *Qué sospecha tengo* (What suspicion I have - 2001). In 1985 Luis Rafael Sánchez wrote monologues included in a work entitled *Quíntuples* (Quintuplets), influenced by Brecht and Pirandello which was well received by the public and has been widely disseminated in the United States up to the present.

The *teatro colectivo* (group theater) of the late 1960s, perhaps sparked in part by an attitude of rejection and protest against the Vietnam War, marked the beginning of a theatrical revolution that lasted until the mid-1970s. The so-called *Theater of the 60's* organized on the Island in 1974 presented a play entitled *Puerto Rico Fuá*, written by Argentine-Puerto Rican Carlos Ferrari which played in New York with exceptional montages as with the collective piece entitled *La verdadera historia de Pedro Navajas* (The true history of PN). Also worthy of mentionis a group organized by the Avelo Puerto Rican Youth Defense Committee, founded by actress playwright Piri Fernández de Lewis, who in 1968 wrote and assembled a collection of works entitled *El grito en el tiempo* (The scream inside time) and *Tributo* (Tribute). Subsequently, some playwrights belonging to these groups began to work on their own and their creations were successfully presented, such as works by Jaime Carrero, Samuel Molina, Jacobo Morales, José Luis Ramos Escobar, Edgar Quiles and Rosa Luisa Márquez.[164]

---

164 - This period produced outstanding, actors, writers and set designers who helped make theater groups such as *El Tajo del Alacrán* (the scorpion's gash) and other works such as *Brecht to Brecht* in 1967, *Estamos en algo* (we're into something), then *La nueva vida* (new life) in 1969, and finally

Another of the most original and important Puerto Rican dramatic expressions in the United States in the 1960s and 1970s was the so-called New York Movement whose activities were mostly staged at the Newyorican Poets' Cafe. This New York theatrical group is not just theater but rather an eclectic set of dramaturgical expressions ranging from street theater to monologues or other such productions in some of the aforementioned theaters such as *el Teatro Rodante Puertorriqueño* (The PR traveling theater), which presents Spanish-language productions of classics, such as works by Cervantes and other greats at Joseph Papp's New York Shakespeare Theater Festivals and productions presented at Broadway theaters. As early as the 1960's Jaime Carrero recognized the special identity of Puerto Rican neighborhoods in New York and created and applied the term 'Newyorican' to literary and theatrical expressions that synthesize stylistic and thematic presentations of certain of his works such as *Noo Jall* and *Pipo Subway no sabe reír* (P.S. doesn't know how to laugh). Exceptional among the group of playwrights in the New York Movement are Miguel Algarín and Lucky Cienfuegos, with her *America Congo Mania*; also Tato Laviera and Pedro Pietri, with their previously-noted Spanish-language creations.

Some of these authors wrote their works while in jail, as was the case with Lucky Cienfuegos and Miguel Piñero. All their works reflect the reality of the *'barrio'*, life on the streets and other realities such as crime, drugs, sexual misbehavior and other activities looked upon as 'abnormal'. More recently, exponents of this movement have produced works such as those coming from theatrical workshops, university campuses and student residences. Some are worthy of special mention such as *Bodega* (Cellar) by Federico Fraguada and *Family Scenes* by Ivette M. Ramírez which was translated in Spanish; *Ariano*, by Richard V. Irizarry; *First Class*, by Cándido Tirado and Eduardo Gallardo—works that have been collected in an interesting anthology by John Astush, published in 1991. In addition to presentations at the *Newyorican* Poets' Cafe, the works of these writers have been presented at Aquarius, Latin Insomniacs, The Family, *Teatro Otra*

in 1970 and 1971, they presented short outdoor plays, such as *La tumba del jíbaro* (the Jíbaro's tomb), *La venta del bacalao rebelde* (selling rebellious codfish), *Las huelgas* (strikes), *La despropiación* (expropriation) and *¿Qué importa un muerto más?* (what can one more death matter?) The piece *Gloria, la bolitera* (Gloria the ticket lady) by Lydia Milagros González - 1971), lasted beyond the group. The theatrical group Anamú, which was together for three years, from 1972 to 1975 premiered *Este solar es mío y tú lo sabías* (this piece of land is mine and you knew it - 1972) by Jorge Rodríguez and Emanuel Logroño; *Bahía Sucia-Bahía Negra* (dirty bay-black bay -1972), also written by the above-mentioned. And there were others: *Ya los perros no se amarran con longanizas* (the dogs are no longer on sausage leashes - 1973) by Jorge Rodríguez and José Luis Ramos, and *Pipo Subway no sabe reír* (PS doesn't know how to laugh), by Jaime Carrero. Also of note were to Moriviví Theater, the Guerrilla Theater and the *Colectivo Nacional* (National Collective); as well as the aforementioned Theater of 60's.

*Cosa* (something else theater) and at the Puerto Rican Bilingual Workshop founded in 1973 by Carla Pinza who in 1975, working with Woody King Jr., produced *Mondongo* (Tripe)—a 'musical *salsa*' written by Ramón Ramírez, which also premiered on Broadway in 1979.

In the final decades of the 20th Century and early in the 21st, despite the crisis surrounding theatrical productions in the 80's and 90's both on the Island and on the continent, Puerto Rican dramaturgy gained strength and expanded, in spite of interruptions but there were no creations of significant literary importance.

*El Teatro Repertorio Español* (Spanish repertoire theater)—one of the most active Hispanic theatrical groups in New York City—staged *El Huésped* (Guest) in 1990 at the Gramercy Arts Theater in Rhode Island, which has also served as a venue for Pedro Juan Soto's Puerto Rican Theater. *El Huésped* (The guest) is a play about tragedies suffered by a New York Puerto Rican family. They also staged *Los Jíbaros progresistas* (Progressive *Jíbaros*)—a kind of musical presentationabout the old rural Puerto Rico some 130 years in the past by the local composer Manuel González with a libretto based on a work by playwright Ramón Méndez Quiñones.

In New York, in the year 2000 the Hispanic theatrical group *Pregones* (Announcements)—undoubtedly one of the most prominent in the United States—continued to present Puerto Rican theatrical pieces with such works as *En Tres Actos* (In 3 acts) by Janis Astor del Valle and Tere Martínez; *Los ángeles se han fatigado* (The angels are overcome with fatigue) by Luis Rafael Sánchez; In 2001, *The Ballad of Maria Sabida*, based on a short story by Judith Ortiz Cofer, (2001); and *Gení y el Zepelín*(G and the zeppelin)—a piece by José Luis Ramos Escobar. In 2005, *Pregones* opened the doors of their new venue by staging *La Rosa Roja* (Red rose), a piece written and directed by Rosalba Rolón, with Jesús Colónas the main protagonist in this work symbolizing the Puerto Rican migratory experience. Jesús Colón (1901-1974) had come to New York in 1917where he participated in and created civic, cultural and political groups that helped the development of the local Puerto Rican community, working in parallel in different kinds of literary creations. In 1959, he faced down the U.S. Congress's Anti-American Activities Committee. This was followed by the presentation of *El bolero fue mi ruina* (the bolero was my ruin), based on a story written in 1997by Manuel Ramos Otero, and the premiering of the musical *Betsy*. In the 2006-2007 season,*El último rosario de Medea* (Medea's last rosary) was presented—a work created by award-winning Puerto Rican poet and playwright José Manuel Torres Santiago, with actress Lupita Ferrer in the role of Medea. The theatrical group *Pregones*, founded in

1979 by three Puerto Rican actors, under director Rosalba Rolón, began performing a compilation of scenes from Puerto Rican theatrical productions in addition to the ones mentioned previously, namely: *Joel Rose, A Battle Report Direct from the Lower Depths, Bienvenido* (Welcome) *don Goyito*by Manuel Méndez Ballester; *La carreta* (The wagon) and *Carnaval afuera Carnaval adentro* (Carnival outside, carnival inside) by René Marques, directed by the acclaimed director/writer, Víctor Fragoso. They also experimented with collective works and Latin American dramaturgy centered on specific struggles, such as the play *Voces de acero* (Voices of steel -1989), highly acclaimed by critics, about the mistreatment of Puerto Rican political prisoners in U.S. prisons.

Also, in recent years, the *Teatro del 60* (60's theater) enriched its trajectory of the presentation of Puerto Rican works in New York with the play *Quíntuples* (Quintuplets), by Luis Rafael Sánchez in 2001-2003, and the play *Recital*at the *Newyorican* Poets' Café in September of 2004, as well as *Tiempo muerto* (Dead time)by Manuel Méndez Ballester, also in 2004. Here, as in other theatrical spaces, U.S.-born Puerto Rican playwrights, along with others who travel between Borinquen (i.e. Puerto Rico) and Manhattan, have very often followed a scenography that include newer and older generations with such names as Rosalba Rolón, Pedro Pietri, Alfredo Mantilla, Myrna Casas, Orlando Rodríguez, Pedro Juan Soto, Miguel Piñero, Eduardo Iván López, Ruben González, Eva Cristina Casas, Carlos Vega Abreu, Janis Astor del Valle, Tere Martínez, José Luis Ramos Escobar, Cándido Tirado, Migdalia Cruz, Carmen Rivera, Nancy Nevárez and other previousl mentioned authors.

The new generations of playwrights which include many groups, producers, actors and directors still at work, persist in their search for new forms and novel content. In the long run, the competition among theatrical forms will diminish, although imagination will never be exhausted, and content, insights and questionings will be accentuated—all of which will motivate the public to want to see these dramatic productions—one of the most ardent expressions of the rich, complex and changing Puerto Rican identity. And this on-going history has just begun to be written.


### Cuban Theater

We will now refer to some essays written by Matías Montes Huidobro, an expert on the subject, especially from his extensive chapter on Cuban theater appearing in the *Enciclopedia del Español en los Estados Unidos* (the previously referenced *Encyclopedia of Spanish in the United States*, pp. 743-768). Huidobro, being aware of the difficulty of dealing with the dramatic genre in its textual complexity, publication and montage, noted that the early instances of Cuban dramaturgy in the United States were in what was called *Teatro Bufo* (Snort theater), presented in Miami, although its history dates back to the 19th century, at the time of the independence movement in performances at the *Mambí* Theater in Tampa, Florida, at venues New York and other places with some contributions by José Marti himself. These beginnings include the play *Dos cuadros de la insurrección cubana* (2 paintings of the Cuban insurrection - 1869) by Francisco Víctor y Valdez.

In a cursory documentation of truly generational Cuban productions stemming from the immigration flow following the 1959 Revolution and up to the Mariel Exodus of the 1980's, for reasons of space and now skipping over to Los Angeles, we shall concentrate on the main centers of activity, beginning with New York in the 1960's where, according to Beatriz J. Rizk, "any historical review of Cuban immigrant theatrical creativity must start with María Irene Fornés' arrival in the United States in 1945. This playwright occupies a significant place in New York's off-Broadway scene, where she received Obie Awards—seven in total. It was the highest award bestowed by *The Village Voice* periodical for off-Broadway creations for her works such as *Promenade* (1965), *The Successful Life of Three* (1977), *Feju and her Friends* (1979), and other productions, to the most recent in 1988 for *Abingdon Square*."[165] With support from local institutions like INTAR (international arts relations) and others, the works of Cuban exiles and resident authors such as those by José Cid: *El primer cliente* (The first client - 1965), *Su última conquista* (His/herfinal conquest - 1968), *La rebelión de los títeres* (The puppets' rebellion - 1977), *La comedia de los muertos* (Comedy of the dead); Eduardo Machado's *Las damas modernas de Guanabacoa* (The modern ladies of G. - 1986), *Revoltillo* (Little uprising - 1988); Gloria González's, *Café con leche* (Coffee with milk - 1985); *Padre Gómez y Santa Cecilia* (Father G. and Saint C. -1988), Dolores Prida's *Botánica* (Botanist- 1991), put on by the Spanish Repertoire Theater and Manuel Martín Jr. with *Swallows* (1980) and *Union City Thanksgiving* (1983); Ana María Simóu's *Exiles* (1982) and *Alma* (Soul - 1988); Dolores Prida's, *Savings* (1988) and Luis Santeiro's, *Our Lady of the Tortilla* (1987) and *The Ladies from Havana* (1990). Of course we must not overlook the outstanding works of the Mariel exile playwright Reinaldo Arenas, with his

165 - In "The Latin Theater of the United States," *Tramoya* 22 (1990), p. 18: which can also be accessed in its digital version: http://cdigital.uv.mx/bitstream/123456789/3826/2/199022P5.pdf, as well as the article that we have referred to throughout this section, "The Theater of Latino Communities in the United States and its relationship to a particular social context" (New Theater Research Center), pp. 179-193, which can be obtained in digital version at http://dspace.uah.es/dspace/bitstream/handle/10017/4460/El%20Teatro%20de%20las%20Comunidades%20Latinas%20en%20Estados%20Unidos%20y%20su%20Relaci%C3%B3n%20Contexto%20Social%20Determinado.pdf?sequence=1p. 190.

work *Persecución* (Persecution) writtenin New York in 1985 and presented in 1986, consisting of five experimental theatrical pieces entitled *El traidor* (Traitor), *El paraíso* (Paradise), *Ella y yo* (She and I), *El reprimero* (The oppressor) and *El poeta* (The poet).

The *Teatro Dúo* (Duo Theater), founded by Magaly Alabau and Manuel Martín, is another New York institution that promotes works by playwrights from the Hispanic community such as those by the aforementioned Dolores Prida who, influenced by Anglo theatrical productions, wrote musicals such as *Beautiful Señoritas* (1977),*The Beggars Soap Opera* (1979), which Beatriz J. Rizt points out "were based on *The Three Penny Opera*, by B. Brechtand Crisp (1981), which in turn was based on *Los intereses creados* (Vested interests) by Benavente."[166] One of her best remembered creations was *La era latina* (Latin era) co-written with Víctor Fragoso and presented in New York City parks and squares in the summer of 1980 as part of *Teatro Rodante*'s programs. Other authors worthy of mention in this field are José Fernández, with *El bravo y Fame* (The rough guy and Fame - 1988) and in the non-musical genre *El súper*(the super guy) by Ivan Acosta, which premiered at the Cuban Cultural Center in New York in 1977. This work—like most other Cuban productions—addresses issues of identity, culture shock, generational conflict, the going back and forth, the to and from here to there. With a long "etcetera" we conclude this segment on the Cuban theatrical presence in metropolitan New York by including the names of four additional well-known Cuban playwrights, namely, Manuel Pereiras, Randy Barceló, Renaldo Ferradas and Pedro Monge.

The history of Cuban theater in Florida—particularly in Miami—is lengthy and impossible to include adequately in this summary. One who was a nexus between New York and Florida was José Yglesias, a journalist, writer and sometime sailor, born in Ybor City near Tampa. He composed his nationally recognized works in English while living in New York. Early Cuban theater in Miami, most probably appeared with the premiere of the now little-remembered work entitled *Hamburguesas y sirenazos* (Hamburgers and blaring sirens) by Pedro Román, which at one time was performed internationally. The *Teatro Avante* in its forty-year history had a presence and leadership enabling it to organize thirty international drama festivals under the direction of Mario Ernesto Sánchez, presenting works like *Alguna cosita que alivie el sufrir* (Some little thing to relieve the suffering) by René Aloma which, although originally written in English, went beyond local audiences with presentations in Spanish in New York and elsewhere. There was also the *Teatro Prometeo* (Prometheus Theater) founded in 1972.

---

166 - Beatriz J. Rizt, Op. Cit., p. 190.

But looking back at the previous decade, worthy of mention are the names of Leopoldo Hernández, Matías Montes Huidobro (who resided in Miami but also Hawaii) and Raúl de Cárdenas (who at one point resided in California). Specifically, I refer to a 1969 premiere of the realistic piece by Hernández entitled *940 SW Segunda Calle* (940 SW 2nd St.) and *Guáimaro, Lección de Historia* (G, history lesson) and *Liberación* (Liberation). Playwright and renowned drama student, Matías Montes Huidobro in his essay entitled *El teatro cubano* (Cuban theater), which we will summarize in this brief review, stated: "In the early 1960s, black face and Galician humorous presentations continued on Miami stages with Federico Pineiro, Alberto Garrido, Leopoldo Fernández and Rosendo Rosell, among the most popular actors in Miami and in nearby Hialeah, where Néstor Cabell acted in the 1964 blackface production entitled *Bijirita*. Other artists acted in folk theater with popular blackface and Galician characters. On Miami's *Calle 8* (8th Street), Chela Castro successfully starred in *La Nalgada*. Less successful was Miguel Ponce with his *Teatro 66* and *Teatro 67*."[167]

The above-mentioned Leopoldo Hernández wrote *Hollywood 70, Hollywood 73* and other works such as *No negocie, Sr. Presidente* (Do not negotiate, Mr. President - 1976), and the monologues *Nadie* (Nobody) and *Tipit* (1973), and was a finalist for the 1988 Gala Prize. He also wrote *Retorno* (Return - 1978), *Cheo* (1975) and *Los pobres ricos* (The poor rich - 1979)—his most important work—as well as *Siempre tuvimos miedo* (We were always afraid -1981). Matías Huidobro pointed out that theatrical activity in the 1970's increased "with the founding of numerous theatrical groups with productions ranging from popular subject matter to more ambitious projects, such as *Las Máscaras* (Masks) by Salvador Ugarte and Alfonso Cremata (1970); In 1971, *Teatro Marti* by Leopoldo Fernandez; in 1972, *Los comediantes* (Comedians) performed by Mario MartinOsvaldo Calvo, Norma Zúñiga and Aleida Leal; in 1973, *La Comedia1* (Comedy 1) by Ernesto Capote); From 1973 to 1975: *Teatro Carrusel* (Carousel theater by)Enrique Beltran; in 1976: *Repertorio Español* (Spanish repertoire) by Mario Arellano); in 1977: *Teatro Experimental* (experimental theater); the Dance Studio by Armando Navarro; 1978, *Teatro Blanquita Amaro*; 1979, *Teatro La Comedia 2* (Comedy theater 2) with Ernesto Capote, *Teatro Versailles* with Fermín Borges;*Café Teatro Cabell* with Nestor Cabell and *Teatro Avante* with Mario Ernesto Sánchez and Alina Interian."

As an example of something that has frequently happened with Cuban playwrights in their going back and forth to and from that geographic, political and thematic Island, I want to emphasize the name of Victor Varela, who in 1988 created experimental theater in Cuba with his production of

---

167 - In the Encyclopedia of Spanish of the United States, p. 805-806.

*La cuarta pared* (The 4th wall) and later attempted something similar in Miami at the *Teatro Obstáculo* (Obstacle theater), with the staging of his *Melodrama cuarta pared II* (Melodrama 4thwall No. 2 - 1998), *Aplaude con una mano* (Applaud with just one hand - 2001) and *Nonato en Útero* (Unborn in the womb - 2003).

There were other important productions, that were the subject of a scholarly analysis by Matias Huidobro including *Una caja de zapatos vacía* (An empty shoe box) presented at the *Avante* Theater, *Dos viejos pánicos* (2 panicky old men) presented by the Acme Acting Company, and *Falsa alarma* (False alarm) staged at the *Prometeo* Theater—works by the acclaimed resident Cuban playwright Virgilio Pinera; *El Chino* (The Chinaman) by Carlos Felipe was also staged at the *Prometeo* playhouse as well as several presentations of *La noche de los asesinos* (Night of the assassins) performed at the *Avante* and *Garabato* (scribble) theaters. According to Matias Huidobroin his referenced articles[168] the works by Cuban playwrights residing in the U.S. written in Spanish and staged mainly in Miami, were as follows: *La navaja de Olofé* (Olofé's razor) by Matías Montes Huidobro presented at the *Teatro Nuevo* (New theater); *Juego de damas* (Checkers) by Julio Matas at the *Teatro Nuevo*: *Los tres cerditos y el lobo carnicero* (The three little pigs and the butcher wolf) by René Ariza staged at the *Avante* theater; *Invierno en Hollywood* (Winter in Hollywood) by Jesús Hernández Cuéllarat the State of the Arts Theater; *Café con leche* (Coffee with milk) by Gloria González at the *Repertorio Español* (Spanish repertoire) theater; *El extravío* (The misplacement) by Julio Matas at the *Avante*; *Patio Interior* (Interior courtyard) by José Ignacio Cabrera at the *Taller del Garabato* (Scribble workshop); *Ojos para no ver* (Eyes not for seeing) by Matias Montes Huidobro at the *Prometeo*; *La época del mamey* (The time of the lazy guy) by Andrés Nóbegras at the *Avante*; *Matacumbe* by Mario Ernesto Sánchez at the *Avante*; *La Peregrina* (The female pilgrim) by Héctor Santiago; *Lola*at the *Avante* by Rafael Blanco; *Oscuro total* (Total darkness), by Matias Montes Huidobro at the *Trigolabrado* and *Pro Teatro Cubano*; *El hombre inmaculado* (The immaculate man) by Ramón Ferreira at the *Avante* and *La mujer de Antonio* (Antonio's woman) by Frank Quintana at the *Maderamen*; *La pequeña intrusa* (The little lady intruder) by José Vicente Quiroga at the *Chicos* theater; *Esto no tiene nombre* (This has no name) and *Los quince de Yaniré* (Yaniré's 15th birthday) by Julio O'Farril at the International Art Center and *La sorda* (The deaf lady) by Andrés Nóbregas, at the same venue; *A quien pueda interesar* (To whom it may concern) by Miriam Acevedo (played at the *Avante* and presented by the Italian Committee for Cuban Human Rights); finally *Desde la orilla* (From the shore), staged by Grisel Pujala Soto, Lilliam Vega and Sandra García.

---

168 - Noted in the Encyclopedia of Spanish of the United States, pp. 743-768 and pp. 805-815.

In addition to the above-mentioned Miami Cuban playwrights included in Matías Montes Huidobro's list, we must add: Marcos Miranda, Raúl García Huertas, Maricel Mayor Marsán, Jorge Trigoura, Rolando Moreno, Antonio Orlando Rodríguez, Victor Varela, Carmen Duarte, Ernesto García, Eddy Díaz Souza, Armando Roblán, Néstor Cabell, Alfonso Cremata, Roberto Antinoo, Orlando Rossardi, Tomás Fernández Travieso, José Enrique Puente, Pedro Román, Cristina Rebull, Jorge Valls, Guillermo Hernández, Nena Acevedo, Uva de Aragón, Mary Calleiro, Julie de Grandy, Concepción T. Alzola, Ivonne López Arenal, Miguel González Pando, Evelio Taillacq, Rafael Blanco, Orlando González Esteva, José Ignacio Cabrera, Mario Ernesto Sánchez, Fernando Villaverde, José Carril, Rafael Blanco, Frank Quintana, José Vicente Quiroga, Julio O'Farril, Teresa María Rojas, Felix Lizárraga, Federico Piñeiro, Alberto Garrido, Alfonso Cremata, Salvador Ugarte, María Julia Casanova, Vivian Ruiz, Luis G. Basurto, Ángel Nodal, Blanca Pereda, Ivonne Martín, Marily A. Reyes, José Sánchez Boudy, Jorge Valls, with the following opportune observation: "'and many more.' This phrase that protects me from any involuntary omissions"[169] and excuses me from writing about their creations in more detail regarding plot, audience reaction, montage, text and author analyses, as well as other historical and anecdotal information.

## Theater of Spain, Central and South America andHispanic Theatrical festivals in the United States

Continental Spanish theatrical works starts in United States territory, since the previously mentioned staging of *Moros y Cristianos* (Moors and Christians), by Marcos Farfán de los Godos—a captain the historic Oñate expedition. It is fitting to begin this section with Beatriz J. Rizk's general observation that "the first wave of emigration included the upper and middle bourgeoisie, from among whom arise several of the promoters of culture who still today are at the head of institutions such as Max Ferrá, director of INTAR (International Arts Relations), and Rene Buch, director of the Spanish Repertoire Theater. Both organizations have been active in New York City since the late 1960's and for many years they were involved in preserving and promoting Hispanic heritage with Spanish and Latin American classics. The Spanish Repertoire Theater, for example, continues to actively promote the *zarzuela* genre with one or two presentations a year, which the Thalia Spanish Theater has also promoted during the last decade in Queens, New York, under the direction of Silvia Brito. INTAR has also been active in experimentation by presenting new montages of classi-

---

169 - Matias Montes Huidobro *La Dramaturgia Cubana de Miami* (Cuban Dramaturgy in Miami), lecture given on November 3, 2010 during TEMFest activities that can be read at: http://www.ellugareno.com/2010/11/la-drama-turgia-cubana-de-miami-por.html.

cal works such as the adaptation of *La vida es un sueño* (Life is a dream), by Calderón, starring Maria Irene Fornés, (1981)."[170]

In studies by Gerardo Piña-Rosales[171]on which we base this summary, he stated that "At the beginning of the 20th Century Spanish dramas were popular in the United States. The works of Jacinto Benavente, Martínez Sierra, the Alvarez Quintero brothers (Serafín, 1871-1938, and Joaquín, 1873-1944) and later on, Federico García Lorca (1898-1936), achieved considerable success on North American stages. In 1920, the Theater Guild staged *La malquerida* (The bad luck lady) by Benavente (translated by John Garrett Underhill), and had significant box office success. The play *Canción de cuna* (Cradle song) by Martínez Sierra was also quite successful, presented for the first time in Times Square Theater in 1921. Another work by Martínez Sierra, *El reino de Dios* (Kingdom of God), first played at the Ethel Barrymore Theater. In New York's1929-1930 seasons, no fewer than three comedies by the Álvarez Quintero brothers were staged. Another work often performed at the time was *El gran Galeoto* (The great Galeot) by Echegaray. Garcia Lorca's works were presented frequently and with great success: *El amor de don Perlimplín con Belisa en su jardín* (The love of don P. with B.in her garden), *Bodas de sangre* (Blood weddings), *Yerma*, *La casa de Bernarda Alba* (Bernarda Alba's house), and *Doña Rosita la soltera y la zapatera prodigiosa* (Maiden doña Rosita and the prodigious female shoemaker)."[172]

As previously mentioned, the leading venue in this New York activity was the Spanish Repertoire Theater founded in 1968 which now operates together with the Gramercy ArtsTheater. In Queens, Silvia Brito founded the Thalia Spanish Theater in 1977 which has put on hundreds of plays and *zarzuelas*, starring famous actors such as Antonio Gala, Jaime Salom and Jerónimo López Mozo. According to Gerardo Piña Rosales "one of the most interesting Thalia productions was the bilingual production of Picasso's *Guernica* in 2000, by Spanish director Gil Orrios." The works of Spanish playwrights have also been presented at the *Duo* Theater in Manhattan along with more recent works by Hispanic playwrights living in the United States. Also, there is the *Amistad* (Friendship) World Theater founded on 1981, the *Circulo* (Circle) Theater Company (1994), the Proshansky Auditorium at the Graduate Center of the City University of New York which has presented three short plays by Miguel de Cervantes—*El juez de los divorcios* (The divorce judge), *El viejo celoso* (The jealous old man) and *Los*

---

170 - From his earlier article, "The theater of Latin communities in the United States and their relationship to a particular social context" (New Theater Research Center), pp. 189-190.

171 - In his article "Spanish Theater", in the Encyclopedia of Spanish in the United States, pp. 818-821.

172 - In his article "Spanish Theater", in the Encyclopedia of Spanish in the United States, pp. 818.

*habladores* (The gossipers)—groups which in 1995 successfully took part in and received acclaim at the 20th Golden Age Festival in El Paso, and in 1996 inaugurated the 21stFestival of the Golden Age with its presentation of *La dama duende* (The lady gnome). In the autumn of that same year *La celosa de sí misma* (Jealous of herself) a play by Tirso de Molina premiered in New York. Like other theatrical companies in the United States, they also put on works by other contemporary Spanish and Spanish-American playwrights such as *Zanahorias* (Carrots) by Antonio Zancadaat the Duke Theater on Broadway in 2001; *Divinas Palabras* (Divine words) by Ramón del Valle Inclán at the *Centro Dramático Nacional* (National Drama Center) in 2007 under the Lincoln Center's Rose Theater.

As in New York (and what we have already covered in Florida, the Southwest and California) other cities in the United States have vibrant Hispanic theatrical activity. I confirm this assertion by referring to such activities in the U.S. Capital Washington D. C. where there are two very active theaters which I have attended regularly for nearly four decades: the Gala Theater (Latin American Artists Group), founded in 1976 by Hugo Medrano and Rebecca Read, with roots in the *Teatro Doble* (Double theater) and the *Teatro de la Luna* (Theater of the moon) founded in 1991 and since then under the direction of Mario Marcel. Since 1984, the Gala Theater preeminently and frequently has been offering presentations of Spanish classics with such works as *La casa de Bernarda Alba* (Bernarda Alba's house) by Federico García Lorca; in 1985 with *El caballero de Olmedo* (The gentleman from Olmedo) by Spain's Lope de Vega during its season of traditional classics and repeated in 2010; then in in 2008, *Bodas de sangre* (Blood weddings) and in 2010 *El retablillo de Don Cristóbal* (Don Cristóbal's altarpiece)—both by Federico García Lorca, to mention just a few. The *Teatro de la Luna* (Theater of the moon) offered *El Público* (The public) also by Lorca, among the many plays I remember enjoying—all these in addition to works by renowned Spanish playwrights and others from Hispanic American countries. Among the contributors to the Hispanic Theater Festivals from Spain sponsored by the Theater of the Moon we cite some samples: In 1993: *Noche de primavera sin sueño* (A sleepless spring night) by Jardiel Poncela; *Los sirvientes* (The servants), by Alfonso Paso (1994); *La barraca de Federico* (Federico'shut) by Cervantes, works by Casona and Lorca respectively (1998); *Trafalgar* by Agustin Iglesias (1999); *Entremeses del Siglo de Oro* (Golden century side dishes - 2000); and *El paso del cometa* (The passing comet); *Chiquilladas* (Little girls), by Raymon Cousse (2001); *El hombre gato-gallo* (The cat-rooster man) by Darío Cardona (2003); in 2005, *Ñaque o de piojos y actores* (Odds and ends or of lice and actors) by José Sanchis Sinisterra (2005); in 2007, *Que nos quiten lo bailao* (Let them stop our dance) by Laila Ripio (2007).

In both these theaters the works by Hispanic-American authors are too numerous to include. For example, on the many occasions that I have personally enjoyed: *La nona y El saludador* (The *nona* and The greeter) by Roberto Cossa; *Lejos de aquí* (Far from here) also by Roberto Cossa and Mauricio Hartun, *Quererte como te quiero* (To love you as I do—a collage of works by García Lorca by Mario Marcel; *La caja de sorpresas* (Box of surprises) by Juan Enrique Acuña. The reader can find the details of their montage, authorship, names of directors, casting, and the names of production personnel in the histories contained in their web pages.[173]

To give another example, in Miami the renowned playwright Fernando Arrabal, with the theatrical group *Prometeo* presented *Picnic en el campo de batalla* (picnic on the battlefield). At Miami-Dade College in 2007, students from the Actor's Arena workshop performed *Los dos verdugos* (The two hangmen), *Oración* (prayer) and *Picnic*. Earlier and later many of their works were presented, among them, *El Jardín de las delicias* (The garden of delights), *El arquitecto y el emperador de Asiria* (The architect and emperor of Assyria) and *Los verdugos* (The hangmen). At International Hispanic Theater Festivals they have also staged classical works sponsored by the *Avante* Theater such as *Yerma* by Federico García Lorca and others at the Miracle Theater in Coral Gables, the *Abanico* (Hand-held fan) Theater in Miami and at other theaters throughout the southeastern United States.

In this context, by way of illustration, we have the following information from Gerardo Piña-Rosales "the Association for Hispanic Classical Theater of Arizona has had the following website since March 2002: (http:// www. trinity. edu/ora/comedia/textlist. html/), where the reader can consult theatrical texts prepared by specialists at *Siglo de Oro español* (Spanish golden age)."[174]

We conclude this segment by adding the names of Theatrical Festivals and Theaters with Spanish-language montages, as an example of this dynamic Hispanic dramaturgical presence in the U.S. For detailed information about the participants in some of these Festivals you may consult, among others, an extensive article entitled *Los Festivales de Teatro* (Theatrical festivals) written by Esther Sánchez Gray in the *Encyclopedia of Spanish of the United States*.[175] The previously-mentioned Chicano Theater, organizes a series of festivals in California,New York, Colorado and Seattle with over a dozen performances, occasionally including the Puerto Rican New York*Teatro Cuatro*, as was the case in Season 6, and the following

173 - For the Gala Theater: http://www.galatheatre.org/system/file.php?id=1029 and, for the Theater of the Moon: http://www. teatrodelaluna.org/homes/obras.htm.
174 - In his article "Spanish Theater", in the Encyclopedia of Spanish in the United States, p. 821
175 - Pp. 822-845.

they year participated in the First Festival of Popular Latin American Theater along with 40 other theatrical groups. As early as 1972 a festival was held at the San Clemente Church in New York in which works by Argentine, Peruvian, Chilean and Colombian playwrights were presented,

Of special significance in this chronicle are the International Hispanic Theater Festivals that have been held annually in Miami since 1986 at different venues as well as another places of Florida with excellent presentations of works by theater companies from around the Hispanic world, including the 30th Festival held from July 7 to 24 in 2016, sponsored by the *Avante* Theater, and also now by the Adrienne Arsht Center, the Prometheus Theater and Miami-Dade County. In the metropolitan Washington D. C. area the Gala Theater has established the National Center for Latino Performing Arts in addition to the already referenced seasonal theatrical events, annual Flamenco Festivals and tributes to poets such as Pablo Neruda. There are popular performances, courses of instruction in dramatic arts given by and for actors, directors and scenographers including by the community Theater of the Moon which also offers workshops and classes at various levels at local schools—activities that most of the aforementioned Hispanic theaters promote as part of their activities.

The *Teatro de la Luna* has so far held 17 International Hispanic Theater Festivalsas well as 22 poetry marathons plus numerous other activities during its 24-year history. To illustrate its variety and scope, in the first Festival that took place in 1998, it presented *El Amateur* by Argentina's Mauricio Dayub, *Don Quijote y Sancho Panza* by Miguel de Cervantes Saavedra (staged at the Dominican Republic's Gayumba Theater), *Más se Perdió en Cuba* (More was lost in Cuba) by Agustín Iglesias (presented at Spain's Guiriguay Theater), *Calisto* by Julio Salvatierra Cuenca (presented at Portugal's *Meridional* Theater), *Quimera*(impossible dream) by Roberto Ramos Perea (by Puerto Rico's *El Cemi* Company), *Las cosas del cantar* (The things about song) by Dahd Sfeir of Uruguay; *Monte Calvo* (Bald mountain) by Jairo Aníbal Niño (at the U.S. *La Tea*theater), *Comegato* (Cat eater) by Gustavo Ott of Venezuela; *Las Fórmulas del Abuelo* (Grandfather's formulas) by Daniel Dimauro and Raul G. Aguirre (at Venezuela's *La Pareja* [The couple] Puppet Theater,). In the 17th annual Festival which took place in 2014, the following works were presented: *Gracias Por Todo* (Thanks for everything) by Julio César Castro of Uruguay; *Loca la Juana* (Crazy Juana) by Juana Estrella of Ecuador; *Pasos al Azar* (Random steps) byÁngeles Páez of Spain, *Mea Culpa* (My fault) by Felipe Acosta (presented by the Honduran BAMBU Theatrical Group), *Vegetal* (Vegetable) by Claudio Pazos of Argentina; *The Tsunami* by Manuel García Cartagena (staged by the Guloya Theater, Dominican Republic). In the Children's Theater at the same Festival, the U.S. *Theater of the*

*Moon* group staged *Siempre Amigos, Sanos y Contentos* (Forever friends, healthy and happy) by Neher Jacqueline Briceño as well as *Platero y Yo* (Platero and me)—a theatrical adaptation by Claudio Rivera of a book by Juan Ramón Jiménez Guloya of the Dominican Republic.

And so in large brush strokes we have painted this panorama of the literary and theatrical Hispanic-American presence in the United States with some specific examples to portray what is happening here and now in the places mentioned and also at the same intense level throughout the United States with passion and respect for dialogue, with different and shared identities in the face of common problems and their potential cultural, political and social solutions represented in these presentations and activities.

## Flagship Institutions and Activities

Before concluding this book, we wish to mention a number of organizations, and I would like to start with one of the pioneering institutions in the area of documenting and promoting Hispanic literature, history and culture (including poetry in Spanish) in the United States. I am referring to the Hispanic Division of the Library of Congress under the leadership of Dr. Georgette Dorn, who in her literary archives has not only included more than six hundred Spanish-speaking poets, both those residing in the United States as well as those from other countries,including Spain and the Americas (and laureates such as Pablo Neruda, Octavio Paz, the author of this book, and many more), but also sponsors an active program of presentations, panels and poetry recitals in Spanish as well publishing the *Latin American Handbook* which contains critical collaborations on the literature, sociology, and humanities in the countries of Latin America.

Another preeminent coalescing entity of cultural and literary activity in Spanish has been the North American Academy of the Spanish Language one of whose founders and directors was the poet, critic and eminent Spanish linguist Dr. Odón Betanzos Palacios. Together with other great poets and academicians such as Cuban Eugenio Florit, also embracing the prestigious poets of "Generation 27" and the present generation, now operated under the leadership of author, essayist, linguist, novelist and poet of photography, Dr. Gerardo Piña-Rosales. The Academy, based in New York and with regional delegations, inspires and congregates its member devotees, issues publications and provides leadership, not only through the attentive cultivation of the Spanish language but also its literary and poetic expression. The Academy's most important contribution to date has been the *Encyclopedia of Spanish in the United States*—a pioneering document published by Santillana; a Cervantes Institute yearbook (in 2008) and the Academy's Journal

216

RANLE which also includes poetry in its pages. In this context we should mention ALDEEU (Association of graduates, doctors and other Spanish-speaking professionals in the United States) under Gerardo Piña Rosales, Nicolás Toscano, Rafael Corbalán and other Hispanists and authors who collaborate with their contributions, such as poets Mordechai Rubín of Columbia University and Fernando Opere of the University of Virginia. This association published *Hispanic Poetry in the United States* (2011), edited by Ana Valverde Osán. The *Ranle* magazine published by the North American Academy of the Spanish Language which contains important literary creations, reviews and interviews with current well-known Hispanic authors, under the editorial direction of Dr. Carlos Paldao. We also include the American Association of Teachers of Spanish and Portuguese (AATSP) and its magazine *Hispania y Albricias!* (Good news) published by the Honorary Hispanic Society, with essays in Spanish about poets and poetry, as well as pedagogical linguistic articles on the Spanish language.

Many universities have Hispanic programs and organizations of Spanish-language writers based on and inspired by outstanding contributors and academics specializing literature in Spanish. (As examples of this we mention the University of Maryland with professor Juan Ramón Jiménez and, more recently, José Emilio Pacheco; Harvard, Princeton and Yale, with numerous representations of poets referred to herein; Columbia University, Boston College, the University of Virginia, Georgetown, Duke University, the Universities of California, Florida, New York, Houston, Iowa, the University of Pittsburg with its prestigious Department of Hispanic Literature and its publication the *Revista Iberoamericana* (Ibero-American magazine) that includes numerous essays on Hispanic poetry and poets; Indiana and Purdue Universities, the University of Indianapolis and its Center for Latino Studies under Dr. Rosa Tezanos-Pinto; and there is a lengthy etcetera). And, not to forget the Cultural Literary Hispanic Institute, founded and directed by Dr. Juana de Arancibia, which sponsors more than 40 International symposiums and produces publications including the *Alba de America* (Dawn of America) magazine. If I were to be specific and inclusive in the contributions made by all of these centers, it would occupy another entire volume. With regard to every work of poetry, every literary movement, every Hispanic writer, every defined period and/or poet/writer mentioned (or omitted) herein, detailed critical studies have either been made or are waiting to be made in the future. This is the challenge facing other current and future researchers.

**Summary of the thematic and aesthetic characteristics of Hispanic literature**

In the U.S., Hispanic literature and Spanish literary language in general (but particularly poetry), exhibits peculiarities with respect to how the language is used and spoken all the way from Patagonia to Alaska. It is portrayed in diverse genres (poetry, prose and drama) throughout its prolonged and multifaceted history by multicultural richness, by old and new words—a poetic creation constituting a reverse dialectic in which thesis is desire, antithesis is experience and synthesis of the present is memory, a unification of idealized memory, an opening up into the future, as described by Yves Bonnefoy.[176]

Different linguistic codes are used (Spanish, English and "Spanglish"—a combination of the two) which is often blended in a natural way, giving the language a peculiar and idiosyncratic dimension to its poetic memory, to the plurality of its polyphony within textual plurality, figures and formal expressions, so that, although its roots are Hispanic, there are influences from the native languages of the Americas and of course the English of the United States.

It is a legacy, a memory, a unique and valuable literary language. The style, the images, the discursive hubs that reflect the dynamism of this prefiguration (i.e. history), configuration (i.e. experience) and multi-cultural re-figuration (i.e. desire) in its diverse forms of conquest, struggle, oppression-oppressed-oppressor, struggle for survival, identity, abandonment, race relations, immigration, exile, pilgrimage, melancholy, resentment, desertion and nostalgia in a generationally, geographically and coincidentally diverse voice addressing acculturation, the desire to overcome—in the end a question of love and death in the defining context of a constant search for a better world.

It contains instances of all literary movements, from Baroque to post-globalization[177] with an increasingly predominant feminine presence that has questioned, resisted and liberated itself from those experiences and expressions with a literature that is dialogical and relational, expressing solidarity in the face of dogmatic subjugation, violence, warfare mentality, virile power and patriarchal domination, as I have documented in other essays.[178]

---

176 - *Sobre el origen y el sentido* (regarding origins and meaning), Córdoba, Alción Publisher: 2011. Translation by Arturo Carrera and Silvio Mattoni, pp. 58-59.

177 - I have documented this approximation in more detail in the article *Representantes de los movimientos literarios en la poesía escrita en español en los Estados Unidos: Modernismo, Pre/Post/ Neo y otros ismos* (representations of literary movements in poetry written in Spanish in the United States: Modernism, Pre / Post / Neo and other isms) in: *Alba* (soul) *de América* Vol. 30, Nos. 57 and 58, 2011. Pp. 214-227.

178 - As I emphasized in my essay *Voces femeninas en la poesía escrita en español de los Estados Unidos* (feminine voices in poetry written in Spanish in the U.S.), Plenary lecture given during the 36th International Symposium of Literature, Asunción Paraguay, Universidad Uninorte, August, 2011.

Others have critically studied or will study some of the writers, poets and literary works mentioned herein, aware of Octavio Paz's constant and valid observation that poets and their poetry are"the product of a history and a society, but their historic nature is contradictory. Even though it is not a poet's intention, his poetry is a machine that creates anti-history." (325).[179] This is also true of prose and the theater. This long summary of literary names and capricious generational attributions and movements has been an ambitious effort to document—even if summarily—certain relevant con-tributors to poetry, prose and theatrical works written in Spanish in the United States in the universe of Latin American literature, in line with the postulates of Hans Robert Jauss in his essay entitled *From Literary History as a Challenge to Literary Theory* (1406-20).[180] In addition to the genius of individual authors it is important to recognize the historical context in which any literary work is created and received. In this way literary histo-rians organize the works of authors they write about with a certain degree of objectivity; however, such methods are dialogical because perceptions and classifications change with the passing of time, and although their presentations look like a collection of permanent monuments, the dynam-ics undergo mutations according to the expectations and changing so-cio-political perceptions of readers, audiences and critics. This constant game—the vital dialectic of creation—faced with the artifice of the different "isms" (pre-, post-, and neo-modernism as well as others) by which we try to define and encapsulate in specific time frames and aesthetic canons, all of which, in the irrepressible genius revealed in Spanish-language works created in the United States, at once represent, establish andtranscend.

But beyond time periods, generations and theorists, in a synchrony inside a diachrony, the discursive and aesthetic hubs of this literary memory in its different forms, share certain characteristics: (1) their intimacy with the preserved language, with identifying roots and the general environment by which they are formed and explained, in a re-creation of the lives of real and imaginary people of today and remnants of the past, of multifaceted souls, hybridity and duality, beyond mere tradition; (2) social, political, re-bellious and independent commitments; a questioning of and resistance to the dominant culture; (3) revolutionary, transgressive literature, not only in its contents but also through its expression in vernacular populism, some-time seven purposely vulgar ("fetishism"), the overlapping readings of an innocuous and even humorous appearance, but always in a bilingual and multicultural synthesis in both form and substance beyond the innovative techniques of 20thcentury poetics. (4) More recently, exile poetry and liter-

---

179 - Octavio Paz, *Los hijos del limo* (the silt children), Seix Barral, Barcelona, 1974.
180 - Essay translated by Timothy Bahti and published in The Norton Anthology of Theory and Criticism, Second Edition, edited by Vincent B. Leitch, New York, W. W. Norton & Company, 2010, pp. 1406-20.

ature contain the sap of cross-fertilization, shows distance and yet has a critical presence. It is a tug of war around spiritual and material adaptation and a bustling loneliness which are expressed in reincarnations replete with good-byes practically without repercussions in the beauty and diversity of the crying out. (5) Always, in any case, there is a clinging to the essence of language, culture, family, loved ones, and native idiosyncrasies in order to identify the essence of that imaginary realm, as Zulema Moret points out in the introduction to her anthology entitled *Mujeres mirando al sur. Antología de poetas sudamericanas de USA* (Women looking south. Anthology of South American poets in the U.S.[181] Within each literary body's peculiarity and expression—voices rich in nuance and struggle—we find the chorus of "the deserved voice," not yet fully acknowledged, as encapsulated by Juan Armando Epple, under Salinas'[182] *Hispanic literary memory in the United States*, which this chapter simply attempts to summarize and pay homage to. It is a journey of names, literary works, and subject matter to document their creators' presence and to stimulate future studies devoted to each and every one of them, onlyalluded to here.

I bring this chapter to a close bearing in mind Juan Gelman's reference to the invocation that "the poet speaks through what he writes", with a poem that I wrote in an attempt to express my sentiments about the U.S. Hispanic presence—a poem which I have recited in many places around the world, including in the "muses temple"—a sacred precinct of the cultures found in all the United States (at the Library of Congress), as a representative voice of Hispanic America residing in the United States:


**United States landscapes**

*If each brick could speak;*

*if each bridgecould speak;*

*if the parks, plants, flowers could speak;*

*if every chunk of pavement could speak,*

*they would speak Spanish.*

---

181 - Madrid, *Ediciones Torremozas*, S. L: 2004.
182 - Juan Armando Epple, *La voz a ti debida: la Poesía Hispánica de los Estados Unidos* (the voice you deserve: *Hispanic Poetry in the United States*) by Lilianet Brintrup, Juan A. Epple, Carmen de Mora, editors., *Hispanic Poetry of the United States*, Seville, University of Seville: 2001 , p. 19. An important book on the critical evaluation of various aspects of Hispanic poetic creations in the United States by resident poets and essayists in this country and other countries at a symposium on the subject at the University of Seville in Spain.

*if the towers, roofs,*
*the air conditioners could speak;*
*if churches, airports, factories could speak,*
*if every furrow in the country could speak,*
*they would speak Spanish.*

*if the toils could bloom with a name,*
*they would not be called stonesbut Sánchez,*
*González, García, Rodríguez, José or Peña.*

*But they cannot speak.*
*They are hands, works, scars,*
*that for now keep silent.*
*Or perhaps not anymore.*
*2003.*

# Coda

## Perspectives on the Future

SONIA SOTOMAYOR

Although I would like to, I don't know if I fully agree with Daniel Ureña's assertion that "the future of the United States is Hispanic", but I do know that the country's future cannot be envisioned without a broad, deep and essential Hispanic component, not only because of demographic growth, but also because of the way in which U.S. Hispanics have been forging ahead in all areas: in commerce, academia, the media, in cultural affairs, in politics and in significant other areas that point to a note worthy prognosis in all aspects of Hispanic inclusion in the nationality and civic life of the United States.

This is not totally surprising because a Hispanic presence exists in the very base of the country's history. It is an acknowledged, meaningful and valid centuries-long existence including some nearly forgotten facts such as, for example, the contribution of Pedro Casanave—a merchant and real estate agent originally from Navarre, Spain, who just a few years after arriving in the United States in 1785, attained a privileged position in Georgetown high society, became its fifth mayor and, in this capacity, was given the honor of laying the cornerstone for the White House, known at the time as the President's House. Notably, the date chosen to begin construction—October 12, 1792—was not random; it was the third centenary of the discovery of the Americas. The country's capital—Washington, DC—was founded two years earlier in 1790, east of the existing village of Georgetown. Its name "District of Columbia" (DC) was chosen precisely in honor of the discoverer of the Americas, Christopher Columbus, whose statue adorns the main train station near U.S. Congress buildings. Casanave, a Freemasonry leader and friend of George Washington, was instrumental in having his uncle, Juan de Miralles, appointed liaison between the Spanish Crown and the American revolutionaries during the War of Independence.

From Washington, and with regard to the White House, the Supreme Court, the Capitol building—all so beautiful—beyond the stonework, the permanent buildings such as the museums, it should be noted that in the course of the present decade, in addition to the factor of the previously-mentioned Hispanic vote which is not yet adequately represented in the nation's demographics, we pay tribute to the first Hispanic member of the U.S. Supreme Court: Sonia Sotomayor.

The history of Hispanic participation in the United States Congress dates from 1822 with the election of Florida congressman Joseph Marion Hernández. Three decades later José Manuel Gallegos was elected New Mexico's congressional delegate. In 1877, Romualdo Pacheco, representing California, became the first Hispanic to preside over a congressional committee. In 2016, Ted Cruz became the first Hispanic member of the Republican Party to run for President. Another member of that same party, Cuban-American Senator, Marco Rubio, was also a presidential candidate. The only current Hispanic Democratic senator is Robert Menéndez of New Jersey. Three years previously, we witnessed a historic first with Tim Kaine, a Virginia Senator and former governor of that State who became Hillary Clinton's vice-presidential running mate. He is fluent in Spanish, and is the president of the Spanish American Council. He was the first to give a speech in Spanish in the United States Congress during a legal debate on immigration reform on June 11, 2013.

On the other side of the aisle (as they say here referring to where members sit in the Congressional Legislative Houses according to their party affiliation), Presidential candidate Jeb Bush resides in Miami where he proudly practices his bilingualism (English-Spanish); but clarified to the press that he is not Hispanic. However, he did choose HispanicDanny Diaz to manage his 2016 presidential campaign. Senator Marco Rubio, whopresidential candidate Mitt Romney considered as a possible vice-presidential running mate, speaks of his family's admiration of Cuban poet José Martí, whom his father would read,and told the *Diario de las Américas* (Journal of the Americas), of his love for the Cuban culture and how he was exposed to racism and discrimination, and although he spoke Spanish very well . . . he did so only at home. Now, however, he uses the language daily with his Hispanic friends. Hispanic Congressman Mario Díaz-Balart was elected to the Florida Senate when he was only 31 years old and was the youngest person in the State's history to be elected to the Senate. He was also the first Hispanic head of the all-important Appropriations and the Ways and Means Committee Finances and Taxes (and chairman of the combined Appropriations Ways and Means /Finance and Tax Committee). In 1992, Congresswoman Nydia Velázquez (D) was the first Puerto Rican to be elected to the U.S. House of Representatives. Another Puerto Rican, José Enrique Serrano (D) was also elected to this body, as well as Luis Gutierrez (D) of Illinois, Mexican-American Loretta Sánchez (D) of California and others, so that as this book was written there were more Hispanics than ever—a total of 23 Democrats and five Republicans in the

226

House of Representatives. To show the breadth of this representation and presence, their diverse origins are worthy of note. In 2015, California was the State with the most Hispanic members of Congress, both as Representatives and Senators, with a total of nine, followed by Texas with seven, Florida with four, Arizona, New Mexico, New Jersey and New York with two each and the States of Washington, Illinois and Idaho, one each. It is also of note that one of Idaho's two representatives is Hispanic, namely Republican Raúl Salvador, and that the Hispanic population is only slightly over 10% of that State's total. Despite comments to the contrary regarding the importance of the Hispanic vote for the Republican Party (GOP), they learned lessons from their defeats in the 2008 and 2012 presidential campaigns as they seem not to have heeded their own preaching. I imagine that the Party was making an effort to please the dominant right, since only one presidential candidate, Ben Carson, (an African-American neurosurgeon) of the 16 Presidential candidates in the 2016 campaign attended the NALEO convention (National Association of Latino Elected and Appointed Officials) in Las Vegas in June, 2015. Ted Cruz, Marco Rubio, Jeb Bush, Rand Paul and the remaining 12 potential Republican candidates were left to explain their non-attendance at that Convention. This was in contrast to the Democratic Party candidates, Hillary Clinton and Senator Bernie Sanders who did attend that Convention. However, both parties did appeal to the Hispanic vote and Hillary Clinton promised that if she were elected President she would end deportation efforts, but she lost the election. Candidate Jeb Bush announced that he would choose Brian Sandoval, governor of Nevada, as his vice presidential running mate. Cristóbal Alex, president of the Latino Triumph Project, stated that he had never seen such priority given to seeking the Latin vote so early in the campaigns and in such significant ways. Daniel Garza, Executive Director of the LIBRE association, who had the backing of Republican David Koch, also expressed his intention to redouble his efforts to win Hispanic votes for the Republican Party. For both parties, it was just one more indication of the growing political importance of the country's Hispanic population.

Among the many Hispanics who have served in the executive branch is Julian Castro, the Secretary of Housing and Urban Development during Barack Obama's second term, preceded decades earlier by Henry Gabriel Cisneros, former Mayor of San Antonio, Texas.[183]Hilda Solis is a former Secretary of Labor and Ken Salazar was Secretary of the Interior. Several other Hispanics served under President Obama, following in the footsteps of earlier Hispanic Democrats in different areas of government, such as

183 - He was preceded in this position 140 years earlier by the historic figure Juan Seguín, who fought for Texas in the battle of the Alamo together with Davy Crockett and was the first Hispanic Mayor of San Antonio, serving several terms, until being violently removed from office by Hispanophobic armed men in 1842 who promulgated hatred Mexicans in Texas—another fact ignored in official histories.

Lauro Fred Cavazos Jr. who was Secretary of Education under the Ronald Reagan and George H.W. Bush administrations from 1988 to 1990. Dionisio ("Dennis") Chávez, a New Mexico Democrat, was the first Hispanic ever to hold a Cabinet position as a member of Congress from 1931 to 1935 and served as a Senator from 1935 to 1962. Ezequiel Cabeza de Baca, the first Hispanic ever elected in New Mexico in 1912 served as lieutenant governor of the State, and was its second governor in 1917. Under the Bill Clinton administration, Aida M. Álvarez, was the first Hispanic woman to hold a U.S. cabinet position. William "Bill" Richardson III became the governor of New Mexico after serving as a congressman and served as the U.S. Ambassador to the United Nations and as Secretary of Energy during the Clinton administration.

Among Republicans there have also been some important firsts: Alberto R. Gonzáles was the nation's first Hispanic Attorney General under the George Bush Presidency and that of his father. Puerto Rican Antonia Coello Novello became the nation's first Hispanic Surgeon General. In 1877, Romualdo Pacheco, the first Hispanic congressman was later elected governor of California. Cuban-American Iliana Ros-Lehtinen became the first Hispanic Congresswoman and has been in office since 1989. She is the only female to have chaired the powerful Congressional Foreign Affairs Committee. Many yeas earlier, in 1928, Mexican-born Octaviano Larrozolo, became the first Hispanic Republican Senator for the State of New Mexico and later was elected governor of that State. More recently, in 2010, Susana Martinez of New Mexico became the country's first female Hispanic governor. Benjamín Fernández, a World War Two veteran, who resided in Kansan and Nevada, was the first Hispanic American to run for President in 1980.

It is of interest to note that Los Angeles Mayor Antonio Villaraigosa presided over the 2012 Democratic Convention, a year in which the cover of the *New YorkTimes Magazine,* in its February 4, 2012 edition,with a montage of Latin faces bore the title "Why Latinos Will Pick the Next President ". At the time, Victor Fuentes wrote, "All these signs point to a growing role for the Hispanic community in the political, cultural and artistic life of the United States."[184]Richard Blanco was the first poet of Hispanic origin chosen to participate in a presidential inauguration ceremony, and he did this for the newly re-elected President Obama in 2012. He is an esteemed friend of this author. Through his poetry, although written in English (with Spanish incursions), expresses himself in the context of his Cuban-American identity and culture. As I mentioned in the previous chapter, Together with him, as Hispanics, we were the proud representatives of American cultural diplomacy under the motto *Estamos Unidos* ("we are united" – rhymes with

---

184 - Op.Cit., p. 184.

*Estados Unidos*) at the 2015 International Poetry Festival held in in Grana-da, Nicaragua, where we recited poetry and shared other presentations. The Democratic Party also promoted the candidacies of other leaders such as Ángel Taveras, the first Hispanic mayor of Providence, Rhode Island and a candidate for Governor of that State in the legislative elections held in November, 2016. Lucy Flores, representing the state of Nevada, is also an aspiring gubernatorial candidate. Amanda Rentería—a California Dem-ocrat—has talked of becoming a candidate for congresswoman for that State. Thus, influential organizations such as the *Congressional Hispanic Caucus* and other similar, such as the *Congressional Hispanic Leadership Institute*, the Republican Congressional Hispanic Conference (CHC) and others, will continue to prosper. Of course, becoming a Hispanic repre-sentative does not guarantee in all cases that that person will fight for their interests or defend the dignity of their presence in the United States. For example, Congressman Henry B. González of Texas, voted against the inclusion of Mexican-Americans in the text of the Electoral Rights Act, opposed the establishment of MALDEF (the Legal Defense and Education Fund for Mexican Americans) and declined to join the above-mentioned *Congressional National Hispanic Caucus.*

The future of the Hispanic American community's political influence is in-creased by the number of potential voters of Hispanic origin in the U.S., whether they be Spanish-speaking only or bilingual. According to the Pew Research Center by the year 2030 they will number 40 million individu-als—nearly double the current number.

In addition to their history and presence, Hispanics take pride in and are in-spired by the achievements of activists like the heroic César Chávez and his colleague Dolores Huerta, one of the founders of *La Causa* (The cause) in defending the United Farm Workers (UFW), whose work Martin Luther King blessed in the following words contained in a telegram to César Chávez:"I am deeply moved by your courage in fasting as your personal sacrifice for justice through non-violence... You stand today as a living example of the Ghandian tradition with its great force for social progress... My colleagues and I commend you for your bravery, salute for your indefatigable work against poverty and injustice, and pray for your health and your continuing service as one of the outstanding men of America;"[185] And in another tele-gram, he wrote: "We are together with you in spirit and in determination that our dreams for a better tomorrow will be realized."[186]Robert and John F. Kennedy also supported and stood by César Chávez in his efforts and during his hunger strikes.

---

185 - (March 5, 1968)
186 - September, 1966.

The positive outshines the negative, although Hispanics have a long way to go and many areas in which they must advance. With optimism Mexican-American Silvia Puente of Chicago, who began working as a member of the United Farmers Workers (UFW) and is now the director of the Latino Policy Forum proclaims that "the culture of *we* will prevail."The classic musical *West Side Story*, deals precisely with the problematic coexistence of an Hispanic culture (in this case, Puerto Rican) with the predominant white culture in a New York neighborhood with all the attendant stereotypes, resentments and mistrust in the process of integrating into the U.S. culture, a romantically tragic resolution to the dilemma is acted out. Incidentally, in such very American productions as Hollywood cinema and U.S. TV shows, the Hispanic presence has made itself increasingly felt and continues to grow, but for directors to even use Hispanic actors is still something they avoid for portraying the role of Hispanic characters most of whom have traditionally been presented in a negative light.

To overcome these disappointments, we highlight some positive accomplishments in this field and recall the performances and influence of actor pioneers such as Antonio Moreno, Desiderio (Desi) Arnaz (Cuba), Chita Rivera, Rita Moreno (Puerto Rico)—the first Hispanic to win an Oscar in her role as "Anita" in *West Side Story.* She also starred in other films such as *The fabulous señorita*, and*Latin Lovers*. Currently and previously in Hollywood and in other mass media there have been and are many Hispanic actors such as José Ferrer, the first Hispanic to win an Oscar for his role in *Cyrano de Bergerac*, Eugenio Derbez with his great success in the movie *Instructions Not Included*, Javier Bardem, a Spanish actor and Oscar winner for his performance in *No Country for Old Men*, Michael Peña, Gael García Bernal, George López, John Leguizamo, Antonio Banderas, Diego Luna, William Levy, Andy García, Jennifer López, Salma Hayek, Benicio del Toro, Eva Longovia, Sofia Vergara, Spain's Penélope Cruz who won an Oscar for her role in *Vicky Cristina Barcelona*. Currently, dozens of Hispanic actors, directors, composers, photographers, writersand designers reside and work in Hollywood, the so-called movie mecca and dream factory and have captivated the world for more than a century with memorable performances, special effects and other innovations aimed at inspiring the imagination while achieving huge box office successes. Names like these and many others come to mind, including Cameron Diaz, Eva Mendes, the award-winning directors Alfonso Cuarón and Alejandro González Iñárritu, photography director Emmanuel Lubezk who for two consecutive years (2014 and 2015), surprised Hollywood with their excellent work. In 1978, Spanish-Cuban Néstor Almendros received an Oscar for his contribution as director of photography; and director and scriptwriter Rodrigo García, the son of Gabriel García Márquez, is an outstanding U.S. TV producer, having directed episodes of popular series such as *Six Feet Under, Carni-*

*val* and *The Sopranos*. Additionally, there are legendary figures like the Argentine composer Gustavo Santaolalla who received an Oscar two years in a row for the soundtracks of *Brokeback Mountain*(2005) and *Babel*(2006). The well-known director Pedro Almodóvar received an award in 1999 for his film *Todo sobre mi madre* (Everything about my mother), which seems to me as though I saw just yesterday. His compatriot Alejandro Amenábar won the Oscar in 2004 for *Mar adentro* (Into the sea); and the Spanish film *Belle Epoque*, directed by Fernando Trueba won an Oscar in 1993. *La historia oficial* (The official history), by Argentine film director Luis Puenzo, received an Oscar in 1985, and Jose Luis Garcia of Spain with his film *Volver a empezar* (Starting over), was honored with an award in 1982. In concluding this segment I call to mind the master of masters, Luis Buñuel whose film *El discreto encanto de la burguesía* (The discrete charm of the bourgeoisie) was the first Spanish film to receive an Oscar in 1972. This is just a brief summary of what Roberto Fandiño and Joaquin Badajoz detailed in their above-cited articles on Spanish cinema in the United States[187] in which Fandiño states, "Spanish cinema has not had the presence or force that our language has achieved in other fields such as literature and television." Then Joaquin Badajoz came forth with his revelatory documentary "The 21st Century Latin boom in Hollywood" (p.904).

Furthermore, journalist Jossette Rivera's article "Hispanics—the secret to Hollywood's blockbusters?" was referenced on a BBC World program on October 1, 2013, with a comment that "Hollywood seems to have found an increasingly effective commercial formula for the box office success of its films—marshal the Latinos. Movies like *Paranormal Activity* seem to bear this out. It was the fifth in a series of the terror genre that owed much of its success to the large numbers of Hispanics who went to see these movies—many shown in Latin neighborhoods. With gross earnings of more than $350 million, the film studio decided that a sequel would portray a typical Latino family in the United States and even have some of the dialogues in Spanish, without subtitles. Journalist Ben Fritz wrote an article in the *Wall Street Journal* in which he stated, "This bilingual movie produced by Viacom Inc., (a division of Paramount), marks the first time a major studio has taken a mainstream franchise targeting general audiences and centered it on Latino characters and their culture. A Nielsen study reveals that Hispanics—who make up just over 16% of the U.S. population—purchase one quarter of movie box office tickets yearly. In this regard, proportionally they outnumber Anglos, African Americans and Asians."

This optimism and progress are seen in many other fields as well. For example, the case of Willie Velázquez who was the recipient of the Presidential Medal of Freedom in 1995—the highest award granted to civilians—for

187 - *Enciclopedia del Español en los Estados Unidos*, pp. 867-911.

his success in promoting voter education programs, including his work in helping millions to register to vote. In 2012 President Obama also honored the previously mentioned Dolores Huerta for her life of activism in support of workers' rights. Conservative social activist Linda Lou Chávez, the most influential woman in Ronald Reagan's White Houseand the wife of Christopher Gersten, was a defender of the equal and civil rights of Hispanic Americans, but with sometimes seemingly contradictory positions. Another woman, Linda Chavez-Thompson was the vice-president of the National Democratic Committee for many years and became the first president of the Confederation of Labor Unions of the Americas.

All of the individual achievements and advances summarized here serve to show an awareness of the positive reality of the U.S. Hispanic presence in counteracting that immense universe and vast territory of ignorance, racism, discrimination, stereotyping and prejudices that are promoted by, among others, neo-Nazi groups, the Ku Klux Klan, and other racist groupings, with their terror tactics that fuel hate crimes against Hispanics—the community that most suffers from such crimes in the United States. Consider the actions of a man accused of several wrongdoings and abuses—the Arizona Sheriff Joe Arpaio and his racial profiling and who, in his own words, talked about setting up "concentration camps." We also have Donald Trump's statements and actions in organizing his Republican candidacy for President in 2016, expressing extreme right-wing positions and denigrating Mexican immigrants by labeling them with insulting generalizations which, because of their spuriousness, are so repugnant to me that I choose not repeat them here. In my own experience of over half a century interacting with this dynamic Hispanic population in the United States, I can affirm that the great majority are hard-working, decent, sacrificial people who make positive contributions to this country. There is, of course, still much to be "conquered" (although this is not my most preferred term). The citizens of the United States should not tolerate such negative actions and attitudes or (so as not to forget) the oft-repeated negative thoughts of people like politician and historian Newt Gingrich, who once proclaimed Spanish to be the "language of the ghetto." (Perhaps he thinks that the entire country is a ghetto?), or the shameful, offensive and equally ignorant claims of one Samuel Huntington expressed in his article, "The Hispanic Threat to the American Dream". He cannot be more wrong. The paradox is that his way of thinking is the real threat to the American dream. For example, he argues with ethnocentric blindness that "There is no *americano* dream, but only the American Dream created by an Anglo-Protestant society, and that. Mexican-Americans will share in that dream and in that society only if they dream in English" Or consider the ethnocentric anguish expressed by Richard Lamm in his book *The Immigration Time Bomb*[188]

188 - New York, NY: Truman Talley Books, 1985

which ignores the true make-up and multicultural evolution of this country. I have many Anglo friends and acquaintances who already dream in Spanish as well as their native English. Individuals in a truly multilingual, multicultural and open-mined society are like the man who was inspired to create the architecture of the Immaculate Conception Basilica which shines resplendent in Washington D.C. near the campus of the Catholic University with its chapels of Anglo Virgins, the Virgin of Guadalupe, Asian and Afro-American Virgins—in a significant expression of religious inclusion by that Church which played an important role in the formation of Hispanic identity (but not excusing any negative issues). At that university (which I consider my own), professor Enrique Pumar speaks out for the humanization of immigrants who—more than just mere workers—are family, personally contribute to the makeup and development of this nation which is a country of immigrants in its very roots and which, therefore—as it has been observed—cannot be anti-immigrant. The importance of the IRCA Immigration Reform Act, signed in 1986 by President Reagan must not be minimized. While it is not perfect and has some serious snags, yet it paved the way for the legalization of millions of immigrants (mostly Hispanic), who were already part of the life of this country, even though without legal status.

In this context, and with "the American dream" in mind, it is of note that the famous project for supporting young immigrants desirous of and qualified for legal U.S. residency, has been called the "Dream Act" (based on the acronym 'development, relief and education for alien minors') and that in 2012 President Obama under the DACA program (deferred action for childhood arrivals) ordered a stop to their being deported after hearing the voices of the American people and the "dreamers" themselves. I am filled with optimism and I prefer the solutions suggested by Aviva Chomsky in her book *Undocumented. How Immigration Became Illegal* [189] which envisions a future in which the country's attitude toward immigration (mainly affecting Hispanics) will be formulated by changing the discriminatory requirements of citizenship, eliminating referents to illegality based on elitist and exclusivist criteria which create boundaries and differences and impose impossibly difficult documentation requirements designed to protect the interests and prosperity of the privileged few who take advantage of the majority, so that Hispanic immigrants will instead be welcomed and will integrate as a population who has contributed, contribute now and will continue to contribute to the unceasing development and advancement of the nation. So I proclaim "Yes, we can" to the dignity of the 2006 marches that triumphed over the Sensenbrenner anti-immigration proposal and raised the

189 - Boston: Beacon Press, 2014

country's appreciation and acceptance of immigrants to the United States, presaging an auspicious future for the Hispanic community.

To adapt to these new realities will require a twofold approach. On the one hand those of the predominant Anglo culture must make an effort to accommodate the U.S. Hispanic culture and on the other hand this growing population, without losing or belittling their own identity, ancestry and legacy, must involve themselves in the Anglopopulation and culture and those of other U.S. community minorities by adding to—and not subtracting from—all their respective contributions.

In view of this perspective of progress, of greater gains and the implications of the Hispanic reality in this country, the responsibilities and activism of this community need to increase and become more dynamic; for example, to create high quality museums in the nation's Capital and in other cities that display Hispanic history, culture and contributions to this country, as well as making substantial investments in other cultural aspects, such as preserving the Spanish language as a national treasure for Hispanic families and the community at large, to stimulate a process of growth while at the same time supporting diverse initiatives to enrich not only the Hispanic community but to show the United States' multicultural identity, to increase the number of voters and the value of their vote as a community presence and capacity in all positions of citizen leadership, to invest in and promote education in the community as a factor of enrichment and progress and, united in their diversity, assert this community's demographic import by taking pride in their history, culture, language and presence, persisting in efforts to recover and make known not only the reality of the Hispanic sector of the United States, but as a decisive part of the multicultural U.S. national identity which can no longer be understood or explained without incorporating this fundamental element. All this within and beyond professional associations leading this endeavor such as the U.S. Hispanic Chamber of Commerce, (USHCC), the Society of Hispanic Professional Engineers, the Society of Hispanic Engineers and Scientists, the National Association of Hispanic Doctors (NHMA), the National Association of Hispanic Nurses, the National Association of Hispanic Lawyers, the National Society of Hispanic MBAs, the Association of Latino Professionals in Finance and Accounting, the National Association of Hispanic Journalists (NAHJ), the Society of Hispanic Professional Engineers and the National Association of Real Estate Professionals (NAHREP).[190] With these we should include other political, social and community institutions such as LULAC and the National Council of *La Raza.* There is also CARECEN (now known as the Central American Resource Center), the

---

190 - More information on these organizations can be obtained at: http://www.impactony.com/las-diez-asociaciones-profesionales-latinas-mas-valiosas/#sthash.RUGGqrl8.dpuf

National Association of Latino Elected and Appointed Officials, the "We are America" Alliance, the "My Family Votes" Educational Fund, *DemocraciaU-SA*, the aforementioned Congressional Hispanic Leadership Institute, the Congressional Hispanic Caucus Institute, as well as previously mentioned academic, cultural associations etc., such as university departments, the Hispanic Society of America, the Spanish Institute, the Cervantes Institute (all 3 in New York), the Cervantes Institutes of Chicago, Albuquerque, Seattle and Harvard University, the Spanish Cultural Center of Miami, the United States Hispanic Culture Foundation, the Association for Hispanic Classical Theater (ACHT), the Cervantes Society of America (CSA), the Latin American Studies Association (LASA), the National Association of Hispanic and Latino Studies, the numerous Cultural Centers of Hispanic countries or Hispanic groups such as Cubans in Miami, the Puerto Rican Cultural Center in Springfield, Mass., the Hispanic Cultural Centers (NHCC) in Albuquerque, New Mexico, Cleveland, Miami, San Marcos, Texas, New York, Connecticut, Idaho and numerous other locations; art-related organizations such as NALAC (Association of Latino Arts and Cultures), the Smithsonian Latino Center and the National Hispanic Foundation for the Arts. This long list is by no means exhaustive and serves only to indicate the effervescence of the Hispanic presence in the United States. It should also be noted that this expansion and many of these associations have emerged in the last thirty years—a promising sign of the increasingly expansive flowering of the U.S. Hispanic community.

As I have suggested in abundant detail, currently and future Hispanic writers, artists and leaders need not deny their origins, nor abandon the use of their language in this country, because it is theirs and they belong to it, as do all citizens, and we Hispanics are among them in this United States. One of the most influential poets of the Twentieth Century—William Carlos Williams—the son of a Puerto Rican mother who insisted on his having a bilingual and bicultural upbringing, stated: "In many ways, Spain and the Spanish of the 16th and 17th centuries are closer to us in the United States today than England perhaps ever was." It is a point at least worth considering. The United States, in terms of latitude and climate, is closer to Spain than to England, and in the volatility of our spirits and our racial mix we are much more similar to Gothic and Moorish Spain." Because beyond Spain, as U.S. founding father Thomas Jefferson emphasized, we are a part of Hispanic America which reaches from pole to pole and is inhabited literally by individuals from all these backgrounds—as current and future citizens of this Hispanic America.

In the future, in this country's commitment to develop and prosper, there is a shield at the United States Embassy in Nicaragua that boldly proclaims: ESTAMOS UNIDOS (we are united). [191] UCLA's Dean of Education, Marcelo Suarez Orozco stated, "Unless there is a happy future for our Latino commu-

191 - The phrase rhymes with Estados Unidos (United States)

nity there can be no happy future for the United States"—words quoted at the conclusion of a roundtable of a group of professionals who took part in *The Future is Today* Forum, in 2013, attended by, among others, the outstanding actress and activist Eva Longoria, and moderated by TV personality Jorge Ramos.

At the 2012 Hispanic American National Summit, it was stated that "This is a critical moment for our country and for the role of the Hispanic-American community in our nation. The NAA (New American Alliance) National Summit has two purposes: first, to change the tone and content of the discourse regarding U.S. Hispanics from a narrow focus to a broader and more accurate definition of who Hispanics are and what their contributions represent with regard to global leadership and the continuing prosperity of our nation" (Words of the Honorable Roel C. Campos, former United States Securities and Exchange Commissioner and NAA's Chairman of the Board.) Now, we celebrate our country year-round, every day and will do so in the future, not just during Hispanic Heritage Month, which was established by President Lyndon B. Johnson in 1968 when he set aside a week in September as National Hispanic Heritage Week. Later, in 1988, according to official government documentation, this observance was extended to an entire month, from September 15 to October 15, "to honor the Hispanic heritage of this country. During this month, the United States celebrates the cultures and traditions of those U.S. residents who have roots in Spain, Mexico and the Hispanic countries of Central and South America and the Caribbean ... Today, more than ever, Hispanic Americans play an integral role in the country's development and growth. More and more Hispanics are attaining leadership positions in government, the legal system, aeronautics, commerce, the military, sports, the health and environmental sciences, the arts, and many other key occupations in helping to promote the economic growth and social development of the country. The influence of this culture is reflected in many aspects of the daily lives of the people of this country by contributing to their progress and diversification." The "culture" industries see promising growth in Hispanic-American life in the areas of radio, TV, music, cinema and publishing, all of which contribute to and sustain this growth, not only in consumer-based economics, but also in bearing the responsibility of shaping the future in light of the present and the past by touching on identity, culture, issues of the day and national concerns, as well as the configuration of the U.S. Hispanic community whose presence here makes the United States the second largest Spanish-speaking country in the world. With regard to matters of identity, I allow myself, as an example, to refer to the history of cinema in which, in spite of persistent discrimination and racism, reveals a rich reality of coexistence with the more "famous" dominant culture. Musician Víctor Fuentes recalled that the national Hispanic organization known as "The Congress of Spanish-Speaking People", was created by activists, among them Luisa Moreno, Josefina Fierro

236

de Bright, Roberto Galván and Carlos Montalvo to promote campaigns for social justice, human dignity and to combat fascist and extremist rhetoric, and has been financially and politically supported by such outstanding figures as Anthony Quinn, Dolores del Río, Orson Welles, and other famous Hollywood actors like Gary Cooper, Judy Garland and John Wayne. The latter was an admirer of President Roosevelt and progressive causes, and during his marriage to Josefina Alicia Sáenz, he gave an Hispanic name to one of their daughters—María Antonia—and later on requested that his own epitaph read "Ugly, strong and formal."

There is another interesting aspect that allows us to be optimistic about the future. In 2015 the U.S. Centers for Disease Control (CDC) announced that, statistically, the U.S. Hispanic population is healthier than the non-Hispanic white population, suffering 35% fewer cases of heart disease, 49% fewer cases of cancer,has fewer Alzheimer's victims, fewer cerebrovascular diseases, fewer cases of pneumonia, etc. According to the CDC, despite socio-economic disadvantages, the Hispanic-American population lives an average of two years longer than the white population. There are several factors including lifestyles, having a lower percentage of smokers and being an average 15 years younger than the white population.

It is worth noting that, in addition to the free and accelerating presence and expansion of the Spanish language of and in the United States, the outstanding, courageous and unbridled journalist Geraldo Rivera, author of *HisPanic ~ Why Americans fear Hispanics in the U.S.*[192], among others, has pointed out that the Hispanic community is forging ahead in using English and is doing so at all levels with pride in their own heritage within the predominant Anglo community, in response to the former President's call,"Yes, we can!", in fighting discrimination, racism, antagonism, mistreatment of Hispanic immigrants who simply ask for respect for their history, culture, language and contributions to this great, inclusive United States, and that they be recognized and accepted-throughout the nation for their vigor, skill, courage, compassion, adaptability, sense of social justice, human dignity and openness in the nation's domestic life and in carrying out its international commitments. This English presence of the Hispanic community must occur at all levels: in government, the economy, education, the digital world, mainstream radio and TV, in social circles, history, in future planning and, finally, to repeat the words of Walt Whitman, as "one of the most necessary parts of that complex American identity" (he also added the word "grandiose").

The statistics given herein taken from different years and decades will be updated in a positive evolution. A rich Hispanic history and reality will consolidate in a positive way. That is why in view of all of the foregoing and all

---

192 - New York, *Celebra*, Penguin Group, 2009.

the curious ramblings, before, with and after "The Pilgrims", there will be a vigorous Hispanic presence in this nation and happily the vision expressed in my poem "The Official Version" will become a reality.

*That history is already written*

*in the unalterable stone of time*

*which defies storms and temperaments*

*and to those who wish to dictatorially*

*play with the facts.*

*Solid history is there*

*with the sober eloquence*

*of its solemn presence*

*of that past that has not allowed silence*

*nor could be forced into it.*

*History contains the eternity of*

*man and the complicity of the universe.*

(May 13, 1987)

And so, we will celebrate now and ever more the **Hispanic United States of yesteryear, today and forever!** The intention of these pages has simply been to serve as a stimulus, a testimony, an invitation to recognize and promote the 500-year Hispanic presence—in an exclamation of pride and hope.

238

# BIBLIOGRAPHY

Alegría, Fernando, Jorge Ruffinelli. *Paradise Lost or Gained?: The Literature of Hispanic Exile*, Arte Publico Press, 1991.

Ambroggio, Luis Alberto. "La poesía puertorriqueña". *Enciclopedia del Español en los Estados Unidos*. Humberto López Morales, Coordinador. Madrid: Ed. Santillana, 2008. 672-77.

"Poesía de Estados Unidos en Español". *Hispanos en los Estados Unidos*. Gerardo Piña et al, Ed. Nueva York: Columbia University, 2004. 197-213. Updated at www.ildialogo.org/poesia/islanegra128especialeupoen.pdf -

"Poesía del exilio argentino en los Estados Unidos". *Isla Negra* 3:128, Febrero 2008, 21-28 at www.ildialogo.org/poesia/islanegra128especialeupoen.pdf

"Poesía mexicano-americana en los Estados Unidos". *Correo Cultural Guanajuato*, Julio 2007, at

http://www.correo gto.com.mx/notas.asp?id=33442 .

*Homenaje al Camino* (Tribute to the road), Córdoba: Ed. Alción, 2012.

*Poemas Desterrados*. Buenos Aires: Allicia Gallegos Ed., 1995.

*Al pie de la Casa Blanca. Hispanic Poets in Washington, D.C.*, co-edited with Carlos Parada Ayala, Nueva York, North American Academy of the Spanish Language, 2010.

*En el jardín de los vientos (In the garden of the winds). Poetic Works 1974-2014*. Carlos Paldao and Rosa Tezanos-Pinto editors. North American Academy of the Spanish Language, 2014.

Anzaldúa, Gloria. *Borderlands/ La Frontera (Border): The New Mestiza (Mixed blood)*. San Francisco: Aunt Lute Books, 1999.

Bloom. Harold. *The Anxiety of Influence: A Theory of Poetry*. New York: Oxford University Press, 1973; 2nd edition, 1997.

Brintrup, Lilianet, Juan A. Epple, Carmen de Mora, eds. *La Poesía Hispánica de los Estados Unidos*. Sevilla: Universidad de Sevilla, 2001.

Crespo-Francés, J.A. *El legado de Juan de Oñate: los últimos días del Adelantado* (The legacy of J.O.: the last days of the advanced one) , Seville: Arboleda, 2003.

*Don Pedro Menéndez de Avilés: deuda histórica con un soldado ignorado de Felipe II* (Historic debt with Felipe II's ignored soldier) . Madrid : J.A. Crespo-Francés, 2000.

*Juan de Oñate y el Paso del Río Grande: el Camino Real de Tierra Adentro* (JO and RG pass: the royal inland road – 1998), edited with Mercedes Junquera, Madrid: Defense Ministry, 1998.

*La expedición de Juan de Oñate: 30 de abril de 1598*. Madrid : Sotuer, D.L. 1997.

Cota-Cárdenas, Margarita. *Noches despertando inConciencias* . Tucson: Scorpion Press, 1975. 2nd edition, 1977.

de Arrieta Martinez, Mónica (2005), "Cuando escribir también es recordar": Michel Tournier y Jorge Luis Borges. de Martíni, Cristina Elgue et al, editors. Espacio, *Memoria e Identidad, Configuraciones en la Literatura Comparada*. (Space, memory and identity, configuratrions in comparative literature) Vol. II. Córdoba: Comunicarte Publishers, 2005. 865-78.

De Martini, Cristina Elgue et al, editors. *Espacio, Memoria e Identidad, Configuraciones en la Literatura Comparada*, Córdoba, Comunicarte Editorial, Vol. II. Córdoba: Comunicarte Editorial, 2005.

Dumitrescu, Domnita, *El español en los Estados Unidos: E Pluribus Unum? Enfoques Multidisciplinarios* (Colección Estudios Lingüísticos), Nueva York: North American Academy of the Spanish Language, 2013.

Falconí José Luis and José Antonio Mazzotti, Eds. *The Other Latinos*. Nueva York: David Rockefeller Center Series on Latin American Studies, 2008.

Fernández-Armesto, Felipe, *Our America: A Hispanic History of the United States*. Nueva York, W.W. Norton and Company, 2014.

Fuentes, Víctor, *California Hispano-Mexicana*, Nueva York: North American Academy of the Spanish Language, 2014.

García Canclini, Néstor. *Culturas híbridas. Estrategias para entrar y salir de la Modernidad* (Hybrid cultres. Strategies for entering and leaving modernity). México: Grijalbo, 1990.

García, Jorge, *Hispanic/Latino Identity. A Philophical Perspective*, Malden, MA: Blackwell Publishers, 2000.

González, Ángel, *Palabra sobre palabra* (Word over word), Barcelona: Seix Barral, 2005 (complete poems).

González, Juan, *Havest of Empire, A History of Latinos in America*, Nueva York, Penguin Books; Revised edition, 2011.

Grüner, Eduardo, *El sitio de la mirada* (The place of the look), Buenos Aires: Norma, 2002.

Halliday, E.M., *Understanding Thomas Jefferson*, New York, Harpers Collins Publishing: 2001.

Hayes, Kevin J., *The Road to Monticello, The Life and Mind of Thomas Jefferson*. Oxford University Press: 2008.

Jefferson, Thomas, *The Life and selected writings of Thomas Jefferson*, edited by Adrienne Koch and William Pedren, New York, The Modern Library: 1998. (Quoted in Life:1998).

*The Papers of Thomas Jefferson*. Colecction of 32 volumes initiated by Julian P. Boyd et al., Princeton N.J., Princeton University Press: 1950 (Quoted in Papers).

*The papers of Thomas Jefferson, Retirement Series*. J. Jefferson Looney et al, editors., Princeton: Princeton University Press: 2004. (Un volumen publicado hasta la fecha. Citado en las notas "Papers").

*The Jeffersonian Cyclopedia, a comprehensive collection of views of Thomas Jefferson*. John P. Folley, ed. New York: Funk and Wagnalls Company: 1900. (Quoted in Cyclopedia notes).

Jiménez, Juan Ramón. "Diary of a Newlywed Poet," a bilingual edition of *Diario de un poeta recién casado*, Translation by Hugh A. Harter, Cranbury, NJ: Associated University Presses, 2004.

*Tercera antología poética* (Third poetic anthology -1898-1953). Madrid: Editorial Biblioteca Nueva, 1957.

Enrique Díez-Canedo. *Cartas literarias*. Ciudad Publishers, 1943

Kanellos, Nicholas, Editor. *En otra Voz. Antología de la literatura hispana de los Estados Unidos*, Houston: Arte Público Press, 2002.

Leal, Luis. *Las cuatro presencias en el patrimonio literario del pueblo chicano. *Antología de literatura latina, Cruzando puentes II, Ventana Abierta*. (The 4 presences in the literary patrimony of the Chicano population. Anthology of Latin Literature. Crossing bridges II. Open window) 7.25 (Autumn 2008): 8-18.

Lipski, John M., *El español de América*, Madrid: Cátedra, 1996.

Lomeli, Francisco, Nicholas Kanellos and Claudio Esteva-Fabregat, Eds. *Handbook of Hispanic Cultures in the United States: Literature and Art*. Houston: Arte Público Press, 1993.

López García-Molins, Ángel, *El español de Estados Unidos y el problema de la norma lingüística* (Spanish in the U.S. and the problem of linguistic norms). New York: North American Academy of the Spanish Language, 2014.

López, Heriberto. *Canclinización de la frontera. Lo post-transfronterizo (The "canclinizatión" of the border. Post trans-borders)*. Literal. Latin American Voice (summer, 2010): 26-28.

López-Luaces, Martha. "Nueva York como motivo de ruptura estética en la poesía española (NY as a reason for the aesthetic ruptura of Spanish poetry): Juan Ramón Jiménez, García Lorca and José Hierro", in **Fundación Carolina**, June 2007, pp. 1-6.

López Morales, Humberto, edition chairman. Enciclopedia del Español en los Estados Unidos North American Academy of the Spanish Language, Madrid: Santillana publisher: 2008.

Mapp, Alf J. Jr. *Thomas Jefferson: A Strange Case of Mistaken Identity*, Lanham, Madison Books: 1987.

*Thomas Jefferson: Passionate Pilgrim*, Lanham, Madison Books: 1993.

Mier, Matt S. and Ribero, Feliciano, *Mexican-American/American- Mexican. From Conquistadores to Chicanos*, Hill and Wang; Revised edition, 1994.

Mora, Pat. *My own true name: new and selected poems for young adults*, 19841999. Houston: Arte Público Press: 2000.

Nagy, Silvia *El arte de vivir: Aproximaciones críticas a la obra poética de Pedro Lastra* (The art of living: critical approximations of PL's poetic works). Co-edition with Luis Correa-Díaz. Santiago de Chile: RIL/La Biblioteca Nacional de Chile, 2007.

O'Connor, Kathleen. Curso Modernism and the Avant-Garde Movements in Latin America. SUNY Old Westbury College, Spring, 2010.

Palau de Nemes, Graciela. *El fondo del exilio de Juan Ramón Jiménez. El exilio de las Españas de 1939 en las Américas. ¿adónde fue la canción?* (Background of the exile of JRJ: the exile of 1939's Spains in the Americas. Where did the song go?): José María Naharro Calderón, ed. Madrid: Anthropos, 1991.

Piña-Rosales, Gerardo, ed. *Escritores españoles en los Estados Unidos* (Spanish writers in the U.S.). New York: North American Academy of the Spanish Language, 2007.

Randall, Willard Sterne, *Thomas Jefferson. A life*, New York, Henry Holt and Company: 1993.

Rivera, Geraldo, *Hispanic. Why Americans fear Hispanics in the U.S.* Nueva York, Celebra, Penguin Group, 2009.

Rizk, Beatriz J., *El teatro latino de Estados Unidos* (Latin theater in the U.S.), Tramoya, 22, 1990, 7-20.

Latino Theater in the Unites States: the Importance of Being the Other, by Luis Ramos-García *The State of Latino Theater in the United States: Hibridity, Transculturation, and Identity*. Ramos-Garcia, Luis, Routledge, 2002. 2002, pp. 1-13

El teatro de las comunidades latinas en Estados Unidos y su relación con un contexto social determinado. (Latin community theater in the U.S. and its relationship to a particular social context) (Centro de Investigaciones del Nuevo Teatro), pp. 179-193.

Silva-Corvalán, *Carmen, Sociolingüística y pragmática del español* (Spanish language socio-linguistics and pragmatic aspects), Washington DC, Gerogetown University Press, 2001.

Soldán, Paz y Fuguet, Alberto, *Se habla español: voces latinas en USA* (Spanish spoken: U.S. Latin voices), Alfaguara, 2001.

Solís, Pedro Xavier. *Pablo Antonio Cuadra Itinerario*, Academia Nicargüense de la Lengua, Managua: 2008.

Stevens, Wallace. *El elemento irracional en la poesía* (The irrational element in poetry). Córdoba: Alción Editora, 2010.

Suárez, Ray, *Latino Americanos: El legado de 500 años que dio forma a una nación* (Latin Americans: the legacy of 500 years in forming a nation). Nueva York, Calebra, Penguin Group, 2013

Tezanos-Pinto, Rosa. *El exilio y la palabra. La trashumancia de un escritor argentino-estadounidense* (The exile and the word. The migration of an Argentine writer) Buenos Aires: Ed. Vinciguerra, 2012.

Zeleny, Mayra, Editor. *El cuerpo y la letra. La poética de Luis Alberto Ambroggio* (The body and the word. The poetry of LAA) New York: North American Academy of the Spanish Language, 2008.

# ABOUT THE AUTHOR

LUIS ALBERTO AMBROGGIO (born in Argentina, 1945), was described by the Magazine *Casa de América* as "A prominent representative of the vanguard in Hispanic American poetry in the United States." He is a member of the American Academy of the Spanish Language, the Royal Spanish Academy and the PEN literary organization.He is a United States citizen and has resided here since 1967. He has a PhD in Philosophy and has completed doctoral studies in the Social Sciences (PhD, AbD) and has an MBA in Business Administration.He has given seminars as a guest lecturer at universities in Massachusetts and at Florida Gulf Coast University.He was the winner of TVE's (Spanish Television) award for "poems of solitude" in 2004, won the international Simón Bolivar Prize, was honored with a Fulbright Hays scholarship and is a member of the Hispanic National Honor Society. Other awards and recognitions include an *Honoris Causa* Doctorate from WAAC Israel and he is a member of literary institutions such as the Academy of American Poets, *Prometheus* and the Canadian Association of Hispanists.He was appointed by the U.S. State Department as Cultural Envoy to Nicaragua and El Salvador and as curator of the Smithsonian Institution for poetry events.

To date he has more than twenty published books covering more than half a century of his creations including *Poemas de amor y vida* (Poems of love and life - 1987), *Hombre del aire* (Man of the air - 1992), *Oda ensimismada* (Self-absorbed ode - 1992), *Poemas desterrados* (Poems of exile -1995), *Los habitantes del poeta* (The poet's inhabitants - 2005), *Por si amanece: cantos de Guerra* (In case the morning comes: war songs - 1997), *El testigo se desnuda* (The witness gets naked - 2002), *Laberintos de Humo* (Labyrinths of smoke - 2005), *Los tres esposos de la noche* (The 3 husbands of the night - 2005), *La desnudez del asombro* (The nakedness of astonishment - 2009), *Homenaje al Camino* (Tribute to the road -2012), *Todos somos Whitman* (We are all Whitman - 2014) and the critical edition published in 2014 by the American Academy of the Spanish Language under academicians Carlos Paldao and Rosa Tezanos-Pinto, entitled *En el Jardín de los vientos* (In the garden of the winds).*Obra poética* (Poetic works - 1974-2014) was chosen as one of 2014's most important books in a survey of ten of the best known Argentine writers. *Cross-Cultural Communications* of New York published his bilingual anthology entitled *Difficult Beauty* edited by poet Yvette Neisser Moreno (2009) with a prologue by Pulitzer Prize winner Oscar Hijuelos which was also published by *Vaso Roto* Editions in Barcelona and Mexico.*La arqueología del viento* (archeology of the wind – 2011 – 2013), translated by poet Naomi Ayala, was the winner of the International Latino Best Book Award.In addition to English translations, his poems have also been translated into French, Hebrew, Korean, Chinese, Japanese, Catalan, Portuguese, Italian, Turkish and Romanian and are included in Internet Anthologies in Europe, the Middle East, Latin America and the USA, among them: *Antología de la Nueva Poesía Hispanoamericana, Muestra del siglo XXI* (anthology of New Hispanic poetry, a 21$^{st}$ Century showing], the *Tigertail*annual Southwest Florida Anthology *Prometeo* [Prometheus], *Tejedores de Palabras* [Word weavers], Poetic Voices Without Borders, D.C. Poets Against the War, Red Hot Salsa and Cool Salsa described by Publishers Weekly as "Spicy as jalapeños and smooth as jazz serving 'English with sauce'"], appearing in numerous magazines (*Linden Lane Magazine, Hispanic Culture Review, International Poetry Review, Beltway Poetry, Alba de America* [Dawn of America], Scholastic, *La Pájara Pinta* [Good- looking female bird] *La Urpila* [The urchin], *O Boemio* [Or Bohemian] and cultural supplements (*El Universal de Caracas* [Caracas Universal], *La Prensa* [The press] and *El Nuevo Diario de Nicaragua* [Nicaragua's new daily], *La Gaceta Iberoamericana* (The Iberoamerican gazette), *La Gaceta de Tucumán* [Tucuman gazette] and in literature texts such as *Pasajes* (Passages), *Encuentros* (Meetings) and *Bridges to Literature*. He has been invited by official and private institutions to participate in congresses, festivals, gatherings in Europe, the Middle East, Central America, South America, Mexico, the United States and Canada, giving lectures at over 30 universities and at national libraries.

The American Academy of the Spanish Language has also published a volume of critical studies his poetry entitled *El Cuerpo y la Letra* (The body and the letter) edited by Mayra Zeleny (2008), the Center for Latino Studies at Indiana University under the direction of Dr. Rosa Tezanos-Pinto has published his *El exilio y la Palabra* (Exile and word). *La trashumancia de un escritor argentino-estadounidense* (The migration of an Argentine-American writer - 2012) and at the National University of Tucumán, Argentina *La metáfora del poder en la lírica de Luis Alberto Ambroggio* (The metaphor of power in the lyrics of LAA) by Dr. Adriana Corda. (2015).

Luis Alberto Ambroggio has compiled anthologies: *Argentina en Verso* (Argentina in Verse - 1993) *De Azul a Rojo* (From blue to red). *Voces de poetas nicaragüenses del siglo XXI* (Voices of 21$^{st}$ Century Nicaraguan poets - 2011) and *Labios de Arena* (Lips of sand - 2014).Together with Carlos Parada he co-edited *Al pie de la Casa Blanca* (At the foot of the White House), *Poetas*

*Hispanos de Washington D.C.* (Hispanic poets of Washington D.C. - 2010), published by the North American Academy of the Spanish Language.He is included in the Anthology *Festival Latinoamericano de Poesía* (Latin American Poetry Festival), in New York City, 2012 by *Urpi* Publishers, together with Carlos Aguasaco et al. in a multilingual anthology, (Americas Poetry Festival of New York, Poetic Art Press, 2014).Among other works, he has done Spanish translations of poems by D.H. Lawrence, Dylan Thomas, William Carlos Williams and he compiled selected poems by Robert Pinsky in a bilingual edition entitled *Ginza Samba*, published by *Vaso Roto* in 2014.

His work as a critic focuses on poetry written in Spanish in the United States with articles appearing in a volume entitled *Los Hispanos en los Estados Unidos* (Hispanics in the United States) at Columbia University and in *Fondo Documental de Prometeo de Madrid* (Prometheus documentary fund of Madrid) and in a special edition of the *Enciclopedia del Español de los Estados Unidos* (Encyclopedia of Spanish in the U.S.), published by the Cervantes Institute and Santillana. Also in the areas of philosophy and poetry, he wrote *Thomas Jefferson and Spanish—the Hispanic element in Walt Whitman's poetic democracy*, and published essays entitled *El arte de escribir poemas* (The art of poetry writing). *Apuntes para no llevar necesariamente el apunte* (Notes not necessarily for taking note - 2009) and the narrative *Cuentos de viaje para siete cuerdas y otras metafísicas* (Tales of travel for 7 strings and other metaphysics - 2013) with a prologue by Lauro Zavala.

He has contributed essays on Canadian bilingualism and identity and on major poets such as Jorge Luis Borges, Gabriela Mistral, Pablo Antonio Cuadra and Rubén Darío they appear in the Central American *Decenio* (Decade) cultural supplement of the Nicaraguan newspaper *La Prensa,* the literary magazine *Carátula* under the direction of Sergio Ramírez; was recognized for his critical work as an honorary member of the Rubén Darío Cultural Heritage Institute of Nicaragua, of the Colombian Poetry Center, the University of California's Hispanic Cultural Literary Institute among others.His articles have appeared in books and periodicals such as *El Universal de Venezuela*, the *Chicago Tribune*, *La Gaceta Iberoamericana*, *Conscientization for Liberation*, *Gabriela Mistral y los Estados Unidos* (Gabriela Mistral and the U. S.), among others. As a PEN member, he has written essays on literature and some of its most outstanding present-day exponents such as Mario Vargas Llosa, Umberto Ecco, Salman Rushdie and other internationally recognized writers.

His poetic works have been selected to be included in the Hispanic-American Literature Archives of the United States Library of Congress.

# GLOSSARY

abuelita – little grandmother

adelita – a synonym of soldaderas, female soldiers defending the Mexican Revolution

al garete – (slang) messed up, go to hell

alurista – Refers to Alberto Baltazar Urista Heredia, known as Alurista, a Chicano poet and activist born in Mexico City and moved to San Diego, CA with his family at age 13.

americano/a – this term often applies to a citizen of the U.S. but can be applied to anyone living in North, Central or South America

America – All of the territory in North, Central and South America as well as the Caribbean; often used to refer to the United States

Americas – (see above definition)

Andalicán – during the era of conquest and colonial times in Chile, the name of the high hill in the middle of two ravines and site of a fortress.

boricua – a Puerto Rican, especially one living in the United States

Borinquen – another ancestral name for Puerto Rico

cachivache – object or utensil, usually in a strange or complicated way, that you do not know how to name or designate.

campesino – peasant, coutry dweller

candela – candle, also refers to a badly behaving child.

CEPI – Circle of Ibero-American writers and poets

chicana – female Mexican in the U.S.

chicano – male Mexican in the U.S.

chicanito –diminutive of chicano

chole – a friendly girl who is loved by everyone

chupacabras – literally, "goatsucker" – a mythical animal believed to prey on livestock and drink their blood

Colón (Cristobal) – Christopher Columbus

corrido – a kind of ballad or type of theater

cristiano/a – Christian

décima – a stanza consisting of ten octosyllabic verses.

desangrar – bleed to death

Diasporripocano/a (or Diasporican) – new Puerto Rican poetic generations, later called "Neorrians" published in anthologies and magazines

diepalismo – an avant-garde movement that proposed to replace logic with phonetics by resorting to sounds and onomatopoeia.

don – natural gift

Don – Mr.

Doña – Ms, Miss, Mrs.

español – Spanish (language and nationality; if referring to a person, a Spaniard)

española – Spanish (female gender); see also "español"

Estados Unidos – United States

estadounidense – a citizen or resident of the United States (no caps in Spanish)

fronterizo/a – having to do with a national border

frontera – border

gringo/a – slang term for a foreigner, usually a U.S. citizen

habanero/a – resident of Havana

hispano/a – from Spain or related to Spain; also used to refer to a person of Latin American origin

hispanoamericano/a – Hispanic-American (U.S.)

hispanoparlante – Spanish-speaking

iberoamericano/a – Iberoamerican (i.e., of Portuguese, Spanish or Latin American descent)

indita – diminutive term for a native or tribal woman

inglés – English

inglés/a – English national

jíbaro – a term commonly used in Puerto Rico, and other Latin American countries, to refer to mountain-dwelling peasants, but also has a nobler, cultural meaning

jibarismo – the clandestine sale of illegal drugs

latinoamericano/a – Latin American

Latinoamérica – Latin America

letrilla – a kind of short poem

libertad – freedom, liberty

libre – free

libro – book

lírica – lyric, lyrics

literatura – literature

literario/a – literary

Malinche – also known as Malinalli, Malintzin or Doña Marina, was a Nahua woman from the Mexican Gulf Coast, played a role in the Spanish conquest of the Aztec Empire, acting as an interpreter.

matachín – originally, a Spanish sword dancer (in its plural form Matachines refers to a native and Hispanic dance tradition in the SW United States

Matacumbe – refers to geographical area of the Florida Keys

Mejico – Mexico

mejicano/a – Mexican

mestizo/a – a person of mixed European and native/tribal ancestry

migra – derogatory slang for Immigration/Border Police

Navidad – Christmas

navideño/a – relating to Christmas

negro/a – black

neomanierismo – Neomanierism Postmodern movement, characterized by being a transvanguardist and neo-expressive tendency, seeking to express the cult of a particular figure

Niuyorricano (Nuyorican) – "Spanglish" name meaning a Puerto Rican living in New York (New Yorker-American)

Noismo – "No-ism" – The belief that to be in the opposition means to say no to everything

partido – political party, game

pastorela – a play about the infant Jesus

pocho/a – person of Mexican origin who lives in the United States and has adopted American customs or speaks Spanish with an English accent.

puertorriqueño/a – Puerto Rican

quinceañera – a 15-year-old girl; a special birthday party to celebrate a girl's 15th birthday

salsipuedes – (expression) "get out if you can"

Santa Fe – (literally, "Holy Faith") a major city in New Mexico

silva – Renaissance Spanish versification—a strophe, consisting of eleven- and seven-syllable lines

soldadera – a female soldier of the Mexican Revolution

258

sudaca – South American (derogatory term)

sudamericano/a – South American

taíno – Taino (indigenous group and language)

trashumancia – migration

trovo – poetic duel

Edit on August 15, 2017
in Suffolk County, Long Island, New York,
by Long Island al Día Editores
33 Chestnut Street
Central Islip, New York 1172
Telephone (631)241-0913

12186087R10146

Made in the USA
Lexington, KY
19 October 2018